WRITING WELL

BOOKS BY DONALD HALL

BOOKS OF POETRY

Exiles and Marriages, 1955
The Dark Houses, 1958
A Roof of Tiger Lilies, 1964
The Alligator Bride: Poems New and Selected, 1969
The Yellow Room: Love Poems, 1971

BOOKS OF PROSE

Andrew the Lion Farmer, 1959
String Too Short to Be Saved, 1961
Henry Moore, 1966

EDITED WORKS

New Poets of England and America, (with R. Pack and L.
	Simpson), 1957
The Poetry Sampler, 1961
New Poets of England and America (Second Selection) (with
	R. Pack), 1962
Contemporary American Poets, 1962
*A Concise Encyclopedia of English and American Poetry and
	Poets* (with Stephen Spender), 1963
Poetry in English, 1963
The Faber Book of Modern Verse (New Edition with
	Supplement), 1965
The Modern Stylists, 1968
A Choice of Whitman's Verse, 1968
Man and Boy, 1968

WRITING WELL

DONALD HALL
UNIVERSITY OF MICHIGAN

 LITTLE, BROWN AND COMPANY
BOSTON

LIBRARY OF CONGRESS CARD NO. 72-11457

THIRD PRINTING

Published simultaneously in Canada
by Little, Brown & Company (Canada) Limited

PRINTED IN THE UNITED STATES OF AMERICA

ACKNOWLEDGMENTS

James Agee. Quotation on pages 84–85 from "Southeast of the Island: Travel Notes." Reprinted from *The Collected Short Prose of James Agee* (Boston: Houghton Mifflin, 1969) by permission of Houghton Mifflin Company and Calder & Boyars Ltd.

The Ann Arbor News. Quotation on pages 200–201 from the editorial page of *The Ann Arbor News,* July 4, 1972. Reprinted by permission.

R. P. Blackmur. Quotation on pages 238–239 from "New Thresholds, New Anatomies" in *The Double Agent* by Richard P. Blackmur. Copyright 1935 by Richard P. Blackmur.

John Malcolm Brinnin. Quotation on pages 240–241 from *The Sway of the Grand Saloon* by John Malcolm Brinnin. Copyright © 1971 by John Malcolm Brinnin. A Seymour Lawrence Book/Delacorte Press. Used by permission of the publisher and Macmillan, London and Basingstoke.

Robert Coles. Quotation on pages 23–24 from *Children of Crisis: A Study of Courage and Fear* by Robert Coles, by permission of Atlantic-Little, Brown and Co. Copyright © 1964, 1965, 1966, 1967 by Robert Coles.

John Collier. Quotation on page 170 from *Indians of the Americas* by John Collier. Copyright © 1947 by John Collier, Reprinted by arrangement with The New American Library, Inc., New York, New York.

James B. Conant. Quotation on pages 245–246 from "Athletics: The Poison Ivy in Our Schools" by James B. Conant. Reprinted from *Look Magazine,* January 17, 1961 by permission of Cowles Communications. Copyright © Cowles Communications, Inc., 1961.

Frank Conroy. Quotation on pages 14–16 from *Stop Time* by Frank Conroy. Copyright © 1967 by Frank Conroy. All rights reserved. Reprinted by permission of The Viking Press, Inc. and The Bodley Head Ltd.

Hart Crane. Quotations on pages 238–239 from *The Collected Poems and Selected Letters and Prose of Hart Crane* by Hart Crane. Permission of Liveright, Publishing, New York. Copyright © 1933, 1958, 1966 by Liveright Publishing Corp.

James Dickey. Quotation on pages 195–196 from *Deliverance* by James Dickey (Boston: Houghton Mifflin Company, 1970), pp. 184–186. Reprinted by permission of Houghton Mifflin Company and Hamish Hamilton, London.

David Finn. Quotation on pages 199–200 from *The Corporate Oligarch* by David Finn. Copyright © 1969 by David Finn. Reprinted by permission of Simon and Schuster.

Robert Frost. Quotation on pages 236–238 from "Acquainted with the Night" by Robert Frost. From *The Poetry of Robert Frost,* edited by Edward Connery Lathem. Copyright 1928, © 1969 by Holt, Rinehart and Winston, Inc. Copyright © 1956 by Robert Frost. Reprinted by permission of the publishers, Holt, Rinehart and Winston, Inc. and Jonathan Cape Ltd., and the Estate of Robert Frost.

Germaine Greer. Quotation on pages 247–248 from *The Female Eunuch* by Germaine Greer. Copyright © 1970, 1971 by Germaine Greer. Used by permission of McGraw-Hill Book Company and MacGibbon & Kee, Ltd.

To Gerard McCauley

AUTHOR'S NOTE

The people from whom I have derived my ideas of style are the writers whose work I have loved. I quote many of them here, so that they may speak in their own voices, and not depend upon the articulation of an admirer. I do not quote them all. I owe my *sense* of style, as well as some ideas of it, especially to the modern writers I read and imitated when I was young: Ernest Hemingway, Ezra Pound, George Orwell, James Joyce. I do not mean that I am fit to call myself a pupil.

More immediate help has come from Charles Christensen of Little, Brown, and from the numerous teachers whom he persuaded to read and criticize my manuscript at several stages. I am hugely in debt to Richard Beal, of Boston University, who has helped me to retain my sanity, I am sure at some cost to his own. I am indebted to Lawrence Russ, for considerable assistance, and to David W. Lynch, for adding a second stylistic conscience to my own. I am indebted to Dorothy Foster, as ever, for reading my handwriting, for typing four complete versions, for patience and for accuracy.

Donald Hall

CONTENTS

I

INTRODUCTION

WRITING TO DISCOVER   1
HONEST AND DISHONEST FEELING   2
EXAMINING THE LIFE   5
REVISING THE MAP   6
THEMES AND REVISIONS   7
SOME PROFESSIONAL WRITING   14
DISORGANIZED WRITING, POMPOUS WRITING   17
LEARNING TO WRITE WELL   18
DAILY WRITING   19
    Exercises   21

II

WORDS

THE INSIDES OF WORDS   25
    Words Themselves   25
    No Synonyms   27
    Literalness and Metaphor   30
    Sense Words   31
    Misusing the Insides of Words   31

Avoiding Self-Deceit   34
Collecting Words   35
Words as Blanks   37
Words and Meaning   37
Audience and Self   38
Exercises   39

VERBS   41
Action, and the Choice of Style   41
Verbs with Nouns and Adjectives   42
Verbs with Participles   43
The Passive Mood   43
Particular Verbs   45
Invisible Verbs   46
False Color in Verbs   46
Fancy Verbs   48
Made-Up Verbs   48
Exercises   48

NOUNS   53
Particularity and Choosing a Style   53
Abstract and Particular   55
Abstractions: Beginnings and Endings   56
Invisible Nouns   56
Making Bad Nouns from Verbs   57
Fancy Nouns   58
Revising Nouns   58
Exercises   60

ADJECTIVES AND ADVERBS
AND OTHER MODIFIERS   63
Qualities and Choosing a Style   63
The Adjective and the Cliché   64
The Modifier That Weakens the Noun   64
Modifiers as Weak Intensives   65
Automatic Adjectives   66
Nouns as Modifiers   68
Using Modifiers Well   69
Revising Modifiers   73
Exercises   73

ORIGINAL WORDS: COMPARISONS   76
    The Need for Originality   76
    Overhearing Your Original Self   77
    Looking for Original Images   78
    Simile and Metaphor   78
    Originality and Memory   80
    Analogy   80
    The Unintended Comparison   82
    Looking for Analogies   83
    Revising for Comparison   85
    Exercises   85

III
SENTENCES

STYLE AND THE SENTENCE   89
TYPES OF SENTENCES   89
    Simple Sentences   89
    Compound Sentences   90
    Complex Sentences   91
    Compound-Complex Sentences   91
    Incomplete Sentences   91
    Exercises   93

VARIETY OF SENTENCES   94
    The Uses of Variety   94
    Subordinating for Brevity: Complex Sentences   94
    Long Sentences   96
    Punctuation and Variety: Compound Sentences   98
    Mixing the Types   101
    Revising for Variety and Conciseness   103
    Exercises   105

UNITY   108
    The Need for Unity   108
    Grammatical Unity   109
        Misplaced Modifiers. Conjunctions and Unity:
        Complex Sentences. Agreement. Consistency of Tenses.
    Structural Unity   113

Parallelism. Emphasis. Balance.
Rhythm. Resolution. Concluding the
Sentence.
Unity of Diction   123
Formality and Informality. Formality
Gone Bad. Pompous Language. For-
mal and Informal Sentence Structure.
Informality Gone Bad. Subject and
Audience. Mixing Formal and Infor-
mal Diction. Revising for Unity.
Exercises   133

IV
PARAGRAPHS

THE USES OF PARAGRAPHS   143
FOCUSING WITH PARAGRAPHS   144
LENGTH OF PARAGRAPHS   146
UNITY, SEQUENCE, AND COHERENCE   150
NARRATIVE PARAGRAPHS   154
TOPIC SENTENCES   154
SOME WAYS OF DEVELOPING PARAGRAPHS   157
TRANSITIONS   160
Overt Transitions   160
Repeated Words or Phrases   161
Parallel Constructions   162
Transitional Words and Phrases   163
Implicit Transitions   164
Revising Paragraphs   166
Exercises   166

V
THE PAPER

GETTING IDEAS   180
ACCUMULATING DETAIL   181
SHAPING THE PAPER   182
Cutting Detail   184

Beginnings: Narrowing the Topic   185
Endings: Concluding the Topic   188
Middles: The Structure of Thought   191

EXPOSITION   191
ARGUMENT AND PERSUASION   196
  Clarity in Argument   197
  Reasonableness in Argument   198
  Time for the Opposition   201
  The Order of Argument   203
  Logic and Emotionalism   205
  Common Fallacies of Thinking   206
    Generalizing from a Particular. The Overinclusive Premise.
    Guilt by Association. Begging the Question
    Evading the Issue. Nonsequitur. Sequence as Cause.
    The Argument ad Hominem. Analogy as Fact.
    The General Fallacy of Imprecision.

DESCRIPTION   210
NARRATIVE   212
DIALOGUE AND QUOTATION   214
AUTOBIOGRAPHY   215
WRITING FICTION   218
WRITING RESEARCH   220
WRITING ABOUT WRITING   232
  Exercises   240

GLOSSARY   253
INDEX   315

WRITING WELL

I

INTRODUCTION

WRITING TO DISCOVER

Students write papers and answer questions on tests, scientists write reports on their work, teachers write evaluations of their students, people make lists to remember what they must do, some of us keep diaries to remember what we have done, salesmen write messages from the field to the office, and we write notes and letters to keep in touch with relatives and friends. There are practical reasons for literacy. The reasons for writing *well* are practical also.

But not at first. First, comes the message: "I want milk." Even earlier, "Mmm," to the mother's ear, can mean "I want milk." As our brains grow, our messages become more complicated. We make our verbal messages emphatic by gesture and facial expression, as a guitar solo may borrow some of its rhythmic drive from a drum. Learning to write well is harder than learning to talk, but the results include pleasures deeper than the satisfaction of immediate needs.

A good writer uses words to *discover,* and to bring that discovery to other people. He writes so that his prose is a pleasure that carries knowledge with it. That pleasure-carrying knowledge comes from self-understanding, and becomes the understanding of others. It makes the difference between writing and writing well.

1

Here is a passage from an essay about a short story:

> The usage of these types of image contribute to the overall beauty of the thematic content of this lovely piece.

The writing is pretentious and wordy, but a message comes through. Rewritten well, a message will come through with more information, and more feeling. The first message is swaddled in seven sweaters and three pairs of pants; it can hardly walk. The writer revised the passage:

> These images make the story pleasing to read—you taste the fruit of the orchard, you touch the ripening grape—but also the sensuousness shows us the point of the story.

The rewritten prose names and communicates feeling. A shortened version could have read simply:

> These images contribute to the beauty of the story and its theme.

This version is brief and correct. It is less pretentious than the first version, but it is not good enough. It is dry, and it does not carry the voice of the person speaking. It is a message purified of character and feeling, like a slice of bread purified of nutrition and taste.

The live shape could have taken many forms besides the form this writer gave it. Someone else, writing well about the same story, did it differently:

> This story needs to be read aloud. When you hear the voices of Helen and her husband, gestures and facial expressions seem to accompany the words. I feel as if the author had put invisible stage directions between the lines. The relationship we hear in the dialogue shows the meaning of the story.

One reader saw images, another heard dialogue. Both were eventually able to say what they meant in language that let their own feelings—responses to a work of art, this time—come through with clarity. Writing well is the art of clear thinking and honest feeling.

HONEST AND DISHONEST FEELING

The phrase, "honest feeling," implies an opposite, dishonest feeling, which no one admits to, but which we sometimes see clearly enough in others. We all know that many feelings are falsely expressed. We have all heard people say on the telephone, "I'm *so* sorry I can't come!" when we knew they could but didn't want to. And we have done the same thing. We have grown up on the false laughter of television, the fake enthusiasm of advertising, the commercial jollity and condolences of greeting cards, and the lying assertions of politicians. If some falsity has not entered our prose, we are made of aluminum.

There are a thousand ways to be false. We do it with handshakes and we do it with grunts. We do it by saying outright lies, like "It was good to meet you." But this outright lie is only a formula, and at least we know that it is false if we give it a moment's thought. When we fool *ourselves*—which we do frequently—we are in more trouble. We fool ourselves with words that can mean almost anything. How much have we said when we call someone "straight"? We fool ourselves when we avoid blame by using a passive (the table was knocked over and broke) or sometimes by using personification (the glass fell off the table). We fool ourselves by clichés that have become meaningless substitutes for feeling and thought:

> It's not black and white.
> The situation is very complicated.
> That's more or less what I had in mind.

Clichés are little cinder blocks of crushed and reprocessed experience. Every profession—medicine, law, theater, business in its different disciplines—has its clichés. One set of clichés appears especially at graduations, from primary school through graduate school:

> The future belongs to you.
> The challenge of new . . .
> The most exciting generation of . . .
> Responsibility, good citizenship, service to the community, etc.

One of the great sources of clichés is the university. Here is a paragraph from a prospectus for a Ph.D. dissertation:

> This is not a shocking development, perhaps, since even a cursory familiarity with the history of higher education in the United States reveals a consistently enlarging sphere of concern and influence for colleges and universities whose curricula and programs have expanded to meet a variety of societal needs.

It may seem only natural that as during the past three decades higher education has reached an unprecedented magnitude in terms of numbers of faculty and student participants, resources at its disposal, and social power, higher education as an institution has been wont to take the arts under its protective wing with a theretofore [sic] unparalleled seriousness of commitment and ambition.

It took this academic years and years to learn to write so badly. Every phrase in the passage is a cliché, and the clichés are held together by the mortar of empty words like "is" and "and" and "with." But the edifice is all reprocessed garbage:

> shocking development
> cursory familiarity
> the history of higher education in the United States
> consistently enlarging sphere
> variety of societal needs
> only natural
> an unprecedented magnitude
> resources at its disposal
> protective wing
> theretofore unparalleled

The smoothness of the masonry is exceptional, but the passage is without content and without feeling. The paragraph is "insincere" because it does not represent the feelings of a person. Of course the author did not *intend* insincerity, nor did he feel that he was lying. He felt, we can presume, that he was using the language expected of him.

   The idea of sincerity is tricky. Yet it is a valuable idea, if we can think clearly about it, and it has everything to do with the reasons for writing well. A man named Peter Elbow, quoted in Ken Macrorie's excellent book *Uptaught*, says:

> I warn against defining sincerity, as telling true things about oneself. It is more accurate to define it functionally as the sound of a writer's voice or self on paper—a general sound of authenticity in words. The point is that self-revelation . . . is an easy route in our culture and therefore can be used as an evasion: it can be functionally insincere even if substantially true and intimate. To be precise, *sincerity is the absence of*

"noise" or static—the ability or courage not to hide the real message.

The static is the distance between what the words say and what we sense lies behind them. The person with a pose of sincerity fixes us with his eyes, saying, "I am going to be wholly honest with you. I am a bastard. I cheat on my girlfriend and I fink on my roommate. I hate my father because he gave me a car. I hit a blind man once when nobody was looking." The real message: "Love me, I'm so *honest*."

The distance between the meaning (the apparently stated) and the expression (the really implied) is the sickness. In the Ph.D. candidate's passage above, the meaning has something to do with the arts in the American university; the expression is a continual exhibition of academic smoothness; it is a little dance, a performance of a well-trained educationist seal. It says, "Look at me. Admit me to your ranks. I am one of you."

We cannot take sincerity as a standard if we are going to take the writer's word for it. We can take it seriously, if we listen to his *words* for it. Sincerity is *functional* (Elbow's word) if we believe it, if we hear the voice of a real person speaking forth in the prose—whether of speech or of the written word. And functional (maybe we should call it "convincing") sincerity comes from the self-knowledge that is the result of self-exploration. It is not easy. It requires self-examination, and hard thinking or analysis. It is worth it. Socrates made the commitment: The unexamined life is not worth living.

EXAMINING THE LIFE

By learning to write well, we learn methods of self-discovery and techniques of self-examination. Understanding the self allows us to move outside the self, to read, to analyze, to define. Writing well can be a basis for all thinking. Self-discovery and self-examination are separate things, though they can happen at the same time. Self-exploration finds what we have inside us that is our own. Of course we are stuffed with clichés—we have been exposed to them all our lives—but clichés are not "our own." We have swallowed everything else that has ever happened to us: we dropped the bottle to the floor, at the age of eight weeks, and cried for the loss of it; the telephone did not ring last week, and we cried for the loss of it; the toy shines under the tree, the toy rusts behind the garage; the smell of bacon, the smell of roses, the smell of kittens that have been careless; the flowers and the beer cans emerging from the snow. Everything that ever happened remains on file in our heads. As someone has said: The human brain is a big computer made of meat.

If the brain is a computer, we are all engaged in learning how to operate it. For the Ph.D. candidate quoted above, the task of writing was simple; he was programmed to write that kind of prose; he pushed the right keys and his brain computer turned out preassembled units of educationist jargon. The commencement speaker, or the student writing home for money, presses other keys for printouts of ready-made pseudo-thoughts and pseudo-feelings. But let us suppose that we are interested in something genuine, the voice without static, the utterance in which expression and meaning are the same. We must learn new ways to use the accumulation of words, sense impressions, and ideas that we keep in the disc-packs of the brain.

One of the mottoes of Confucius was "Make it new." "It" was thinking, feeling, expressing, writing. Only by making it new, each time we speak or write, can we make it true. To make it new does not mean to make it merely novel. One can leave out capitals, change typography, mount new rules of spelling—and still write with clichés or other static. Really to make it new, we must avoid the worn roads of conventional associations; we must find what is uniquely our own voice out of our own experience. Then our words will not make rows of identical houses like the subdivision prose of cliché. "New" is "fresh, genuine, ourselves, our own experience."

It is not, however, the predictable result of spontaneity. Spontaneous writing is a good way to start to learn how to write, and a good way to uncover material you didn't know was in you. One important computer key is a sense of freedom in writing. But then there is the second half of genuine expression, the half that applies the map-maker's self-examination to the new country of self-exploration.

REVISING THE MAP

Almost all writers, almost all the time, need to revise. We need to revise because spontaneity is never adequate. Even when we write as quickly as our hand can move, we slide into the emotional falsity of cliché or other static. And we make leaps by private association that leave our prose unclear. And we often omit steps in thinking, or use a step that we later recognize as bad logic. Sometimes we overexplain something obvious. Or we include irrelevant detail. First drafts remain first drafts. They are the material that we must shape, the block of marble that the critical brain chisels into form.

Good writing is an intricate interweaving of inspiration and discipline. A student may need one strand more than the other. Most of us continually need to remember both sides of a piece of writing: *We must invent, and we must revise.* And in these double acts of invention and revision, we are inventing and revising—not just our prose style—but our knowledge of ourselves and of the people around us. When Confucius recommended "Make it new," he meant what Plato called "the examined life." It was a moral position. By our language, we shall know ourselves—not once and for all, by a breakthrough, but continually, all our lives. Therefore the necessity to write well arises from the necessity to understand and to discriminate, to be genuine and to avoid what is not genuine, in ourselves and in others. By understanding what our words reveal, we can understand ourselves; by changing these words until we arrive at our own voices, we change ourselves.

THEMES AND REVISIONS

On the first day of class, the assignment was to write for twenty minutes under the heading, "How I Came to College." Here is an impromptu theme by Jim Beck:

> Education is of paramount importance to today's youth. No one can underestimate the importance of higher education. It makes us well-rounded individuals and we must realize that all work and no play is not the way to go about it, but studies is the most important part, without a doubt. Therefore I decided when I was young that I would go to college and applied myself to studies in high school so that I would be admitted. I was admitted last winter and my family was very happy as was I. Coming here has been a disappointment so far because people are not very friendly to freshmen and everyone has their own clique and the whole place is too big. But I expect that it will get better soon and I will achieve my goal of a higher education and being a well-rounded person.

Repetition at the end of the impromptu gives it some unity. In the lines in which Jim Beck says that "people are not very friendly to freshmen," the reader glimpses Jim Beck and his feelings. But for the most part, the writer is not being himself. You can tell that he is not being himself because he is sounding like so many other people. Jim Beck is assembling an impromptu from the cliché collection in the why-I-want-to-go-to-college box. When he says "paramount importance," does he really know what "paramount" means? Does he mean that "today's youth" is genuinely different from yesterday's or tomorrow's? And how long in history does "today" extend? What does "well-rounded" mean? Why say "individual" instead of "person"? "Important" is vague, and saying it twice makes it vaguer. In the sentence of complaint, where the reader briefly senses an actual writer, Jim Beck would have done better to *show* his loneliness in an anecdote, instead of just *telling*.

Later in the term, when he had a free theme, Jim Beck wrote an essay which was not so much a revision of his impromptu as a new start, and which *really* told how he came to college:

The Race to College
Jim Beck

It's horrible now, and I don't know if it will get any better. The only people who pay attention to me are the people who are trying to beat me out for the track team. My roommate is stoned all day and gets A's on his papers anyway. I hate him because he hates me because I'm a jock. My classes are boring lectures and the sections are taught by graduate students who pick on the students because the professors pick on them.

But I remember wanting to come here so bad! Nobody from Hammerton named Beck had ever been to college. Everybody knew the Becks were stupid. This went for my father, who never got through high school, and for my grandfather, who died before I was born, and who was the town drunk. It went for my two older brothers who went bad, as they say in Hammerton. Steve got a dishonorable discharge from the Marines and he works on a farm outside town and gets drunk on Fridays and Saturdays. Curt stole a car and did time at Jackson and nobody has heard from him since. My sister had a three-month baby and the town liked to talk about that.

I was different. Everybody told me I was. My mother told me I wasn't a Beck. My father told me I was going to bring back the family's good name. (I never knew it had one.) In grammar school the teachers all told me how much better I was than my brothers. By the time I was in sixth grade my father and the school Principal were talking about the University.

My father isn't really dumb. Sometimes people look dumb because it's expected of them. He's worked at the same grocery for twenty years, I guess. Now that I made it to the University, he wants to be called Manager, because he's the only man there besides Mr. Roberts who owns it. (The rest of the help are—is?—kids who bag and an old lady cashier.) When I went back for a weekend everybody treated me as if I won the Olympics.

I said the Principal and my father were talking about my going to the University. All through junior high I said I didn't want to go. I was scared. No Beck could do that. Bad things kept happening to my family. My father had an accident and totalled the car and lost his license and for a year we didn't have a car at all. He had to walk home two miles every night pushing a basket of groceries. When I said I would quit school and get a job, everybody jumped on me.

It wasn't that I was an A student. It was just that I tried hard at everything I did. I got B's mostly. Now with B's, the counsellors kept telling me, I could be admitted to the University, but I wouldn't get a scholarship. I needed mostly A's for that, and then when I got to the University I would lose the scholarship if I couldn't keep the grades up. Then my brother Steve, who was a pretty good athlete once, suggested athletics.

I was too skinny for football, too short for basketball, I could barely swim and my school didn't have a swimming team anyway. There is one sport you can practice with no money and no equipment. I started to run when I was in my last year of junior high. It felt good right away. I ran to and from school. I went over to the high school and did laps. The high school coach noticed me and asked me to go out the next year. Running long distances hurts a lot. Sometimes you get a stitch in your left side and suddenly it shifts to your right side. I didn't exactly mind the pain. I studied it. I studied it in order to go to the University, the way I studied everything else.

In my Senior year I was all-state and held two high-school records (600 and half-mile) and I had an athletic scholarship to the University. Now I am here, the first Beck to make it. I don't know why I'm here or why I ran so hard or where I go from here. Now that I am here, the race to get here seems pointless. Nothing in my classes interests me. I study, just as I did before, in order to pass the course or even get a good grade. I run to win, but what am I running for? I will never be a great runner. Sometimes when I cannot sleep I imagine packing my bags and going back to Hammerton. But I can't do that. They would say, "He's a Beck, all right."

Jim Beck's essay has the two most important features of good writing: it has unity, which means the focus, the point, the coming together of many details; and it has the voice of a real person speaking out of his own experience, using his own language, with a minimum of tired phrases, of borrowed clothing. It has discipline, and it has feeling. Although Jim Beck is discouraged and feels aimless and melancholy, his mind has made an enormous stride toward the ability to know and present itself. Self-knowledge may feel uncomfortable, but in the end it is more satisfying than self-delusion. He revised using his own experience in his own language. *And* he was disciplined; he used tighter sentence structure and he found unity in his experience. He learned about himself while learning to write prose.

The same assignment brought forth this theme from Marian Hart:

I always wanted to go to the University because my Dad went here.

I remember how it got started. I had a job as a car-hop in a drive in, an A & W in Flint where I make my home. Business was slack because it was about 3:30 Saturday afternoon so I was talking away with Barb and Karen who were working there too and I knew them from school of course. We had to wear these very tight stretch pants because Boss said it was good for business. A car came in and because it was my turn I picked up a pad and started out for it, then I saw it was my Dad. He jumped out of the car and hugged me. I knew what it was and so did Barb because we were all waiting to hear about admissions. I told him he could open it and he did and that's why he drove out, to tell me. Barb had to wait until she got off, the Boss wouldn't let her go and there was nobody at home to call up.

So! We got here three days ago, in the same car, only loaded to the roof with my stuff. I was petrified with fear. My Dad kept telling me what to do, and then he kept saying he knew it had changed a lot in 25 years. I wished he'd be quiet. My Mom cried. We couldn't find the dorm. Everybody we asked didn't know either. The boys all had long hair and beards and looked exactly the way I expected them too. My Dad hated it. Then when we found my dorm and we found my room my Dad was all out of breath, and mad, and he just pushed the door open with his shoulder and busted in. There was a naked girl standing there, with no clothes on, my roommate (whose very nice, named Terri, but I didn't know that yet) and he made a funny noise and dropped the suitcase and ran back out into the hall.

The theme needs only revision; it needs focusing, understanding, thinking, and care. When you look over a first draft, trying to find ways to clarify it and bring it together, it is wise to ask yourself, "What is this *really* about?" and see if you can come up with an answer. Jim Beck's first paper was about nothing at all—or about trying to say what you imagine the Institution wants to hear. His second paper was about social class, and trying to escape a family social pattern, and the empty feelings of success. Marian Hart's paper is mostly a playful account of her feelings for her father and his for her, with evidence of some jealousy and flirtation.

"I always wanted to go to the University because my Dad went there."

The word "because" begs questions. Probably thousands of high school graduates *don't* want to go to some University precisely because their Dad went there. And this one-sentence paragraph does not really introduce the reader to the action. It does not set up what follows in an intelligible or unifying way. Of course at the same time it is exactly what Marian Hart had to say, and thus is the first clue to the real content of the paper. For her, it *was* true that she wanted to go to the University because her Dad went there. But because she has not yet examined the implications of her prose—for instance, the literal illogic, and the emotional truth, of her first sentence—she is not ready to write or think with coherence.

Some of the writing is bad. "Where I make my home" is a euphemism for "where I live." (Euphemisms are fancy words for simple things, or soft words for harsh things, like "pass away" for "die.") Barb and Karen are useless details; they add nothing and are only there because they were part of the landscape in the opening anecdote. The story becomes truer when they are omitted, because the outlines become clearer, as the mists of futile detail recede. Another detail, about the tight stretch pants, might seem to be irrelevant also, but, unintentionally, this detail is a prelude to her father's arrival. So later the beards and long hair of the boys, and her father's irritation,

12   *Introduction*

could seem irrelevant, if you didn't understand that her father is as fond of her as she is of him, and therefore jealous of young male rivals. The chance discovery of a naked roommate provides the writer with the perfect, comic moment in which the father faces his own illicit desires and drops the suitcases. The materials are abundant, and this is the place to stop. In her first account the girl ran out of time here, or she would have gone on to have them eating supper at a German restaurant with a dressed Terri, and then waving goodbye as her parents drove off to U.S. 23. Haste saved her from going on too long.

The week after she wrote the impromptu, Marian Hart rewrote the theme for unity and focus. As she learned more about writing and about herself, she returned to it occasionally and rewrote a passage as part of an exercise. Finally, feeling bored with the theme but also determined to finish it once and for all, she rewrote it as a free theme near the end of term.

My Father's Place

It is about an hour and a quarter from my house in Flint to the dormitory in Ann Arbor. All the way, as we drove here last August to move in, my Dad was talking about the class of 1939. I tried to listen. I had heard him talk about the University since I was a little girl, and since I was a little girl I had wanted to come here to college. But in the car I was shy and frightened. I was going to meet a roommate named Terri who was from Detroit. She would be sophisticated and have long hair. All the boys would be crazy about her. I would be the invisible frump from Flint. My Dad was talking about *fraternities* and *dances!* My God.

I tried to think about happy things. I tried to think about how happy I was, as I sat there feeling stupid and ugly. I remembered how happy I was to be accepted. It was a Saturday last Spring when I was working at the A & W, being a car hop in the stretch pants that the boss made us wear "because it's good for business."

It was a slack time of day, and suddenly a car rolled up, parking across two parking places, and rocking with the brakes put on too fast. I picked up an order pad and headed out, and then I saw that it was our car and that my Dad was jumping out at me waving an envelope and grinning. He didn't have to say anything. We hugged and he called me his sweetheart. The three of us went out to dinner that night and celebrated.

Now my mother was sobbing and my teeth were chattering and my father was talking about *corsages!* I groaned a little, and he said—for the twelfth time—that of course he knew that everything was different now, with student rights and politics and ecology and (he gagged a little) co-ed dormitories. But . . . and he was off again. He was as nervous as I was.

When we drove into town my Dad's composure fell apart completely. He didn't know where he was. We asked directions but everyone else was as lost as we were. The whole place had changed, he said; none of the old landmarks were there. And he obviously hated the new landmarks. Girls with overalls and no bras and bare feet and long hair were throwing frisbees with boys with blue jeans and no shirts and bare feet and long hair and beards. My father's jaw went tight, and from the back seat I could see the tenseness of his neck that happened when he was worried or angry.

We found the dorm. My father carried the four suitcases. I carried a portable stereo and a box of indispensable records. My mother had three garment bags full of clothes which I knew I would never wear. Of course my room was on the third floor. Every time we passed a boy in the hallway my father's neck, which was red with carrying four suitcases, got tenser.

When we got to the door of my room, he didn't set down the suitcases to knock. Puffing and snorting, he pushed open the door with his shoulder and strode in, me and my mother close behind. Then he dropped all four suitcases, crash, and made a weird little noise. I thought: My God, he's having a heart attack. Then I looked past him and saw a girl standing facing him with her mouth flopped open in surprise—Terri, I thought, even then, and she's *not* too beautiful—and stark naked.

Notice how Marian Hart has brought in the essentials of the A & W scene, but kept her unity by a judicious use of context; car/car; affection/affection; college/college. Because of these connections, the flashback is not mechanical but organic; it grows naturally out of the scene.

Both of these student writers revised their work by improving their understanding of themselves and their material; and Marian Hart improved by adding unity to her anecdote, cutting unnecessary detail and arranging the rest to give her story dramatic point.

SOME PROFESSIONAL WRITING

The essays were impromptu, and the revisions printed here came two months later. Professional writers often take longer still, and struggle with the same enemies of disunity and evasion. The professional writer differs from the beginner in many ways: he knows that he is likely to fail at first, and why; he is patient, he is adamant, and he expects his writing to be hard work. The comparison of professional models and freshman examples is unfair, of course, but we do not make the comparison in order to emphasize the distance between the two. We bring in the models to give an idea of a goal, to exemplify and make concrete the standards we can otherwise only talk about; to show and not just to tell.

The best way to learn to write well is to read good prose. Gradually we acquire the manners of the good writing we admire. It is like learning a foreign language by living daily with a family that speaks it, shopping in it, and listening to television shows dubbed into it. This book, like the course that uses it, tries to take short cuts—but examples from native speakers (good writers) will be necessary to the student.

Take this passage of reminiscence from a book that appeared recently:

> I was twelve when my father died. From the ages of nine to eleven I was sent to an experimental boarding school in Pennsylvania called Freemont. I wasn't home more than a few days during these years. In the summer Freemont became a camp and I stayed through.
>
> The headmaster was a big, florid man named Teddy who drank too much. It was no secret, and even the youngest of us were expected to sympathize with his illness and like him for it—an extension of the attitude that forbade the use of last names to make everyone more human. All of us knew, in the mysterious way children pick things up, that Teddy had almost no control over the institution he'd created, and that when decisions were unavoidable his wife took over. This weakness at the top might have been the key to the wildness of the place.

Life at Freemont was a perpetual semihysterical holiday. We knew there were almost no limits in any direction. A situation of endless, dreamlike fun, but one that imposed a certain strain on us all. Classes were a farce, you didn't have to go if you didn't want to, and there were no tests.

Freedom was the key word. The atmosphere was heavy with the perfume of the nineteen-thirties—spurious agrarianism, group singing of proletarian chants from all countries, sexual freedom (I was necking at the age of nine), sentimentalism, naïveté. But above all, filtering down through the whole school, the excitement of the *new thing*, of the experiment—that peculiar floating sensation of not knowing what's going to happen next.

One warm spring night we staged a revolution. All the Junior boys, thirty or forty of us, spontaneously decided not to go to bed. We ran loose on the grounds most of the night, stalked by the entire faculty. Even old Ted was out, stumbling and crashing through the woods, warding off the nuts thrown from the trees. A few legitimate captures were made by the younger men on the staff, but there was no doubt most of us could have held out indefinitely. I, for one, was confident to the point of bravado, coming out in the open three or four times just for the fun of being chased. Can there be anything as sweet for a child as victory over authority? On that warm night I touched heights I will never reach again—baiting a thirty-year-old man, getting him to chase me over my own ground in the darkness, hearing his hard breath behind me (ah, the *wordlessness* of the chase, no words, just action), and finally leaping clean, leaping effortlessly over the brook at exactly the right place, knowing he was too heavy, too stupid as an animal, too old, and too tired to do what I had done. Oh God, my heart burst with joy when I heard him fall, flat out, in the water. Lights flashed in my brain. The chase was over and I had won. I was untouchable. I raced across the meadow, too happy to stop running.

Hours later, hidden in a bower, I heard the beginning of the end. A capture was made right below me. Every captured boy was to join forces with the staff and hunt the boys still out. My reaction was outrage. Dirty pool! But outrage dulled by recognition—"Of course. What else did you expect? They're clever and devious. Old people, with cold, ignorant hearts." The

staff's technique didn't actually work as planned, but it spread
confusion and broke the lovely symmetry of us against them.
The revolution was no longer simple and ran out of gas. To
this day I'm proud that I was the last boy in, hours after the
others. (I paid a price though—some inexplicable loss to my
soul as I crept around all that time in the dark, looking for
another holdout.)

Frank Conroy, *Stop-Time*

Notice the careful but subtle ordering here. The brief and stark first
paragraph, then the characterization of Teddy leading to a
generalization, in the last sentence of the second paragraph, which
leads us into the rest of the anecdote. The third paragraph is a series
of examples of "wildness," and then in the fourth paragraph we have
the supreme example: revolution. Here, the writer expresses excitement in rhythmic sentences, in images ("Lights flashed in my
brain."), and in exaggeration that embodies true feeling ("I was untouchable."). But if the anecdote stopped with this excitement, we
would have only a good story. Nothing ends with such ecstasy; both
the rhythm of storytelling, and honesty to our experience, require
that what goes up must come down. "The revolution was no longer
simple and ran out of gas." Conroy's prose imitates the state of mind
it describes.

Or take another example, from fiction this time, a tiny paragraph
only. One of the models of prose style in contemporary literature is
Ernest Hemingway, who worked carefully on rhythm and sound.
When he was young especially, he studied style and practiced and
revised, to learn the way to his own voice. A short story called "In
Another Country," about some wounded soldiers in a hospital in
Italy during World War I, opens with this paragraph:

In the fall the war was always there, but we did not go to it
any more. It was cold in the fall in Milan and the dark came
very early. Then the electric lights came on, and it was pleasant
along the streets looking in the windows. There was much
game hanging outside the shops, and the snow powdered on the
fur of the foxes and the wind blew their tails. The deer hung
stiff and heavy and empty, and small birds blew in the wind
and the wind turned their feathers. It was a cold fall and the
wind came down from the mountains.

Such a simple style! And if you try and write like it, you are likely to lace one shoe to the other. The grammar is simple, yet the length of sentence and clause and unit of rhythm varies continually. The vocabulary is simple—the fall, cold, and wind repeated, wind four times in the last five lines—and yet expressive. The effect of the whole is hypnotic or dreamy; the war is around us but we are not in it. Then the paragraph ends with the corpses of animals, described with a loving detail. Look at the word "pleasant"; normally, we might find this word too general, and want to ask *how*, exactly, did you feel? But here, in the emotional context of the paragraph, the vagueness is an understatement that is accurate; it embodies the emotional restraint of this removal from war, the tentative acceptance that "we" are alive, unlike the animals outside the shops and the unmentioned combatants among whom "we" used to count ourselves.

DISORGANIZED WRITING, POMPOUS WRITING

For a perverse sort of fun, let us rewrite the passage in a couple of bad versions. First, a parody (an imitation of a style, for the sake of mockery) of the disorganized writing that most of us start out with:

> September through December, in the fall, at any rate, the war still went on, but we ourselves weren't doing the fighting by this time. It got chilly then in the Italian city of Milan. It started to get dark earlier in the day. When it got dark they turned on the lights. It was nice to look in the windows of stores. There were a lot of dead wild animals outside of the stores. When it snowed it snowed on the animals' fur too. There was a lot of wind and it blew the animals' fur and it even blew the little ones around. It was really cold because the wind was coming down from the mountains, which were cold.

Maybe even this parody is better than the prose most of us write at first because the writer observes real things. Most bad writing omits anything that might be interesting and expressive. The whole paragraph might be reduced to:

> It was fall in Milan, Italy, one year during World War I. It got colder and the days got shorter.

Or we could try it in Pompous Institutional Moderne:

> During the autumn, the hostilities continued to ensue, but we no longer engaged in them ourselves. The daily temperature declined in Milan as the autumn continued, and the hours

of daylight gradually contracted. When darkness ensued, lights were illuminated. It was altogether agreeable to promenade and investigate the contents of shop windows. There was considerable unrationed meat available at this time, by reason of the prevalence of slaughtered wild animals. Precipitation in the form of snow, as the months progressed, accumulated on the fur of these slaughtered beasts, and the cold breeze that accompanied the snow caused the tails of the animals to wave. Venison was available, as was small fowl. The extreme cold of this autumn is attributable to the fact that the prevailing winds came from the direction of the mountains which, because of their elevation and the snow which had already accumulated thereon, were lower in temperature than the temperature which normally prevailed in the city.

This last writer, if he existed, might be elected chairman of the board, but he would never excite our feelings, or understand his own.

We learn to write well, if we learn, for good reason. Few of us will ever write with the skill of the passage from Hemingway or from Conroy. We don't need to, unless we are writers. But we need to move toward them. If we write, now, with the haphazard chaos of the first parody of Hemingway, or with the pompous institutionality of the second one, we are in trouble, in our heads and our hearts, not just in our writing. If we learn to write well, we will sharpen our wits on the one hand, and point our imagination and expression on the other—both together, or neither at all.

LEARNING TO WRITE WELL

So how do we learn to write well? We can do three things, at least. First, we can read well, which helps slowly, but keeps on helping; second, we can study writing and think about it and discuss it with others; third, and most important, we can write, and rewrite, and rewrite. Because rewriting our own work is most useful, we must have writing to rewrite. Keep your old themes. Keep a notebook. Keep a journal. Keep copies of papers or exams you write for other courses. In this collection of your own prose, you will find ideas for expanding and rewriting. You may notice, the tenth time you reread something, that you have written in order to hide something from yourself instead of writing to discover. After thinking about clichés or paragraph organization or passive verbs, you will find examples in your own prose, and you will see how to revise them.

DAILY WRITING

While you are learning to write, it is a good idea to write something every day. Continual application of pen to paper will ease the work of writing, and will give you a collection of words and sentences in which to look for ideas and for work to revise. Writing is a skill, like an athletic skill, which comes more naturally to some people **than to** others, but which improves with practice for everyone. Practice is a necessity. Maybe the best method is daily dated entries in a notebook. This notebook sounds like a journal, but for most people a journal is like a diary, and records merely the events of the day:

> Had pancakes for breakfast. 9 o'clock boring . . .

Little entries that set out our daily schedule do not help us. Better are memories, whole anecdotes, ideas, and queries. Doing daily writings, the student writes a page or two a day, every day, seven days a week, working rapidly and without trying to impose a direction on himself, without conscious control or focus or an attempt at mechanical perfection. Nor should a daily entry be continuous, necessarily. Some days one has a series of apparently unrelated flashes of thought or memory. Some days one seems to have no ideas at all. On such a day, a student may let his hand flow over the page with disconnected words and phrases. When Henry Moore, the great English sculptor, sits in front of the television set at night, sometimes he lets his hand wander over a page, "sketching" while he pays little attention; and sometimes ideas start, in this way, that later (with direction, control, focus, and attention to mechanical perfection) become works of art.

Many professional writers keep notebooks. Theodore Roethke, the American poet, left two hundred and seventy-seven notebooks behind when he died. Some entries were lines and images for poems; some were used, some were not. Others were prose notes to himself about writing poetry, and might have been the seeds of unwritten essays:

> Get down where your obsessions are. For Christ's sake, shake it loose. Make like a dream, but not a dreamy poem. The past is asking. You can't go dibble dabble in your tears. The fungi will come running; the mould will begin all over the noble lineaments of the soul. Remember: a fake compassion covers up many a sore. . . .

At other times, he made a more conventional journal entry:

> Today, or tonight, I realized finally at the age of 40, for the first time, that it is really possible for me to think, and even get pleasure from the process. Not that my efforts—or effects—are spectacular. Perhaps four consecutive related thoughts at present is the absolute top of my form—and that only just before falling asleep, or just after eating a fine breakfast, when I'm too lazy to write anything down. But still, even this is a beginning. And such excitement!

F. Scott Fitzgerald kept a notebook in which he recorded situations, observations, jokes, and anything else:

> Widely separated family inherit a house and have to live there together.
>
> . . .
>
> Girl and giraffe.
>
> . . .
>
> Family quarrels are bitter things. They don't go according to any rules. They're not like aches or wounds; they're more like splits in the skin that won't heal because there's not enough material.
>
> . . .
>
> Jules had dark circles under his eyes. Yesterday he had closed out the greatest problem of his life by settling with his ex-wife for two hundred thousand dollars. He had married too young, and the former slavey from the Quebec slums had taken to drugs upon her failure to rise with him. Yesterday, in the presence of lawyers, her final gesture had been to smash his finger with the base of a telephone.
>
> . . .
>
> Hearing Hitler's speech while going down Sunset Boulevard in a car.
>
> . . .
>
> Run like an old athlete.

Daily writing can lead to the loosening of minds. Our minds are muscle-bound, not by intellect, but by formulas of thought, by clichés both of phrase and of organization. Our minds do not need to remain restricted. A student going into economics wrote the following entry in a notebook:

> Blue clouds in Arizona. I was hitchhiking last August, at the

edge of the desert waiting for a ride that would take me across state. A little tree, a little shade. Sun so hot it melted turtles. Blue clouds of Arizona. Because there were no clouds at all, just blue glaring and turning white toward the sun. Like an egg only a lot brighter and hotter. Got a ride with a truck driver. "Never went to college myself. The war came along and then I had kids, you know. My daughter's at State." Jiggle. Oil. **Hot.** We had cheeseburgers in an airconditioned diner and I never felt so good in my whole life as when that ice-air hit me. Then the heat outside. Walking into the oven. (cliché.)

There is no point to his story, or maybe no story. No one told him he had to make a point. All he had to do was write a page. He was practicing.

Practice was the first thing for him, sheer practice in putting pen to paper, letting the words follow each other across the page; if the habit of writing remains alien to us, we will never learn to write with any naturalness. Second, he was learning to loosen up. No one was going to correct his spelling, or argue with his logic, or tell him that his clauses were not parallel, so he felt free to let the images follow each other loosely by association. Until the last phrase, his loosened mind provided a fresh series of images. But if he had written a string of clichés, nobody was going to bother him about it. Earlier in his notebook, before he trusted himself to loosen up, his prose had been rigid and trite.

This daily writing helps us to show us to ourselves, but unless the writing becomes directed and shaped toward an end, it does not help us to talk to another person. Unity, clarity, effect, and the disciplines of sentence and paragraph—all are necessary to move the message from the writer to the reader. So once we have found an idea or an image or a secret lode of language, then we must learn to shape and control in order to communicate. For communication, we need the right *words*.

EXERCISES

1. Write a brief impromptu on the events of the first few days of coming to college. Use specific examples and anecdotes. Find some unity or focus to hold your writing together.

2. Argue with the main thesis of this chapter, that there is an intimate relationship between our use of language and our understanding of ourselves and others.

3. Take the following passage and make two (or more) distinctly different parodies of it, trying to stick close to the original but to write with true badness:

The cradle rocks above an abyss, and common sense tells us that our existence is but a brief crack of light between two eternities of darkness. Although the two are identical twins, man, as a rule, views the prenatal abyss with more calm than the one he is heading for (at some forty-five hundred heartbeats an hour). I know, however, of a sensitive youth who experienced something like panic when looking for the first time at some old homemade movies that had been taken a few weeks before his birth. He saw a world that was practically unchanged—the same house, the same people—and then realized that he did not exist there at all and that nobody mourned his absence. What particularly frightened him was the sight of a brand-new baby carriage standing there on the porch, with the smug, encroaching air of a coffin; even that was empty, as if, in the reverse course of events, his very bones had disintegrated.

Vladimir Nabokov, *Speak Memory*

4. In the passage quoted from *Stop-Time* by Frank Conroy, could anything be cut out, to give the story greater unity or focus?

5. Imitate the structure of the *Stop-Time* passage by writing about a group or institution out of your own past.

6. Here is another "How I Came to College" impromptu. (a) Criticize it, for language and for structure. (b) Edit it. Rearrange, and rewrite.

Never Too Late

I just got out of the Marine Corps last May and I couldn't get a job. Thats how I came to college.

I guess that sounds dumb but maybe I am. My teachers back in school said I was an underachiever, even back in kindergarten I underachieved at blocks. The sergeant when I went in the Marines said other things I can't put down here.

When I got out I just hung around. School was a drag, I never learned anything, couldn't get interested. What for? I always thought. Also I was, if you pardon the expression, one smartass. When everybody got put on pro by the principal for long hair I had my head shaved and they sent me home for that. My father was mad.

So I never even finished. The Marine Corps was worse than school, as far as that's concerned. I hated every minute of it. Some times guys would ask me what I was going to do when I got out and I told them I was going to buy a car. Then they shut up.

I never got to Viet Nam, thank God. When I got out I just watched television for about a week. I bought a used-car and worked on it in the back yard. I looked for work but the only thing I could get was parking cars for a dude restaurant and I said no. People kept telling me to get an education. It's never too late, they kept saying.

The reason I came to college is that I had nothing else to do.

7. Here are three paragraphs in which a psychologist tells us the background from which he started his investigations.

I came to the South a New Englander, not only by birth but with over a quarter of a century of living and growing up. At the end of a psychiatric residency I was called to Mississippi to serve my required two years in the military as a doctor, in this case as the chief of an Air Force neuropsychiatric hospital. The Air Force is a memory, but the South has become a real, a fresh part of my life. At first it was a region that I cared little to know, in fact it took me from several assignments I would have preferred. It has become one whose continuing pull upon my mind and heart prevents me from staying away for very long.

It is easy to categorize and give names to experiences once we are done with them. It is often sad that we do, because the effort takes away much of their original and spontaneous character. I suppose we need to try—it helps others understand, and makes us feel less anxious because more in control of our fate. As I look back at the past years in the South, I recall how easily I slipped into its very distinctive life and how pleasant I found that life to be. Only now do I stir anxiously at the thought of just how long (weeks turning to months) it took me to develop the dim awareness that became the vague uneasiness which marked a change in my thoughts and habits while living there.

One way of putting it is that I was a white, middle-class professional man, and so I easily fitted into that kind of Southern society. Only gradually did I begin to notice the injustice so close at hand, and as a consequence eventually take up my particular effort against it. (There would be those various categorical "stages" in such a development, ranging from faint glimmers to horrified, full recognition.) In the South, of course, anyone who begins to discover "injustice" in the world is in fact noticing the existence of a caste system wherein Negroes have an inherited position in a social organization which both needs them and yet notices their skin color before any individual attainments or accomplishments.

Robert Coles, *Children of Crisis*

In these paragraphs, Dr. Coles is beginning a large work. How do you take to the man whose voice you hear? What words seem especially expressive? Do any of his words or phrases seem inadequate to you? Are any words overly familiar or imprecise?

8. Write one or two pages every day for two weeks. Bring your notebook to class, not to hand in, but to read aloud from. Discuss some of each other's daily writing in the classroom, especially looking for anything that is fresh, interesting, and subject to further development.

II

WORDS

THE INSIDES OF WORDS

Words Themselves

The Gospel according to St. John starts, "In the beginning was the Word." When we construct the world of our own prose style, we begin as St. John does. It may seem difficult, at first, to think of words apart from contexts; "salt" does not stand alone; it is part of "salt and pepper," or "please pass the salt." Words seem like drops of water in a stream that has its own wholeness and its own motion. But when you write well, each word is accurate and honest and exact in itself, and contributes its special history to the wholeness of the stream of meaning.

The writer must be able to feel words intimately, one at a time. He must also be able to step back, inside his head, and see the flowing sentence. But he starts with the single word. He starts with tens of thousands of these units, and he picks among them. He may end by writing a passage like this account of the end of man's first day on the moon:

> It was almost three-thirty in the morning when the astronauts finally prepared for sleep. They pulled down the shades and Aldrin stretched out on the floor, his nose near the moon dust.

25

> Armstrong sat on the cover of the ascent engine, his back lean-
> ing against one of the walls, his legs supported in a strap he
> had tied around a verticle bar. In front of his face was the eye-
> piece of the telescope. The earth was in its field of view, and
> the earth "like a big blue eyeball" stared back at him. They
> could not sleep. Like the eye of a victim just murdered, the
> earth stared back at him.
>
> Norman Mailer, *Of a Fire on the Moon*

Until the end, this exposition seems simple and straightforward. Simple and straightforward it is, with the power of visual exactness, "his
nose near the moon dust," and the unexpected detail, "a strap he had
tied around a verticle bar." Norman Mailer cements each word in
place exactly and inevitably, with the help of rhythm and sentence
structure. For now, just look at how he prepares the dramatic emotion of the last image by a series of related words.

This passage, and much of Mailer's book, is about man and machine. The machinery is sophisticated, complex, overwhelming. Men
are frail in comparison. The language begins to embody this idea, by
repeating the names of parts of the body: "nose," "back," "legs,"
"face." We have become accustomed to the jerking motions of the
puffed-up spacesuits, as if we are watching robots. Now suddenly we
see "nose" and "face." We might be a mother looking at a sleeping
child. From "face" we move to the most vulnerable and necessary of
sense organs, the "eye," first by way of the "eyepiece" of a telescope,
then a visual comparison, easy to follow, of the earth to a "big blue
eyeball," which stares. We have departed from the astronauts' bodies, and moved into metaphorical bodies. Then, because the eyeball
stares, we can leap to the emotional crux: the earth is dead, murdered as it were by the astronauts who leave it behind for another
planet, for the beginning of the exploration outward, into the stars.
Mailer makes his point not by telling us about it overtly, but by his
control of language, his understanding of the insides of words, so that
the movement from "nose" to "face" to "eyepiece" and "view" to
"victim just murdered" has an inner and emotional necessity.

Or look at some description from a work of fiction:

> All the warm night the secret snow fell so adhesively that every
> twig in the woods about their little rented house supported a
> tall slice of white, an upward projection which in the shadow-
> less gloom of early morning lifted depth from the scene, made

it seem Chinese, calligraphic, a stiff tapestry hung from the gray
sky, a shield of lace interwoven with black thread.

John Updike

These sentences begin a short story called, "The Crow in the Wood."
Updike exercises the possibilities of our language in rhythm, in variety of sentence structure, and in observation that is dreamy and precise at the same time. He does it with words. Instead of looking at
everything he does, let us look at a few of the words that stand out.
"Adhesively" is a word we all know, from the noun or adjective
"adhesive," as a longer way of saying "glue" or "sticky." Here the
snow "fell" "adhesively." Snow really cannot fall like glue, and so we
have something apparently inaccurate; yet it is right, because the
context prepares us. It is a "warm night," so the snow will be damp.
And "adhesively" rather than "stickily" in this context shows that the
snow is not merely gooey to the fingers, but will actively adhere to
something. "Adhesively" by its unusualness draws the right attention
to itself.

Then look at the word "slice," ". . . every twig . . . supported a tall
slice of white. . . ." Most of us would have said something about snow
"piling" or "accumulating" on branches. But "a tall slice of white,"
besides being pleasing to the ear, is a brilliant image; the sharpness
of "slice," together with the image of whiteness, nearly dazzles the
eye. With the word "slice" is an unspoken "knife," just out of sight.
And I think we have a moment's vision of an upright piece of white-
frosted cake.

There are many more words for praise, in the passages from Mailer
and Updike, and maybe some flaws as well, which we will look into
later. But the character of the excellence is perhaps that of all excellence. These writers are *original, as if seeing a thing for the first
time;* yet they report their vision in a *language that reaches the rest of
us.* For the first quality the writer needs imagination; for the second he
needs skill. Without both qualities, he could not write the passage.
Imagination without skill makes a lively chaos; skill without imagination, a deadly order.

No Synonyms

To appreciate the word—the "eyepiece"/"eyeball," the "slice," the
"adhesively"—the writer and the reader must first realize that there
are no synonyms. Some words are close to each other in meaning,

close enough to reveal that they are not the same. The writer must
know not just the surface definitions of words; he must go deeper,
and realize the families of contexts with which particular words have
become associated—like "slice" with "knife" and even "cake." These
families are the connotations of the word, and the associations we
make with their denotation; "pepper" is not a connotation of "salt"
but it is an association of it. Since the writer uses the whole family, it
does not matter that he discriminates connotation from association.
But he must know the insides of words; he must be a friend of the
family.

The verbs "to emulate," "to imitate," and "to ape" may be listed as
synonyms in a dictionary—and they are synonyms, by definition—but
when we use them in a sentence they carry slight differences of
meaning. "To emulate" sounds fancy; also it usually implies that the
imitation involves self-improvement. "To imitate" is neutral, except
that everyone knows that an imitation is not the real thing; inferiority shadows the word. "To copy" is mostly to reproduce exactly,
though like "to imitate" it states a lack of originality. "To ape" is to
mimic, and to be comical or mocking about it. If you wanted to say
that a young pianist imitated a famous virtuoso, but you carelessly
used the word "ape" instead of "imitate," you would grant his style
the grace of a gorilla. Context is all; the inside of a word must rein-
force or continue the force of the context. When a sportswriter wrote
that another middle linebacker aped Dick Butkus, he was being
witty.

Dictionaries of synonyms and other books, especially *Roget's
Thesaurus*, list words that resemble each other. The experienced
writer can sometimes use a thesaurus to joggle his brain, to find not a
"synonym" but the *right* word. He will be aware of the insides of the
words he discovers. The thesaurus can be useful, not for supplying
words never heard before (we know words only when we know them
in sentences; some dictionaries supply examples of words in use) but
to remind the writer of words he has known in the past, which he
had not remembered when he needed them.

Sometimes an unsophisticated writer finds disaster in such a book.
A thesaurus supplies us with words that *resemble* each other, but we
must recognize the *differences* between them. When I look up "imitation," in my pocket *Roget*, I find under Verbs:

> imitate, copy, mirror, reflect, reproduce, repeat; do like,
> echo, re-echo, catch, match, parallel; forge, counterfeit.

mimic, ape, simulate, impersonate, act, etc. *(drama)*, 599; represent, etc. 554; parody, travesty, caricature, burlesque, take off, mock, borrow.

follow in the steps (or wake) of, take pattern by, follow suit [colloq.], follow the example of, walk in the shoes of, take after, model after, emulate.

The editors separate the verbs into three categories, which ought to help the cautious writer, but it is difficult sometimes to defend the sorting-out. Why does "forge" or "counterfeit" belong among the closer synonyms in the first group, and "emulate" among the phrases in the third group? Why is "represent" among the comic or belittling words? Putting "ape" with "travesty" and "parody," however, reminds us of the comic insides of "ape." The beginning writer should certainly be wary of a thesaurus, because if he believes in the exactness of synonyms he could produce a prose that means something wholly different from his intention.

I walked in the flowers that bordered the garden, sniffing the sweet airs of spring.

could become:

I peregrinated in the flowerets that flounced the orangery, sniffing the saccharin ventilation of the vernal equinox.

Spoken by W. C. Fields, the second version could be perfect for its context. As an example of how people misuse a thesaurus, it is exaggerated.

Using dictionary synonyms, you can test your sensitivity to the insides of words. Put the adjectives "false," "fake," "phoney," "insincere" with the noun "laugh." Everyone has heard laughs that were unreal, laughs for the sake of flattery, laughs that express the laugher's nervousness, or laughs at jokes that are not funny. If we wrote a description of such a laugh, we might want to write, "His laugh was false," or "His laugh was fake," or "His laugh was phoney," or "His laugh was insincere." Each time the exact meaning, dependent on the context of the story or the essay, would differ. "His laugh was false" sounds direct and serious, a stern and objective judgment. "His laugh was fake" sounds harsher, a strong indictment of the laugher; it implies that the falseness was deliberate. "His laugh was phoney" tells us more about the writer of the phrase. The choice of "phoney" over "false" or "fake" or "insincere" makes the speaker imply something like, "I am relaxed enough to be slangy." On the other hand, "His laugh was insincere" sounds pompous in its moral judgment—partly pompous, partly naïve.

These attempts to name the associations of words without the context of paragraph or essay are speculative; but, whatever the context, the words would all be different. Slightly, but genuinely different.

Literalness and Metaphor

Another way to become sensitive to the insides of words is to take them as literally as you can. When you read, "Fog enveloped the city," try seeing a gigantic gray-brown envelope enclosing Los Angeles. There is some silliness to literal images—but it is a silliness that can increase our sensitivity to the wholeness of words. Puns help too, working through the ear. Literal-mindedness, like all exercises that can improve our writing, can improve our reading as well.

Literal-mindedness exposes mixed metaphors, careless phrases comparing things that are comic or gross or inappropriate when we bring them together. Mixed metaphor usually happens when a writer uses clichés—the kind called dead metaphors—without noticing their original meanings. Sometimes people write, "The door yawned open"; the would-be comparison of door to mouth is dead from overuse. Sometimes people write, "The door beckoned," and the dead metaphor has the door turn into a hand that gestures an invitation. Once a student wrote in a paper, "The door yawned and beckoned." Two clichés make a mixed metaphor, if we are reading the insides of words: first the door is a huge, gaping mouth; suddenly an arm emerges, between rows of teeth, and motions us to enter.

When we take words literally, we respond to metaphor. We see the fog *compared* to an envelope. A metaphor is a comparison made without being stated. We *state* a comparison as a simile—"like a big blue eyeball"—and we *make* a comparison when we leave out "like" or "as." Hamlet in his soliloquy wonders if he should "take arms against a sea of troubles." It is futile to fight with the ocean. The futility is what Shakespeare had in mind. If you take the words literally, as they come, you can see something like an armored knight wading into the surf and slashing at the waves with his sword. The image shows an emotion that the abstract word, futility, would only name. The picture—which we receive by literal reading—gives us the emotion, without losing the idea of futility that the picture expresses.

Sense Words

Words that carry feeling most strongly are pictures and smells and touches and tastes and noises. The more sensual words are, the more they reach us and move us. We see how Updike embodies feelings of cozy shelter, and of precise observation of the outside world, by using images, not by using words that *tell* us how to feel (like "cozy") or that abstract ideas from actions (like "observations"). We see Mailer giving us an exact visual image of the astronauts trying to sleep on the moon. We feel the astronauts' cramp and discomfort because of the images; he need not say "cramp" and "discomfort." In the next paragraph, Mailer writes about the failure to sleep, and he writes ideas, but he uses images:

> It used to be said that men in the hour of their triumph knew the sleep of the just, but a modern view might argue that men sleep in order to dream, sleep in order to involve that mysterious theater where regions of the unconscious reach into communication with one another, and charts and portraits of the soul and the world outside are subtly retouched from the experience of the day.

"Theater," "charts," "portraits . . . retouched"—Mailer uses a series of images to make his concept clear by a comparison. Not *all* writing can be sensual and figurative, but *most* writing can be. Of course it is always possible to be safe and boring by stating only the facts, without images and feelings. Mailer could have said that the astronauts arranged themselves to go to sleep but couldn't, perhaps because so much had happened that day. Updike could have said that when his characters woke up, they discovered that it had snowed while they slept.

Misusing the Insides of Words

Just as we can learn to embody feelings by being aware of the whole family of a word, and by using language that appeals to the senses, so we can misuse words to fool ourselves and other people. The poet W. B. Yeats wrote, "The rhetorician would deceive his neighbors,/The sentimentalist himself." Sentimentality means faked or exaggerated feeling, not genuine emotion. Usually, the rhetorician who wishes to deceive others must first become a sentimentalist who deceives himself. In the advertising business, it is well known that you have to *believe* in your product; so grown men ride the commuter trains believing in the superiority of Hotz over all other cold breakfast cereals. To con others, you begin by conning yourself, or you end that way.

Some propagandists deceive by will. The dangerous con sets out to change minds by slanting the senses of words to *seem* objective and yet to carry a disguised subjective content. News magazines (*Time, Newsweek, U. S. News and World Report*) often convey subtle editorial comment within their reporting. So do newspapers, though newspapers often attempt to keep the editorials editorial, and the news objective. The controversy was raised again in the early seventies on the objectivity, or lack of it, in the news media; even when you appear objective, you can select with bias. One photograph of candidate Y looks flattering; another makes him look like an ass.

We will never destroy bias, but we can attempt to learn to see bias, and not to be deceived by reporting that is really editorializing. A few years back, one news magazine was blatant in its support for one presidential candidate over another. It said so editorially. And in its "news" stories it used the associations of words. Candidate A, they said, "in his rumpled suit slouched into the gleaming limousine." Candidate B, on the other hand, "strode smiling into his black sedan."

Now a sedan may sound expensive, but it may also seem to suit the dignity required of a candidate for high office. "Gleaming limousine" is more lavish, more gloatingly rich. "Rumpled suit" and "smiling" are obvious contrasts. The most telling use of the loaded word is the contrast between "strode" and "slouched." Who could vote for a man who slouched when he could pick one who strode instead? Yet in all fairness, can we say that the *news* in each sentence is different? In Dick and Jane language, the sentence would read, "The man got in the car." The rhetoricians of the news magazine, playing upon the separation between meaning and expression, flash us the sign: "Vote for B!"

They seem to be doing it consciously, though no one can ever be sure of another man's consciousness. More dangerous uses of loaded words, for anyone who wishes to be honest, are the words we kid ourselves with. We use euphemism to persuade ourselves that one thing is really another; a janitor still cleans floors, but it sounds more lofty to be a custodian. When we say that someone is "wealthy," we are avoiding the plainer word "rich," which has acquired overtones of vulgarity. If a real estate agent shows you a two-room shack converted from a chicken-coop, he does not call it a "house," he calls it a "home." A Cadillac is never a "used car"; it is "previously owned."

Often, a euphemism is more abstract or general than the plain word. The euphemism not only sounds fancier (mortician/undertaker; route salesman/milkman) but it has less color or imagery. This loss especially happens when we want to conceal something real. When we have a tomcat castrated, we tend not to admit that we have cut off his testicles, or even castrated him; we have had him "altered." We have a tooth "extracted"; it would be more painful to have it "pulled." The rhetoric of the Vietnam War has been full of abstract euphemisms. "Pacification" meant destroying villages, "Vietnamization" meant using Asians for killing Asians, and withdrawing Americans. A "relocation center" looks very like a concentration camp. We used the word "incursion" in order to avoid calling an invasion an invasion. We used "waste" rather than "kill," perhaps because even in war we need euphemisms to con the conscience. "Terminate with extreme prejudice" became a long and high-sounding expression for an order that could have been expressed in one word: kill.

Politics and political acts of destruction always bring forth the worst in our prose, as we struggle to justify ourselves. Hitler euphemistically labeled his genocide of Jews "the final solution." One of the finest essays on style is George Orwell's "Politics and the English Language"; he says, writing in the forties:

> Millions of peasants are robbed of their farms and sent trudging along the roads with no more than they can carry: this is called *transfer of population* or *rectification of frontiers*. People are imprisoned for years without trial, or shot in the back of the neck or sent to die of scurvy in Arctic lumber camps; this is called *elimination of undesirable elements*. Such phraseology is needed if we want to name things without calling up mental pictures of them. Consider for instance some comfortable English professor defending Russian totalitarianism. [George Orwell was British, and was writing after Stalin's execution of the Kulaks, and the mass murders of the Soviet purges of the late thirties.] He cannot say outright, "I believe in killing off your opponents when you can get good results by doing so." Probably, therefore, he will say something like this:
>
> "While freely conceding that the Soviet regime exhibits certain features which the humanitarian may be inclined to

> deplore, we must, I think, agree that a certain curtailment of the right to political opposition is an unavoidable concomitant of transitional periods, and that the rigors which the Russian people have been called upon to undergo have been amply justified in the sphere of concrete achievement."

Meanwhile, the bullet enters the back of the head. Always be suspicious—as Orwell advises—when the words do not call up a picture. "Terminate with extreme prejudice" does not call to mind the prisoner bound, blindfolded, kneeling, the pistol at the back of his head, the sound, the rush of the body forward, the splatter of brains and blood, but this is what it meant in 1967, when spoken by the CIA.

Avoiding Self-Deceit

So sometimes we use abstractions to avoid or suppress feeling. And sometimes we use words of the senses in dishonest ways, not so much to evade feeling as to twist it. "Slouched" and "strode" are both verbs of action that make us see. We must know in ourselves, by using our brains and our sensitivity, whether the difference between two images is literal description or an emotional nudge disguising itself as objective description. We do not complain that emotions *show*; we complain that the emotions are *disguised*. We do not object to laughter or to anger. We object to laughter that hides anger, expressing gaiety while it means hostility. We can learn to sense the falseness in language—our own or others'—as we learn to sense the falseness of a gesture or a facial expression.

On May 4, 1970, National Guardsmen shot and killed four Kent State University students during a student protest against the American invasion of Cambodia. The first news reports were mixed up, giving the wrong number of dead, including National Guardsmen among the dead, and speaking of sniper fire for which evidence has never been found. False rumors started. Gradually, some facts became clear. But when we know a number of facts, the way in which we present them can be fair or loaded. It is always difficult, when the subject is emotional. Here is Walter Cronkite on CBS (*Evening News*):

> Four students at Kent State University in Ohio are dead, two of them coeds. They were shot during protests against the American presence in Cambodia.

A studious neutrality, it seems. Cronkite adopts the government euphemism, "the American *presence*," in order, we can assume, not to seem to editorialize against the government. But why do we have the phrase, "two of them coeds"? It is *news*. Armed soldiers shooting girls, in May, 1970, is more news than armed soldiers shooting boys. Because of the attitudes of male chauvinism, the word "coed" brings with it old feminine stereotypes: "defenseless," "gentle." I do not question Walter Cronkite's motives or suggest that he should not have included the phrase. I mean to say that even an apparently innocuous fact may be loaded; and that we should try to understand language as intimately as we can.

Time (May 18, 1970) was more obviously loaded: "When National Guardsmen fired indiscriminately into a crowd of unarmed civilians, killing four students, the bullets wounded the nation." The facts appear correct. The final phrase is a metaphor; it is obviously a statement of feeling, rather than of fact; it pretends to be nothing but what it is, and so it is not dishonest. But some of the words earlier in the sentence are more devious. That the soldiers "fired indiscriminately" means literally that they did not pick out targets, a claim that nothing in the evidence supports or denies. But the writer accomplishes something other than the literal meaning. To "fire indiscriminately" is somehow, in the rhetoric of violence, more cruel than to fire discriminately. But what would it have meant—to *Time*, to the people killed, and to the wounded nation—if the soldiers had fired discriminately at what *Time* calls "unarmed civilians"? To fire at "unarmed civilians" is already "indiscriminate," and in fact the *Time* writer uses the word without any denotative meaning at all, but with a connotative expression of indignation that—though we may share the horror and the indignation is loaded.

The phrase "unarmed civilians" is a less blatant example of political rhetoric. They were unarmed, except that a few of them carried rocks, and they were civilians. But "unarmed civilians" is a phrase that calls up the wholly passive faces of men and women led to slaughter—Vietnamese at My Lai, hostages before the Nazi firing squad, victims of firebombing. A more objective phrase would have been something like "students protesting against the war." A phrase loaded from the conservative side might have been "long-haired peaceniks" or "armed rabble."

Collecting Words

So we must watch our words to see if we are using them with respect for honesty of expression. It helps to love words, and a love of words is something that we can develop. The growing writer finds pleasure in becoming a word-collector, picking up, examining, and keeping new words (or familiar words that he sees, suddenly, as if for the first time) like seashells or driftwood. Think of the richness of "hogwash," or the exact strength of "rasp." English is thick with short, strong words. You can collect words from books, of course, but you can also find them in speech; a sense of lively speech adds energy to the best writing. A writer listens to speech—others' and even his own—with a greedy ear. Primitive people and children love words as things in themselves and collect them as ornaments. To become a better writer, rediscover some of the pleasures of words-as-things that you had in your childhood but have probably lost along the way. You patrol the miles of speech looking for words like "flotsam."

Dictionaries can help, too. A thesaurus or a list of synonyms has the limitations mentioned earlier. Brief dictionaries have brief definitions, and though they may light up a dark patch in our reading, they often give such a limited definition of the word, so void of context, that we may misuse it when we try to say it in a sentence. Good-sized college dictionaries carry more information, and can be a pleasure to read. The more information, the better. Sometime, when you are in the library, take down from the shelves one of the thirteen volumes of the *Oxford English Dictionary* and browse a little. The English poet and novelist Robert Graves says only one book is indispensable to the writer's library: the OED. In the thirteen volumes, the authors collect almost all the words you are likely to come across (except for very new words, and words that at the time of publication were considered unprintable), but it is not the completeness that makes it so valuable. It is the contexts. The editors of the OED tried to supply the earliest examples of the use of each word for each shade of meaning.

Suppose we look up the word "vegetable." More than three columns of small print chronicle the life of the word, which began as an adjective meaning "Having the vegetating properties of plants; living and growing as a plant or organism endowed with the lowest form of life." The earliest example is 1400. The poet Lydgate, a couple of decades later, wrote of the wind (spelling modernized): ". . . that is so comfortable/For to nourish things vegetable." When Andrew Marvell wrote "To His Coy Mistress" two and a half centuries later (1678), he used the adjective in the same way: "My vegetable love should grow/Vaster than empires and more slow." Six examples (complete with small context) come between Lydgate and Marvell.

Meanwhile, the noun, "vegetable," got started in 1582, when an author named J. Hester spoke of "The Hidden Vertues of sondrie Vegitables, Animalles, and Mineralles." The reader can discover thirty-six contexts for the word vegetable as a noun from 1582 into modern use—and many shades of meaning. If you take pleasure in words, you will find your sensitivity to the insides of words increasing the more you know the history of words. So much of man's history, external and internal, global and psychic, is coded into his words. The more you know, the more you respect the integrity of the word; integrity means wholeness; the wholeness of a word includes all of its possibilities: its family, its insides.

Words as Blanks

A frequent failure of our language, spoken or written, is our use of words that can mean anything the context requires. These words are like blanks for the reader or listener to fill in. Words of vague praise or blame—"lovely" and "terrible"—are frequent blanks. What does "lovely hair" look like? Is it red or blonde or white or black or brown? Long or short? Liveliness is specificity. Vogue words are usually blanks also. "Dig," "heavy," "cool." "Fink" was popular a few years ago as a vogue word of contempt, no more precise than the "jerk" or "creep" of earlier generations. Yet once "fink" meant something exact: a man employed to join a labor union and spy for bosses. Words of complex history suddenly come into fashion and lose all color.

Words and Meaning

Words used as blanks get in the way of writing and thinking and feeling. Words mean things only by our agreement. If we start using "April" to mean "sunset" or "anything pleasant," it will not be of use to us any more. Our agreements about words are coded into dictionaries, which of course change, as the words shift gradually in meaning because of historical change and the literary genius that adapts old words to new conditions. Our agreements about words are also coded into the dictionary from which we really make our sentences—the dictionary (the computer) of the brain. The dictionary of the brain is even more complicated and useful, for our writing, than the dictionary on the shelf. The thirty thousand associations of the word "April" are there to be used in the right way at the right time. The inside of a word is a huge room of possibilities, limited—because "April" does not include "August" or "catsup" for most of us—but multiple: flowers and showers, Easter, spring, seeds, vacation from school, Chaucer and Browning and "the cruellest month" for readers of poetry, ploughing or manure-spreading for farmers.

Someone might associate April with catsup or cats or soup or a girl in the first grade called April. These associations are private; the few phrases I listed at the end of the last paragraph are public or general. A moment's thought will usually reveal to the writer, at least in revision, whether he is using a word privately or generally. "Tulips like catsup" would be a grotesque and inappropriate simile for most of us—despite the real color—though it might be a spontaneous expression of the writer who privately associated April with catsup. Any writer must learn to suppress the highly private, because it is *always* an assumption basic to good style that your writing will be able to get through to an audience; you are talking to someone besides yourself; you have climbed out of the pure autism of the crib, and are trying to make human contact.

Audience and Self

But we must also remember, in our choice of words, that "an audience" is not "everyone." The larger the audience we try to reach, the more limited our associations become, and the more circumscribed our room of possibilities. If we are writing for the readers of a big newspaper, we probably do not assume that most of our readers associate April with Chaucer, Browning, and Eliot. So an idea of audience is crucial to our choice of words. Everyone makes this sort of choice in conversation: You use words with your best friend that you do not use with your grandmother; hitchhiking a ride with a white-haired man wearing a blue suit, your words probably are different from those you would use if the driver wore sunglasses, bell-bottoms, and long hair. If your vocabulary stays the same, chances are that you are being hostile in the sacred name of honesty.

In writing we make the same choices. If we write a letter to the college newspaper, we choose the words from a pool different from the one we use when we write a thank-you letter to an aunt. The term paper in business administration requires a different vocabulary from the term paper in literature.

The difficult, necessary task is to adjust your vocabulary to your audience with tact, humility, and appropriateness—but without hypocrisy, without being false. Sometimes it is merely a matter of common sense. If you are writing for an audience from the southern hemisphere, you must remember that April connotes autumn and leaves falling; not green and seeds sprouting. But common sense is easy, compared to the difficulties of learning the difference between appropriate tact and gross hypocrisy. When Jim Beck wrote his first essay, about "well-rounded individuals" and so on (Chapter I, page 7), he was writing *for* an assumed audience, and *against* himself. Probably at that moment he did not believe that he could write with honesty for an audience that was a teacher. Probably for Jim Beck, no vocabularies were available at that moment except the words of high-minded hypocrisy, and the words of the boys in the locker room or the dorm, which can be just as hypocritical and one-sided as graduation oratory. By learning to write with more respect for himself, for his own feelings told in his own words, he learned to write with honesty, and to face things with honesty. By becoming aware of the insides of words, he learned a lot about the insides of Jim Beck; and he learned to make the inside outside—to *write*.

EXERCISES

1. Find four words similar in meaning, like imitate/emulate/copy/ape, or false/fake/phoney/insincere, and discuss the varieties of meaning. A thesaurus or a dictionary of synonyms will help you find a list.

2. Take two or three sentences of good prose from the Bible or Hemingway, or the sentences quoted from John Updike on pages 26–27, or from Norman Mailer on pages 25–26. Using a thesaurus, rewrite the passage by substituting a "synonym" for each of the words. (See the example on page 29.)

3. Collect five words that interest you, and write a paragraph about each of them, as if you were writing the catalogue of an exhibition of paintings or a museum of dinosaurs.

4. Collect five words used as blanks (see page 37). Find their original meanings in the dictionary. Read the history of the word in the *Oxford English Dictionary*. Write a note on the decline of each word.

5. In the following paragraphs, find words that the author uses brilliantly—the way John Updike uses "adhesively" or "slice"—and defend your choices.

I had thought I should be glad to see France in February, 1954, when I arrived at Calais from England, but, looking out the window of the boat-train in the late winter afternoon, I was seized by a sharp irritation. It was cold in the car, and the weather was dismal: a damp mist over graying snow. This landscape—such a waste in itself—was littered with the wreckage of bombings, which reminded me of the wreckage of Italy in the summer of 1945. Nine years later, in France, these buildings had not been rebuilt nor the rubbish even cleared away. It reminded me, also, of the winter of 1917, when, a soldier in the American Expeditionary Force, I had made the long journey from Le Havre to Vittel in a crowded and unheated box-car through a similarly dismal countryside similarly damp with mist. Later on, I had flopped with my company on narrow army cots in a palatial and freezing chamber, where our breaths went up as steam.

Edmund Wilson, A Piece of My Mind

The top of the hill, pasture for one straggly cow, was clear of brush except for patches of dark juniper, in spreading flat circles ten feet across. Around the tumbled stone walls tall pines and maples held off an advancing army of small gray birch. At one side, by the bouldery path that had once been a town road, a little family graveyard lay on slightly tilted ground. A deer trail ran right through it, bright and twisting between the slate stones, and a birch had fallen and rotted out of its bark, leaving a print like a white hand.

Thomas Williams, Town Burning

6. Using advertising and political writing or any other source handy, find three examples of loaded words. Describe the way the authors use the words to deceive others, or themselves, or both.

7. How honest or direct is the political prose in the following passages about the Kent State killings? Be particular in your argument, and be wary of your own political bias.

Universities Must Oust Hooligans
a. Ohio will no longer tolerate its state universities being used as sanctuaries by lawbreaking hooligans who destroy, terrorize and burn and then seek protection in the academic community.

That was the major message of Gov. James Rhodes, who visited Kent Sunday morning and termed the rioting in Kent as the worst the state has suffered.

. . .

The acts of violence in Kent and on campus during the past two days are so serious as to merit the sternest repression: store windows broken and store owners threatened; a campus building burned, fire hoses cut and firemen and policemen pelted with bricks, stones and bottles. . . .

from the Kent-Ravenna Record-Courier
(published on the day of the killings
but written before them)

b. What is clear, however, is that the KSU massacre fits the pattern of increasing repression at home. Because the U.S. is losing the war in Vietnam, it must run a tight ship at home. The connection between protests against the war and the course of the war itself is inextricable, and this was certainly true at KSU. The U.S. has declared war on black people for many years now. The massacre at Kent State may signal its declaration of war against young people.

Here at KSU, 20,000 sons and daughters of Middle Amerika have been thrust into the belly of the warring monster. For some it will be an unforgettable, yet momentary, exposure, but for others (quite a few thousand others) it will be the beginning of a struggle to destroy that monster.

from the *Berkeley Tribe*, May 8–16, 1970

VERBS

Action, and the Choice of Style

Verbs act. Verbs move. Verbs do. Verbs strike, soothe, grin, cry, exasperate, decline, fly, hurt, and heal. Verbs make writing go, and they matter more to our language than any other part of speech.

Verbs give energy, if we use them with energy. We could have said, "Verbs are action. Verbs are motion. Verbs are doing." But if we had written the sentences in this second way, we would have written dull prose. We could have gone even further into dullness, and written, "Verbs are words that are characterized by action."

Try to use verbs that act. Yet we must realize the implications of this advice. The implications involve commitment to a kind of thought that will not always be possible; and so the exhortation is relative and not absolute; sometimes you will need to write verbs that are less than active. If there are no synonyms, also there are no two sentences that mean the same thing but are different only in style. A change of style, however slight, is always a change of meaning, however slight. Is it, therefore, *possible* to make a stylistic generalization at all? Does it mean anything to ask people to use active verbs, when sometimes active verbs will not mean what people wish to say? The vagueness or approximateness of some weak constructions may represent accurately a reservation in the speaker's mind.

The generalization remains possible, with explanation and with room for exception. Both explanations and exceptions will follow, in these chapters on verbs and nouns, but let us start with a generalized explanation. Passives and weak verbs most of the time evade precision and commitment. Examples follow, in which weak verbs add static to statement, and in which passives avoid being wrong by evading definite statement. These habits fuzz our prose with bad brain fuzz. To recommend, in a book on style, that we use active forms of active verbs, is to recommend energy and clarity, definite statement and commitment.

Verbs with Nouns and Adjectives

Usually, a single verb is stronger and better than a strung-out verb-and-adjective or verb-and-noun combination. People say, "I am aware of this fact," or even, "I am cognizant of this situation," when they could have said, "I know it." In these examples, we have a weak verb-and-adjective followed by a noun that means little, but appears to end the sentence, to give the verb an object. The phrases mean something different from "I know it," but the difference in meaning is mere pomposity. "I am aware of the fact" differs from "I know it" because it shows us that the speaker thinks well of himself; he sounds like a professor trying to put down another professor who has tried to put him down. "I am cognizant of the situation" is so pompous it may sound ironical; it would usually fall from the lips, or leak from the pen, of someone diffident about his intellectual status, like a television executive.

So look out for the verbs be/is/are and has/have in combination with nouns and adjectives. See if you do not gain by using the verb itself, clear and clean. "He looked outside and became aware of the fact that it was raining" revises easily into "He looked outside and saw that it was raining" or, more simply, "He looked outside. It was raining." Instead of "We had a meeting," try "We met." The meaning is different, slightly, but if the second phrase is accurate, we save three syllables and add energy to our prose; when we cut to the essential motion, we add vitality. Less is more, in prose as in architecture. Instead of "They were decisive about the question of . . . ," try "They decided to. . . ."

Now "to be decisive"—if we look at the insides of words—means something quite different from "to decide." The person who "is decisive" has vigor and intellectual intensity; he cuts through the uncertainties that surround a question, and makes a choice firmly and quickly. If you are describing a committee meeting in which, after long discussion, the members reached a consensus or took a vote and decided to do something, "they decided" is the clearest phrase to use.

"They reached a decision" wastes words, probably; it does imply that it took some work "to arrive at the decision," which by itself would imply more ease, and less struggle, than "reached." So if you feel that the meaning requires "reached" or "arrived," you must use the accurate word. But, certainly, in writing about the committee meeting described above, "They were decisive about . . ." would be misuse of words. They weren't decisive at all. They decided. Most of the time, when we use a wordy noun/adjective-verb phrase, we are merely trying to *sound* more complicated. Most of the time, the shade of meaning in "reached" or "arrived" is not needed. We use the longer phrase just to *seem* to be considering fine points. The sensible rule: Use the shorter, more direct verb ("They decided") except when the longer variation has a precision that your meaning requires. "They talked about lowering the voting age for two days, without coming to a conclusion. Then Senator Jensen returned from a junket. He spoke briefly. He was decisive. The measure carried by a two-thirds majority."

Verbs with Participles

The same advice applies to phrases that use verb forms ending in -ing (present participles). "They were meeting to discuss" can often become "They met to discuss," and "He is clearing his throat" becomes "He clears his throat." But the participle is different in meaning—it makes a different sort of time—and therefore it can be useful when we mean it. "She'll be comin' 'round the mountain" has more incipient motion in it than "She'll come 'round the mountain." Participles imply continuing action. Just be sure that you *intend* the difference, and are not just lazy. Apparently the mind finds it easier to be pale than to be colorful. Or maybe the mind finds it easier to avoid the extra vocabulary of verbs, sticking to "be" and "has" with a complete set of nouns and adjectives. Whatever the reason, when we add little words like "is" and "has" to participles, adjectives, and nouns, usually we thin our prose into impalpability.

The Passive Mood

When most writers use the passive, they usually subtract meaning from their prose. We say, "A message was received," instead of "they" (or "I" or "you" or "we" or "he" or "she") "received a message." We suppress identity, which is a particular, and we put hazy distance between implied subject and definite action. The passive voice avoids responsibility, as we sometimes claim that "a dish was dropped in the kitchen," rather than name the dropper. It diminishes a sentence by omitting a doer. So it can be very useful politically: "Napalm was dropped yesterday on structures in a fire-free zone near the DMZ." And sometimes we use the passive from diffidence, or modesty, or false modesty, or all three. It waters the soup. We sound as if we wrote labels for medicine bottles. "Doses may be administered three times daily. Dosage recommended for adults is. . . ." So a depressed writer on a gray day, describing a scene, might say, "The tree was observed to be an elm. Leaves were seen falling. It was assumed that the season was autumn." Scientific prose uses the passive by convention, establishing an impersonal tone. Sometimes writers on nonscientific subjects achieve a pseudoscientific tone by using the passive.

Occasionally the passive is right, or unavoidable. Passives are used in a textbook that advises against passives.

> The author uses passives in the text.

> The text uses passives.

> Passives are used in the text.

In some context, the third sentence might be best. The second is most terse, but it involves a metaphor—the text must be compared to a person, if it *uses* something—which may weaken it. The first correctly says that the author does the using, but it would be intrusive in some contexts to state the subject when the subject is perfectly obvious; it would be overexplained, and wordy. So it might be better to use the passive in order to avoid the troubles of the other sentences, as the least of three evils.

Sometimes the passive is useful because we do not know the identity of the doer, and the passive (especially if it is rare) can imply this ignorance; and this ignorance is part of the meaning of the sentence. Suppose this were the start of a story:

> He walked into his bedroom. Clothes lay in heaps on the floor. Dresser drawers lay upside down on the rug, their contents scattered.

It is a description of a scene, most of it in the active voice, with inanimate objects (clothes, dresser drawers) doing active things (lay, lay upside down). It is terse, but it implies no reason for the scene, and no response to it. The active voice in this passage is less meaningful than the passive would be:

> He walked into the room. Clothes were heaped on the floor. Dresser drawers were dumped on the rug, and their contents had been scattered.

The scene is the same. We still don't know who did it. But the passive sentences after the active first sentence implies that someone else, unknown, has done the damage. It only *implies* it, it does not *state* it, but the implication is real, and further implies some shock on his part. We sense that the second and third sentences are versions of what happens in his mind as he enters the room: "I've been robbed!" To make this last sentence active would sound artificial: "Someone has robbed me!" It would sound as if the writer were taking as *absolute* the injunction to avoid the passive, which is only a sensible, general rule.

Good writers use the passive for variety of sentence structure, too. Rarely, but they do. In a paragraph about two groups taking opposite sides on an issue, in which the sentences have all used the active mood, the author looking for stylistic variety might insert a sentence, "Arguments were put forward, on both sides, which would make a goat blush." When you decide to use a passive for variety, only be certain that you are not using it for any of the reasons that make passives bad: diffidence, false modesty, evasion of responsibility, or the imitation of scientific respectability.

Particular Verbs

I have been writing all along as if there were two classes of verbs: strong ones and weak ones. Of course language is more complicated than that, and not only because sometimes weak is better than strong, as I have argued. Some strong verbs are stronger than others. "He moved" is stronger than "He was in motion." But in a context that admits it, we might say with greater strength, "he crept," or "he slid," or "he hurtled." We would almost always want to say "He crept" rather than, "He moved, creeping." (A difference of meaning might, once, make the second phrase useful.) The first verbs I listed, in the paragraph that starts this chapter, are general verbs: do, move, act. The second series is particular, and more colorful. Energy lies often in small shades of difference, rather than in the opposites of "She was in motion" and "She slithered."

Invisible Verbs

In the first chapter, we read academic jargon from the prospectus for a Ph.D. dissertation. Later in the prospectus, the candidate wrote a sentence in which he particularly misuses verbs; in fact, he manages to write almost *without* verbs:

> Illustrative of what Kornhauser means by constraint imposed on professionals in organizations are the findings of Leo Meltzer in a survey of 3,084 physiologists in the United States.

The sentence has no strong and active verbs. "Means" is the closest. "Illustrative" is an adjective substituted for a verb. "Imposed" is a past participle that suppresses responsibility. "Are" is boring.

To rewrite the sentence in a language not far from the original, but with more vigor and clarity, we can simply cut and rearrange:

> Leo Meltzer questioned 3,084 physiologists in the United States; his findings illustrate Kornhauser's contention that organizations constrain professionals.

Maybe "surveyed" is more accurate than "questioned," but "surveyed" smells of jargon.

The last sentence of this revision may not mean what the original author had in mind. Did he mean that the institution imposed the constraint, or that something else, unnamed, chose people in organizations, rather than others, to impose restraint on? The ambiguity of the original passage is real, and serves no function; it is merely unclear. The second version is clearer, though without context it still raises questions. What is this constraint? What desires are held back? Does the author mean "constrain" as restraint or as compulsion? Does he mean all organizations—like YMCA's, universities, corporations, fraternities, bridge clubs, and nations—or specifically professional ones, like the American Association of University Professors, the Modern Language Association, or the American Medical Association? The price of clarity is vigor with detail. Verbs are the most vigorous parts of speech; by particularity, they add to detail.

False Color in Verbs

The search for particularity and color can become obvious, and the prose look silly. In the examples that follow, the faults do not lie in the verbs alone, but in the whole style. However, verbs are at the center of the action in our prose, for good or for ill. In the play, *The Owl and the Pussycat*, a would-be novelist reads the first page of his manuscript to the girl who has invaded his apartment. When he starts by saying the sun "spat" on his protagonist, she flies into a rage. So should we. Men's action-magazines are full of examples of Methedrine prose, violence done to language in the name of violence:

> Hurtt scraped the scum from his lips and dug his finger into his nose. He scraped out a hunk of snot and snapped it at her. Then he grimaced, swung his fist, and crunched her teeth into her gums.

Tough writing is not the only kind of bad overwriting. Maybe pretty writing is worse. It is Liberace prose, and it can rely on verbs for its nasty work, too.

> Songbirds trilled out my window, vines curled at the eaves, buds cocked their green noses through the ground, squirrels danced in dandelions, and Spring drenched the day with gladness.

Often a beginning writer tries to make his verbs of dialogue too specific: "he whimpered," "she snapped." Almost always it looks too strenuous. We should use "said," or nothing at all, most of the time. The trick is energy with appropriateness. We may need to learn to do too much before we can learn to do it right. After considering the importance of verbs, one student wrote this passage in his next theme:

> The train slammed to a stop in the station. Steam vomited from all apertures. Passengers gushed through the barriers and hurtled into the night.

It was a useful exercise, because the student was searching through the words available to him for energetic verbs. The color was in excess of the actions colored, like photographs in advertisements for food. Steam gushing out at the base of an engine is not *like* vomiting; "vomiting" is too sick and unpleasant and bad smelling a word; the writer uses it only for the sake of its power, and not for what it contributes to the picture. Though the general advice—to choose color over pallor, energy over lethargy—holds true, one matter overrides all others, in any discussion of style, the matter of appropriateness: context is all.

Fancy Verbs

Some verbs are too fancy for normal use. Writers use them when they think their prose ought to wear fancy clothes. "Depict" is usually inferior to "paint" or "draw" or "describe." "He depicted a scene of unparalleled magnitude." (W. C. Fields/thesaurus talk again.) Maybe that means, "He painted a big picture," or "He told a good story," or half a dozen other things, but its real meaning is its would-be fanciness. It is a sentence admiring itself in the mirror. "Emulate" would usually be fancy for "copy," "ascertain" for "make sure," and "endeavor" for "try."

Made-Up Verbs

Then there are the made-up words, which sound fancy to the people who use them. When we are tempted to say "finalize," we would do better to say "end" or "finish." In general, we should avoid verbs made of an adjective and an -ize; "personalize" is another. Advertising and politics have created many crude verbs, sometimes using nouns as bases instead of adjectives; not long ago, we had to learn to pronounce "Vietnamization." Some good old English verbs end in -ize. "Scrutinize," deriving from the noun "scrutiny," is a useful verb. "Finalize," on the other hand, is used to sound fancier than "finish" or "end," to give false complexity to a simple act. Therefore it is bad style, pretending to be something that it isn't, a form of euphemism. The writer should search the language for the simplest and most direct way of saying and expressing; he should never make up a new word when an old one will do.

EXERCISES

1. Here are seven passages of prose. Analyze their use and misuse of verbs.

a. John was the son of a prostitute and a naval officer. He lived with his mother until he was six, when he was transferred to his father's care. He was transported into a completely different world. His father, who had not married, sent him to a public school where he did well until, unexpectedly, he failed his university entrance exam. Thereupon he was drafted into the Navy, but failed to become an officer. His father, who was a very exacting man, had been somewhat upset by his son's failure at university level, but was much more upset by his failure to become an officer, and it drew from him the remark that he did not think he could be his son at all. When, in the next few months,

John disgraced himself as a sailor in a number of ways, his father told him plainly that he was not his son any more, and that he now knew he never had been. He formally disowned him.

During his early months in the Navy, John was noted to get into states of anxiety, and it was on the grounds of anxiety neurosis that he had been turned down as an officer. Subsequently, however, his behaviour earned the label of psychopathic delinquent, and it was out of keeping with his "character" hitherto. When his father disowned him his deviance escalated to what was called an acute manic psychosis. His basic premise had become: *he could be anyone he wanted, merely by snapping his fingers.*

R. D. Laing, *Self and Others*

b. But there is an aspect of the crystal of our nature that eschews the harness, scorns sublimation, and demands to be seen in its raw nakedness, crying out to us for the sight and smell of blood. The vehemence with which we deny this obvious fact of our nature is matched only by our Victorian hysteria on the subject of sex. Yet, we deny it in vain. Whether we quench our thirst from the sight of a bleeding Jesus on the Cross, from the ritualized sacrifice in the elevation of the Host and the consecration of the Blood of the Son, or from bullfighting, cockfighting, dogfighting, wrestling, or boxing, spiced with our Occidental memory and heritage of the gladiators of Rome and the mass spectator sport of the time of feeding Christians and other enemies of society to the lions in the Coliseum—whatever the mask assumed by the impulse, the persistent beat of the drum over the years intones the chant: Though Dracula and Vampira must flee the scene with the rising of the sun and the coming of the light, night has its fixed hour and darkness must fall.

Eldridge Cleaver, *Soul on Ice*

c. And she lifted her hands and danced again, to annul him, the light glanced on her knees as she made her slow, fine movements down the far side of the room, across the firelight. He stood away near the door in blackness of shadow, watching, transfixed. And with slow, heavy movements she swayed backwards and forwards, like a full ear of corn, pale in the dusky afternoon, threading before the firelight, dancing his non-existence, dancing herself to the Lord, to exultation.

D. H. Lawrence, *The Rainbow*

d. A machine gun lashed at him from across the river, and he ducked in his hole. In the darkness, it spat a vindictive white light like an acetylene torch, and its sound was terrifying. Croft was holding himself together by the force of his will. He pressed the trigger of his gun and it leaped and bucked under his hand. The tracers spewed wildly into the jungle on the other side of the river.

Norman Mailer, *The Naked and the Dead*

e. Kornhauser's is not, perhaps, a very unique theory; it addresses itself, nonetheless, to an abidingly important problem. It is a cliché to note that academe values expertise: Those whose work orientation and professional commitment are to expertise are sought after in the academic community. Unless professional allegiance and commitment to the highest possible standards obtain, professional performance is dampened. A different way of expressing it might be: If the artist-teacher is not more committed to his art and artistic integrity than to the unprofessional practicalities required of him in order to receive his paycheck, then it is doubtful whether he is the kind of exemplar of artistic sensibility and integrity to which the teaching organization wishes its students exposed. On the other hand, there is a level of professional recalcitrance which becomes intolerable to the organization. The goal, then, is to achieve, insofar as possible, a workable reciprocal accommodation between the professional and the organization in which he participates. *Ideally*, one would seek to minimize any dysfunctional strain and tension between the two, while maximizing both professional autonomy and organizational output.

from a prospectus for a dissertation

f. Cohn's book is neither literary nor circumspect—it is for the most part a venture in sheer indignation, which I judge to be deserved. But why is he the perennial target? Cui bono? I have never been satisfied with the thesis that his sometime exposure of the prosecutor's father's shortsighted decision to turn over our dollar-producing engravings to the Soviet Union while he was Treasury secretary at war's end in 1945 was a plausible source for a filial animosity, which is undeniable. Nor is it persuasive to me that because Roy Cohn and Bobby Kennedy came close to a fist-fight during the Army-McCarthy hearings that encounter generated a Catonic resolution by the future attorney-general to come up with the final solution to the Roy Cohn problem.

William F. Buckley, Jr. "Roy Cohn's Book"

How Service Is Delivered

g. The service shall be delivered in the following manner: Immediately before commencing to serve, the Server shall stand with both feet at rest behind the base line, and within the imaginary continuation of the center mark and side line of the singles court. The Receiver may stand wherever he pleases behind the service line on his own side of the net. The server shall then throw the ball into the air and strike it with his racket before it hits the ground. Delivery shall be deemed complete at the moment the racket strikes the ball.

Official Tennis Rules

2. Look through your own writing—old themes or daily writing —and find a paragraph that can be improved by strengthening the verbs. Copy out the old version, and revise it. (You will find yourself changing other words as well as verbs; but pay closest attention to verbs.)

3. Find three objectionable passives in different places: cereal boxes, newspapers, this book, your college catalogue, or any set of directions. Discuss how these passives fail, and rewrite the sentences with active verbs. Then find two passives that are necessary or useful. Explain why.

4. Find—in a book of essays, a newspaper, or any public source —three weak verb-noun or verb-adjective combinations. Rewrite them by substituting a strong verb for each phrase. Then tell how the meaning or effect of the passage changes. Discuss two weak verb-phrases that you believe are justified by their context.

5. Here is a list of fancy verbs. Find simpler verbs that would usually do better.

masticate
cogitate
commence
expectorate
perspire

6. Here is a list of verbs chosen for varieties of tone and degrees of color. With each of them, find alternatives, near-synonyms, that might work better in a specific context. For an example, remember the differences between emulate/imitate/copy/ape discussed on pages 28–29. A thesaurus or dictionary may help you find alternates. Make up a context for each of the verbs—listed and discovered—in which the verb feels appropriate.

clutch
exterminate
rattle
cook
act

7. Take one of the following passages of prose, and write two parodies of it. Be consistent in parodying two of these categories:

(a) pseudo-intellectual jargon, with passives and weak verb-phrases; (b) supercolor, straining for effect, like the examples on pages 46–47; (c) fancy, like a social climber, or like the medicine man using big words to con the small-towners.

a. There under a spotlight, two Oriental gentlemen in natty blue suits were doing some amazing things with yo-yos. Tiny, neat men, no bigger than children, they stared abstractedly off into space while yo-yos flew from their hands, zooming in every direction as if under their own power, leaping out from small fists in arcs, circles, and straight lines. I stared open-mouthed as a yo-yo was thrown down and *stayed down*, spinning at the end of its string a fraction of an inch above the floor.

Frank Conroy, *Stop-Time*

b. Dante put all of the patriotic Italians of his day into Hell, and showed them boiling, roasting and writhing on hooks. Cervantes drew such a devastating picture of the Spain that he lived in that it ruined the Spaniards. Shakespeare made his heroes foreigners and his clowns Englishmen. Goethe was in favor of Napoleon. Rabelais, a citizen of Christendom rather than of France, raised a cackle against it that Christendom is still trying in vain to suppress. Swift, having finished the Irish and then the English, proceeded to finish the whole human race. The exceptions are few and far between, and not many of them will bear examination.

H. L. Mencken, "The Artist"

c. I studied the next shot with care. I took out a pitching wedge, a club I felt easy with; but as I stood over the ball, bringing back the club, my old terror of being an unwieldy machine swept over me, and I *shanked* the shot, dumping it into a trap off to one side of the green. The ball skidded off almost at a diagonal. The silence was absolute until I broke it with a strained cry, as if after the first two superb shots the absurdity of the third was unbelievable—like two graceful ballet steps, and then a splay-legged pratfall, a thump and a high squawk of dismay.

I stalked miserably into the trap, and, not catching enough sand with my wedge, I lifted the ball into a grove of pines on the other side of the green. I was still about 40 yards away, just the distance I'd been two strokes back. The ball was stymied in the pines, and it took me two more strokes to get out.

"Pick it up," Bruno called petulantly. "There's no use." He himself had bogeyed the hole. We had started off the tournament by losing one stroke to par on the easiest hole on the peninsula.

"I'm awful sorry," I said to Bruno.

"I told your caddy to stick that pitching wedge in the bag and leave it there," he said. "You had a clear line. You should've rolled it up there with a four or a five iron—a pitch-and-run shot." He shook his head.

"I'm not so hot on those," I said. "I've always felt comfortable with that wedge."

"We'll get going," he said more cheerfully. "Hell, we've got 53 holes to go."

George Plimpton, *The Bogey Man*

NOUNS

Particularity and Choosing a Style

If verbs supply the energy that makes prose go, nouns are its body. Without nouns, nothing would be doing the going. Nouns are the simplest parts of speech, the words least tricky to use. Nouns are the names of things, "things" in the broadest sense: table, elm, Nancy, rain, noun, Centerville, nation, hunger, nine o'clock.

Many of the generalizations that apply to verbs apply to nouns also. We prefer as a rule the specific, the sensual, the strong, the simple, and the colorful over the abstract, the general, the polysyllabic, and the fancy. We prefer "elm" to "tree," "Nancy" to "girl," and "nine o'clock" to "evening." The more particular the noun, the clearer the pictures we make, and the more accurate we can be in representing feelings. When a student wrote,

> I remembered a group of flowers that grew on some land near a relative's house . . .

he changed it to:

> I remembered a patch of daisies that grew on a meadow near my Cousin Annie's farm . . .

and the particularity is all gain. The first example was not bad style, but it was pale prose. The second by comparison is vivid.

But these generalizations exist "as a rule," and we must express reservations. Sometimes the more general noun is more accurate and honest than the specific one. From a distance, you see "a man" or "a woman," not "a sophomore" or "a mechanic." "Town" may be more appropriate, in the right context, than "Centerville," though it is less specific. We must keep in mind the injunction to be specific; but, as ever, we must be wary that our injunctions do not lead us into absurdity. A student revised some daily writing into:

> On Tuesday afternoon, October thirteenth, I read a sentence half-way down the first page of *War and Peace* which . . .

Maybe in a particular context, such extreme specificity would be useful, but usually it would sound overly precise.

Also, we must remember again that the advice to cultivate one kind of style, at the expense of another, means thinking or seeing things in special ways. *A change of style, however slight, is always a change of meaning, however slight.* So for some types of writing, like a scientific summary, or a paper in philosophy, an injunction to "Be particular!" and "Avoid abstraction!" is worse than useless; it is destructive.

> The existence theorem states, "To prove the existence of a something one must first present evidence of that something and its existence acceptable to other minds." The nonexistence theorem states, "As long as one assumes the nonexistence of a something one will assume that the signals from the something either do not exist, are noise, are created in another human mind, or come from some mindless process in nature." Therefore, if an unknown mind without a visible, detectable body sends signals, we ignore them, repress memories of having received them, attribute them to noise, or attribute them to a mindless but systematically varying source, or say that they are the results of faulty operation of the observer, i.e., projections from the observer's own mind.
>
> John Cunningham Lilly, *The Mind of the Dolphin*

Lilly is writing a vigorous argumentative prose, which must be abstract. So must books about prose style, for that matter.

The wise advice is simply to be as particular as the context allows us. Too often, we are vague and general, when we would say much more by discovering the concrete. Instead of saying,

> When it got cold the animals looked for shelter.

we could convey much more by a particularity:

> In October there was frost; the sheep huddled in one corner of the barn for warmth, the cattle in another.

Abstract and Particular

There are degrees of difference between the noun at an extreme of abstraction and the noun at an extreme of particularity. But I think we can most usefully talk of three degrees, the abstract, the general, and the particular. For example, take "animal, dog, spaniel." One might go further into particularity by adding a proper name, or age, or color, or by naming a breed of spaniel—all requiring more words. One might go higher in generality to "organism" or sideways into scientific classification with "quadruped." These threesomes can be quite relative. We can list three words which are all abstract but which become more nearly specific: "emotion, love, lust." The writer could use "lust" not as one of the seven deadly sins, but as an embodiment of the general "love"; he might have said "desire" or "eros," but "lust" seemed clearer.

The more abstract a noun, the more difficult it is to use well. Words like "emotion" (or "love," for that matter) or "courage" or "hatred" or "responsibility." To make these nouns work, you must provide the context of anecdote or analogy; you must put flesh on the bones. Usually an adjective in front of an abstraction does not do the work. The abstraction is lazy, retrieved by the writer from the attic of Big Ideas, and the adjective strives to do all the work; but adjectives themselves often are weak, and so we have two weaklings failing to open the door that one strong noun could burst open. "Love" is thin and airy; it is pretty, but what is it about? Our affection for a pet salamander? The grandfather for his granddaughter? Bert's obsession with the character of Charles Dickens? Mark and Nancy in the Oldsmobile? Married affection? "Love" is a grab-bag of possibilities, only a bit less abstract than "emotion" or "feeling." If we modify it with the adjective "intense," we narrow its possibilities a little, but we do not really localize it. If we speak of "young love," we are more particular—and yet we move toward cliché. Many clichés are adjective-noun combinations in which the adjective is a desperate, although habitual, attempt to rescue a bland abstraction with a particular adjective; "blind faith," for example.

Abstractions are usually lazy. The writer finds it easier to label the general category of a feeling than to search out the particulars that embody the feeling. Sight, taste, smell, touch, hearing carry feeling from writer to reader—not concepts. (And most writers using abstractions, we should notice instantly, are not using concepts as a philosopher does, but vaguely and inaccurately.) Usually, we talk best about "love" when we do not use the word at all. If we use "Nancy," and "Centerville," and "a 1969 Pontiac," and "rain," and "nine o'clock," and connect them with strong verbs, the reader may know what we mean by the big hazy word "love"—in this time and in this place.

"Time" and "place" are abstractions. Are they used appropriately here? Sometimes the abstract affords a setting for the concrete, as a black velvet background shows up diamonds. In other contexts, instead of "time" and "place" we would want to use more specific words—steering wheel, September, elm, Long Lake Road.

Abstractions: Beginnings and Endings

An abstraction can be explained by a context or an anecdote. Some abstraction or generalization is necessary to any conceptual or argumentative writing. Only fiction, poetry, and autobiography can be free of it, and they do not always stay free. When we revise an essay, we should look most carefully to eliminate abstractions at two points—beginnings and endings. Frequently, we introduce a subject with an abstraction, "I am going to tell a story that illustrates inequality," and then we tell a story that illustrates inequality. If the illustration is clear, the introductory abstraction was unnecessary; what is more, it was probably distracting. When you announce that you are going to tell a funny joke before you tell it, you take the humor away. Let the idea of inequality arise in the reader's mind—by name or not—from the detail of your anecdote, and it will be much more powerful. Telling the reader the meaning of what he is going to hear bullies him; he is likely to resist.

Similarly, we often trail off an anecdote with an abstraction. Having told a perfectly clear story, we end, "which is an illustration of the inequality so prevalent today." Don't nudge your reader in the ribs, saying, "In case you didn't get it, this is what I mean." When we summarize abstractly, we show a lack of confidence in our own writing, and in the reader's intelligence. Of course some stories need interpreting; they are therefore usually less valuable material. If the road is clear, do not put up road markers; they are good only for stumbling over.

Invisible Nouns

So far, we have been talking about degrees of particularity and color, and we have admitted that some prose needs abstractions. The

Preacher could not have said, "All is vanity," if there had been an enforced commandment against abstractions. But some nouns are almost always useless. These nouns are invisible. When someone says, "The snow is gray in color," what is the phrase "in color" doing? It doesn't do anything for meaning or particularity. Maybe it has a connotation that reflects on the speaker, though not on the snow. Maybe it contains a message informing us that the speaker is precise, academic, and pompous.

Words like "nature" and "character," which have perfectly good uses, turn up invisibly in pale prose. Probably the snow was gray in color because of the urban nature of the environment, and the frigid character of the weather.

We use invisible nouns with adjectives—much as we use invisible verbs like "be" and "do" and "has" with adjectives or nouns—to make a sentence *sound* grander than it really is, or because we lack the vocabulary. Whatever the reason, we abuse the language. Some other nouns we render invisible: "sense," "kind," "action," "situation," "respect," "regard," "case," and "element." Look at this piece of prose from the annual report of a large corporation:

> The President is pleased to report that, despite the unusual nature of the fiscal situation in the past twelve months, earnings have risen substantially above the margin foreseen by the Treasurer's Report of March, 1971. In a marketing sense, the profitable character of the corporation proved itself under trying circumstances.

"Circumstances" is another invisible noun—at least invisible as it is used here.

Making Bad Nouns from Verbs

The sensible writer chooses the plain noun, if it is adequate, over the fancy one, and he chooses the old noun rather than making up a new one. In the last chapter I mentioned the verb "finalize," which had been wrenched out of an adjective; it has been wrenched further into a noun; now and then we run across "finalization," when "end" or "finish" or maybe "finality" would do. There are no limits to what some unstylists will say. "Scrutiny" is a fine noun; "scrutinize," is a necessary and traditional verb. But recently a young man wrote on an application form that he submitted documents "for your scrutinization." The word means nothing more than "scrutiny"; it must have sounded more respectable to this writer.

Or maybe his vocabulary failed him. He remembered the verb "scrutinize" but he forgot the noun "scrutiny." So he made up a new noun out of the verb. When you are tempted to make up a new noun from a verb, go to the dictionary first. You know "unify"; when tempted to create "unifization," go to the dictionary and you will find "unity" and "unification"—and clarity, and a more eloquent prose.

Fancy Nouns

Reading bad prose, we find thousands of common examples of pomposity or fanciness, either neologisms like "scrutinization," or polysyllabic alternatives to simple words, like "domicile" for house or "cessation" for "end." These words parallel verbs like "masticate," substituted for "chew." The fanciness may arise from diffidence or ignorance or pretension or whatever; the result is the same; fanciness separates the thing described and the mental act of perceiving it. Feelings keep their distance. It is by fancy abstractions and by clichés that Orwell's Communist professor is able to discuss without feelings the murder of innocent people.

Revising Nouns

In revising, we should look for the lazy abstraction, as well as the invisible noun, the neologism, and the merely fancy noun, and remove them when we find them. Removing them leaves a hole, which we can fill with other nouns, or with phrases, to specify and bring down to earth the airiness of the word we started with. Lazy abstractions are like clichés and jargon—and the three are usually discovered together—because they are instantly available to the tongue; they lie heaped together with clichés in the foreroom of the brain; we do not have to search for them with our intelligence, or dream for them with our imaginations. Here is a passage from a paper:

> Financial problems were coming to a head in my family last spring and we didn't know if my sister and I could have the benefit of higher education. Then my grandfather got the surprise of his life when a large amount of money came his way when he least expected it. He got a sum from the VA which he didn't know was coming him. Through his generosity, we were enabled to arrange payment for tuition.

As usual with faulty prose, the faults do not lie in one part of speech alone. Some hunks of cliché are ready-made—"coming to a head," "financial problems," "benefit of higher education," "surprise of his life," "when he least expected it," "arrange payment"—and combine with a dozen other signs of lazy thinking and evasion of feeling. Think of the reality of emotion—the anxiety, the jubilation in a family—which these phrases obscure with their familiar haze. Instead of "financial problems," let us forget euphemism and talk about being in debt, or having no money, or losing a job, or payments coming due; *anything* more particular. The ultimate particularity would probably sound as cold as a balance sheet (outstanding indebtedness $27,429.31; assets . . .) but there is a median between the bland, evasive euphemism of "financial problems" and the sterile figures. The median is actual circumstances and anecdotes; the median is stronger than the extremes.

Certainly "go to college" or "go on in school" is preferable to "the benefits of higher education." Then instead of speaking generally of "surprise"—an abstraction that takes the surprise out of surprise—why not show it happening? Have the grandfather opening the envelope, or picking up the telephone. Use dialogue. Or use some new analogy to express his feelings, instead of a useless cliché. He could be as surprised as someone who finds a pearl in his clam chowder. How much is "a large amount of money" or "a sum"? Both seem genteel evasions for saying a specific figure, like "a check for $5,000." But perhaps it seems crass to the writer to name the figure. Then at least some phrase should qualify the idea of numbers, so that the reader can place the figure between five hundred and five million dollars, or so that he can judge the amount of money by what it can do: ". . . received a check for enough money to send us both through school."

The phrase "through his generosity" includes an unnecessary, labeling abstraction. We do not need to be told that he is generous. When we are bullied with the notion, we resist it. Maybe the old man just wants to boast that his grandchildren go to college. Then the last part of the paragraph has a pair of general nouns and a fancy verb in place of simpler and more natural language. It is pretentious to write "we were enabled to arrange payment for tuition" when we could write, "So we were able to pay for college."

The student, in fact, revised the passage into:

> My family was so far in debt last spring that we didn't think my sister and I could go to college. My father had borrowed money to get a fish and chips franchise, and lost it all in six months. My sister and I both took jobs in the summer. I was working

twelve hours a day in the mill, and when I came home at night I was so mad and tired I just drank beer and watched the box. Then my grandfather telephoned my father and I saw my father suddenly start crying. The VA had just sent my grandfather a check he didn't know was coming, and it was enough to pay for us both. That night, we bought a bottle of Four Roses.

He changed verbs and other parts of speech, but the revision of his nouns is most useful of all.

EXERCISES

1. Write a paragraph with a highly abstract title—"love," "idealism," "education"—which does not contain the title word, but which embodies a particular occasion of the word.

2. In the following passages, list each of the nouns as abstract or general or particular, *according to the context of the passage.* Bring your list to class, and be prepared to argue with other students. These distinctions are often tenuous, but a discussion of the distinctions will sharpen your eye for the insides of words.

a. We may therefore entertain the hypothesis that formal logic and the law of contradiction are the rules whereby the mind submits to operate under general categories of repression. As with the concept of time, Kant's categories of rationality would then turn out to be the categories of repression. And conversely, "dialectical" would be the struggle of the mind to circumvent repression and make the unconscious conscious. But by the same token, it would be the struggle of the mind to overcome the split and conflict within itself.

Norman O. Brown, *Life Against Death*

b. He accelerates. The growing complexity of lights threatens him. He is being drawn into Philadelphia. He hates Philadelphia. Dirtiest city in the world they live on poisoned water. He wants to go south, down, down the map into orange groves and smoking rivers and barefoot women. It seems simple enough, drive all night through the dawn through the morning through the noon park on a beach take off your shoes and fall asleep by the Gulf of Mexico. Wake up with the stars above perfectly spaced in perfect health.

John Updike, *Rabbit Run*

c. It was formerly the custom in our village, when a poor debtor came out of jail, for his acquaintances to salute him, looking through their fingers, which were crossed to represent the grating of a jail window. "How do you do?" My neighbors did not thus salute me, but looked first at me, and then at one another, as if I had returned from a long journey.

Henry David Thoreau, "On the Duty of Civil Disobedience"

d. At 15,000 feet, its best operating height, the Kittyhawk IA could fly at a maximum speed of only 354 mph and climb to that height in 8.3 minutes, a longer time than the AGM2 Zero took to reach 20,000 feet. Empty weight was 6,350 pounds, normal loaded weight 8,280 pounds, which was the load carried into combat without drop tank or bombs, and maximum permissible weight was 9,200 pounds. Service ceiling was 29,000 feet. The IA climbed best at lower altitudes, but its best rate was only about 2,100 feet per minute at 5,000 feet.

Pacific Hawk

e. One Hundredth Street was dark, filled with life. I turned off Second Avenue into the street, searching for Number 321. I passed the people, and they were dark too, as seemed appropriate for those who lived in this block. For a moment I imagined that if white men lived here very long, they too would turn dark, by laws as irrefutable as the one that would make them dark if they lived on the beach in Florida—except that here the darkness would not be caused by the sun but by the lack of it.

I passed the dark scar of a vacant lot, blistered with refuse, and came to a building that looked like most of the others. The number was 321. I pushed through the door that was patched with raw board where glass once was, and started up the steps. There were voices, in Spanish, and sounds of frying. An odor like dead cats possessed the stairway. On the third floor I knocked at the door of the front apartment, and one of the girls greeted me.

Dan Wakefield, *Island in the City*

f. In 1945, the 45,000 dead at Sétif could pass unnoticed, in 1947, the 90,000 dead in Madagascar could be the subject of a simple paragraph in the papers; in 1952, the 200,000 victims of the repression in Kenya could meet with relative indifference. This was because the international contradictions were not sufficiently distinct. Already the Korean and Indo-Chinese wars had begun a new phase. But it is above all Budapest and Suez which constitute the decisive moments of this confrontation.

Frantz Fanon, *The Wretched of the Earth*

g. It is a very small office, most of it taken up by a desk. The desk is placed smack in front of the window—not that it could have been placed anywhere else; this window looks out on the daylight landscape of Bergman's movies. It was gray and glaring the first day

I was there, dry and fiery. Leaves kept falling from the trees, each silent descent bringing a little closer the long, dark, Swedish winter. The forest Bergman's characters are always traversing is outside this window and the ominous carriage from which they have yet to escape is still among the properties. I realized, with a small shock, that the landscape of Bergman's mind was simply the landscape in which he had grown up.

James Baldwin, *Nobody Knows My Name*

3. In the passages just quoted:
   a. Is there a best style among the five? A worst? Or is there simply an appropriateness of style to different contexts? The first is from a philosophical and psychological book, the second from a novel, the third from Thoreau's essay, the fourth from a book about the air war with the Japanese from 1941 to 1945, the fifth from a book about Puerto Ricans in New York, the sixth from a polemical work by a revolutionist, and the seventh from an essay by an American novelist.
   b. Discuss each author's use of verbs, and how it agrees or disagrees with the nouns he uses.
   c. Can you find places that might be improved? Try improving one phrase in each passage.

4. Look at the textbook from another course you are taking this term, and find a paragraph in which you can improve both nouns and verbs. Bring in the original (five to ten lines of print will do) and your revisions. Defend your changes in discussion or in writing.

5. Rewrite a passage of your daily writing with special attention to making nouns less abstract and more particular—and to making sure that whatever abstraction you use is well earned.

6. Take each of the following general nouns and find two other words to go with it, one more general and one more specific. If you can't find a word, use a short phrase:

   rodent
   student
   lily
   day
   business

7. Collect seven clichés that combine an abstract noun with an adjective, like "blind faith," "basic need," and "conflicting desires." See how many you can find alternative words and phrases for,

always realizing that a different context will require a different substitute for each of these filler phrases. Thus, "basic needs" in seven contexts might well be revised into seven distinct phrases. Provide brief contexts, if you need them for clarity.

8. In an essay, book, or newspaper, find examples of the abstraction that explains or labels uselessly, as described on pages 55–56. Explain what you mean.

9. Find examples of lazy abstractions (like those in exercise 7 above) in published writing. See if you can substitute more concrete phrases, if the context allows you to understand what is missing.

10. In published writing, find five examples of nouns used to sound fancy or complicated, for which you can supply simple alternatives.

ADJECTIVES AND ADVERBS AND OTHER MODIFIERS

Qualities and Choosing a Style

Modifiers—adjectives, adverbs, participles, and sometimes other words—give quality to nouns and verbs. "The *huge, green* lion"; "leapt *slowly.*" Adverbs and adjectives *modify* nouns and verbs. Participles and sometimes nouns work in the same way: "the *grinning* lifeboat," "the hypothesis *constructed* on Thursday," "*rock candy* mountain," "*mouse* music." Used well, modifiers create distinctions of meaning, and add particularity to the particular. They discriminate and add precision.

But modifiers give us the greatest trouble of all parts of speech. The beginning writer, especially when he tries to write colorfully, may stuff his style into obesity with a diet of fat adjectives.

We have already talked about the misuse of adjectives and adverbs, when we talked about some bad examples of prose in general, and about verbs and nouns: the verb-adjective phrase—like "was decisive"—which is weaker than the verb alone, and the adjective-noun phrase—like "basic ingredient"—in which the noun is vague or abstract and the adjective tries to add vitality.

Overuse or misuse of adjectives and adverbs—*even particular ones*—makes prose weak and lethargic. Because they are qualities rather than actions or things, adjectives and adverbs are inherently weaker parts of speech. Yet once more, the choice of a style *means* something. *A change of style, however slight, is a change of meaning, however slight.*

To choose vigor in writing is usually to work with fewer modifiers. A few great writers, like Faulkner, use as many adjectives as any beginner—but use them well, and with great originality. Most of the best writers use them sparingly and then make them count. We are not saying that adjectives are unimportant to writing. They are important. But verbs and nouns carry the sentence; if they take charge properly, they liberate adjectives, adverbs, and other modifiers to do their proper work, to make the exact final discriminations necessary to honesty and fullness of meaning.

The Adjective and the Cliché

In our minds we associate certain adjectives and nouns. Our minds are not only computer dictionaries, they are junkyards of cliché. If we think "grass," we probably think "green." We move in worn tracks. If we think "snow," we think "white." These weary associations are not really thinking; they are automatic responses to stimuli. The more ourselves we can be, the less we will resemble a machine. If we remember more closely the grass and the snow we are describing, we will describe it precisely, out of our own memories, not out of the sad memory-bank of other people's words. We might find an unexpected adjective for grass that is accurate to the grass of that place and that time. We might think of "harsh grass." Or we might not describe the grass at all, or we might describe it in a clause or in a whole sentence. But we must avoid the description that repeats familiar association. Only the distinct particular takes our attention. Green snow is news.

Other nouns summon their cousin adjectives by bookish associations. The word "sentinel," for many of us, carries with it the adjective "lonely"; "the lonely sentinel" is a cliché. Some of these combinations become comical from overuse or inherent absurdity, like "inscrutable Oriental." Others have sources not so bookish: "responsible citizen," "gracious living." Whenever you use an adjective that sounds habitual to its noun, try omitting the adjective, or recasting the phrase. In avoiding cliché, we have to *think*. We have to decide what we mean by a phrase like "fundamental truth."

The Modifier That Weakens the Noun

An adjective gives us the quality or type of a noun: *white* snow. An adverb relates to a verb in the same way: he grinned *happily*. But each of these examples would be bad style in most contexts. In each, the modifier diminishes the word it should strengthen. "Snow" is whiter than "white snow." "Snow" is white in the computer-dictionary of the brain, so why do we need to color it in our sentence unless we are suggesting its opposite? To say "white snow" must bring to mind snow that is gray with dirt. At a moment in a description, this suggestion might be just what the writer wanted: "White snow fell, that morning, on the trash of the old city." The contrast is part of the meaning; "white" takes its place, modifying "snow," because of the later words "trash" and "city." But most of the time, when a writer adds "white" to "snow," he subtracts from his sentence. He adds "white" in an uneasy search for particularity; he lacks confidence in the insides of the word "snow." The adjective overinsists on a quality already firm in the word.

In the example of the adverb, if we know that the character grinned, must we be told that he "grinned happily"? It can only bring to mind that he *might* have been grinning unhappily, which is a nasty thought; the author reassures us that this supposition is not so, but without the reassurance, there would have been no supposition.

A beginning writer often goes through stages with adjectives, and different people have different problems with them. With some beginners, the only adjectives are predictable ones.

> It was a long trip from the high mountains of the frozen north to the desert wastes of sunny Arizona, but it was highly educa tional and well worth while.

Or remember Jim Beck's original theme on going to college:

> Education is of paramount importance to today's youth. No one can underestimate the importance of higher education. It makes us well-rounded individuals and . . .

The problem is not primarily adjectives and adverbs, but thinking (or not thinking) in the old tracks.

Modifiers as Weak Intensives

We misuse adjectives and adverbs as weak intensifiers. We say "she moved gracefully" when we might say with more gusto that "she danced" or "she swept" or "she glided." We use vague adjectives in place of specific ones or in place of clauses that could add color and precision. We say "a tremendous amount"—when "amount" is vague and "tremendous" is a weak and unspecific intensifier—or "really huge," when we might say "ten million" or "as long as a supertanker." Here the specific number or the comparison carries color; the precision is one of feeling, not of dimensions.

Automatic Adjectives

Another misuse of adjectives and adverbs, a more advanced or sophisticated misuse, appears in writers when they suddenly appreciate bright colors in writing, and appears frequently when we begin to write stories and poems. In this misuse, the symptom is not cliché but multiplicity. Nearly every noun carries its adjective, like a tote bag, and every verb wears the cape of an adverb. The style is flashy and overdressed. Here is part of a poem from a creative writing class:

> I woke suddenly from a ghost-ridden dream
> of old women, to find myself wandering vaguely
> on the far edges of the raw city where white skulls tipped crazily
> in the western sky, and dirty children ran by
> to the cave shelters of abandoned cars . . .

The lines are improved by the mechanical act of stripping them of modifiers. Is anything lost? Yes. "Abandoned" is necessary to the emotion of "abandoned cars." If it is merely "cars" that are "shelters," they could be comfortable, middle-class vehicles in which one drives to the supermarket with one's mother. The "abandoned" makes the children take "shelter" in something like a dump.

Certainly "old women" is different from "women." The phrase is altered by leaving out the adjective, so perhaps we should restore "old." But the other modifiers are well exterminated. "Suddenly" does nothing but make the line move less quickly. "Ghost-ridden" does little to intensify "dream," and what it does, the later image of the skulls does better; also, hyphenated adjectives are usually bad; John Heath-Stubbs, an English poet, says that one should always be cautious of hyphenated names: it means that the lineage of one of the families is not too sound. In "ghost-ridden," what does "ridden" mean? Is the author really using the insides of the word? Does he know what the inside *is*?

"Wandering" includes "vaguely" the way "snow" includes "white." "Edges" are necessarily "far." "Raw" seems to add something to city, and perhaps the author would want to keep it, but the word adds little to the poem except a harshness that is better expressed elsewhere (in "skulls tipped" and "the children ran/to the shelters of abandoned cars.") And it adds a metaphor that connects with nothing else in the poem. When you call a city "raw," you are making a metaphor; since cities are not culinary objects, they are in reality neither "raw" nor "cooked." When we call a city raw we are comparing it to a steak or a carrot or an egg; "uncooked" is an inevitable inside of the word "raw." But nothing else in the poem comes from the kitchen. The metaphor in "raw" is dropped, unused because the author was unaware that he was using a metaphor. He was using "raw" conventionally, as in "raw deal" and "raw material"—without paying attention to its insides. In a poem, the experienced reader absorbs the insides, and is disturbed by the dead and unfulfilled metaphor. So let us omit the adjective "raw."

"Skulls" are "white" enough without calling them so. If there are skulls tipping in the sky, we don't need an elbow in our ribs commenting "crazily." This adverb appears to specify the action of "tipped"—but would you be able to distinguish between a skull that was tipping crazily and one that was tipping sanely? Really, "crazily" describes nothing; it testifies only to craziness in an image that is already crazy.

"Western" in the context of these lines adds nothing to speak of. West is sunset and death, perhaps, but here it is mostly a pretty noise and a useless specificity. "Dirty" does nothing for "children" that is not done better by verbs and nouns (and by the "abandoned" modifier in the spare version). "By" together with "to" is overly prepositional, wordy. And "cave" adds an image or a metaphor that clutters the final line. It is harsh and moving to find that "shelters" for these children are "abandoned cars." This juxtaposition elicits the emotion. To compare (by way of an adjective) the shelters to caves is to confuse the feeling, and to drag in another world of comparisons, like cavemen, Indians, Neanderthals, and fur clothing.

Here the general noun "shelter" seems to me to work better than the more specific noun "cave," which is used as an adjective. But a good argument could support the choice of "cave" over "shelter," making the last line, "to the caves of abandoned cars." We could argue that the associations of "cave" include darkness, and that the primitive world (cavemen) makes a strong contrast with the technology of the automobile. Whichever word you prefer, "cave" or "shelter," one thing seems clear: either word by itself is better than two words together—"cave shelter," or "sheltering cave," if we wanted to write it that way. The modifier belongs to the same world as the noun—caves are like shelters are like caves—and so adds nothing but the slight confusion of its difference. The noun alone is preferable, here as everywhere, unless the modifier adds something new to a noun that is already precise.

The poet was at a stage in his writing when he used a modifier automatically with every noun and verb. The modifiers were not predictable; the author was past the stage of clichés, or, more accurately, he was at a stage where he could cut them out before he brought his work to class. But he was diffident about his nouns and his verbs. His nouns and his verbs were doing their jobs well, but he lacked confidence in them. And so, to protect the poor things, he sent each of them to kindergarten with an adjective holding its hand.

When he revised it, the poem read:

> I woke from a dream
> of old women, to find myself wandering
> on the edges of the city
> where skulls tipped
> in the sky, and children ran
> to the shelters of abandoned cars . . .

Here there are only two modifiers, not thirteen as in the original version. Certainly the spare revision is better writing, and the revision was accomplished wholly by deleting modifiers.

Nouns as Modifiers

In the phrase, "cave shelter," "cave" was a noun used as a modifier. English uses participles and nouns as modifiers—"sheltering cave," as well as "cave shelter"—with the same dangers, and the same opportunities, which attend plain adjectives. Use them with the same cautions in mind.

It is an advantage of the English language that its grammar is not rigid. In some languages, a noun would have to undergo respelling before it could be used as an adjective. English has the reputation among languages of adaptability and looseness. It can accept change. And because it accepts change, in speech and in writing, the writer or the speaker can make shades of meaning more precise. Using nouns as modifiers, he can say "house party," "religion committee," "death wish."

He can also say "this type grammar," or—in Bergen Evans' example of the tedious multiplication of nouns-as-modifiers—". . . he absconded with the River Street fire house Christmas Eve party funds." Because English lacks the fault of rigidity, it is subject to the faults of chaos and disorganization. "Type" is frequently a filler-noun, and when we use it as a modifier we make even less sense with it than we normally do. With Bergen Evans' example, as with too many sentences that are seriously intended, the proliferation of nouns as modifiers creates heaviness and awkwardness.

So be careful when you use nouns as modifiers. Sociologists are guiltiest of abusing this device. One hears of the "city group research effort." By the time one reaches the third of these noun-modifiers, one begins to feel afloat in a sea of possibilities. What will go with what? It is as if one were suddenly cast adrift in a Chinese sentence, with no inflexions, and with no connectives, and with no tense or number. Instead, confine yourselves to one or two noun-modifiers in a row.

Thus phrases are often two nouns that might eventually become one compound noun, like "rain storm" or "wheel barrow" becoming "rainstorm" and "wheelbarrow." When the combination is more unusual, you have the opportunity to make an original contribution. The precedents include such a great phrase as Gerard Manley Hopkins' "Carrion Comfort."

Using Modifiers Well
Ernest Hemingway is known for using adjectives and adverbs sparingly. Let us look once more at the passage that begins "In Another Country":

> In the fall the war was always there, but we did not go to it any more. It was cold in the fall in Milan and the dark came very early. Then the electric lights came on, and it was pleasant along the streets looking in the windows. There was much game hanging outside the shops, and the snow powdered on the fur of the foxes and the wind blew their tails. The deer hung stiff and heavy and empty, and small birds blew in the wind and the wind turned their feathers. It was a cold fall and the wind came down from the mountains.

Hemingway says, "the war" not "the long war" or "the distant war" or "the bloody, maiming, killing, useless, horrid, revolting war." He uses "always" and "any more" as adverbs in his simple predicates.

"Cold" is an adjective in the second sentence; "electric" is necessary to lights, at a time when electric lights were new; in a country at war they seemed especially unwarlike; "pleasant" is an adjective as restrained as the verbs "was" and "go." Then the eye of the paragraph turns away from restrained thoughts of war, and looks at the dead animals that substitute for the corpses of soldiers; right away the verbs and nouns become stronger and more particular: "game," "shops," "powdered." Then the adjectives, exact and strong, come marching in: "stiff and heavy and empty." The last of the three is especially vigorous. The adjectives used sparingly are used strongly and well.

Let us apply the same standards to the passage quoted before from a story by John Updike:

> All the warm night the secret snow fell so adhesively that every twig in the woods about their little rented house supported a tall slice of white, an upward projection which in the shadowless gloom of early morning lifted depth from the scene, made it seem Chinese, calligraphic, a stiff tapestry hung from the gray sky, a shield of lace interwoven with black thread.

Updike is sometimes condemned by critics for overwriting, for self-indulgence in description, for too much prettiness. Can you find anything here to back up such a charge? We can admire a writer, or a passage of his writing, and still find flaws.

What good does the word "secret" do us? It adds a little to the meaning—a kind of coziness—but to me the word seems to exist mostly to be pretty. I would like the line better if it read, "all the warm night the snow fell so adhesively. . . ." "Warm" is connected to "adhesively," but "warm" would be stronger if as an adjective it were more isolated; if the next noun, "snow," did not carry its adjective also. Then later, in a series of phrases, each noun takes one adjective, and although each adjective is defensible in itself, the effect is monotonously pretty: "tall slice," "upward projection," "shadowless gloom," "early morning." The mixture tastes too sweet. Rearrangement of clauses, putting an adjective after a noun instead of before it, putting two adjectives with one noun and none with the next—any number of minor reworkings could improve the passage.

The modifier in exposition or argument can help you or hurt you, just as in poetry and fiction. E. B. White, in a brief essay on schools, says that he always went to public ones; by contrast, he says, "my wife was unacquainted with public schools, never having been exposed (in early life) to anything more public than the wash-room of Miss Winsor's." The sentence includes several modifiers—"unacquainted," "public," "exposed," "early," and "public" again—and yet it has vigor and clarity. The choice of words expresses a light disdain for the snobbism that White associates with private schools. The verb phrase "was unacquainted with" is preferable to alternatives like "knew nothing about" because "acquainted" is a word we use in social contexts: "No, I am not acquainted with that person." In the small world of White's sentence, the past participle wears a monocle and looks down at the peasants. "Exposed (in early life)" suggests that public schools are a contagious disease, like measles. And the parenthesis "(in early life)" has a mock formality that agrees with the medical metaphor.

But the adjective with which White plays the best trick is "public," which he uses twice: "anything more public than the washroom of Miss Winsor's." "Public" then becomes associated with public lavatories; we wrinkle our nose in disdain. At "Miss Winsor's"—the name sounds snobbish—of course the lavatory would be spotless and relatively private. What's more, it would not be a lavatory, john, W.C., or even bathroom; it would be a "washroom." By a *turn* on the adjective "public"—from schools to implied lavatories—White makes his point most clearly.

In expository prose, adjectives usually narrow the generality of a noun, to make the statement more specific. But if we do not watch ourselves carefully, the adjective drifts into one of its characteristic errors. Here is a generally good passage of exposition from an article about Naples that appeared in *Gourmet*:

> Naples was ruled by eight royal houses, ending with the Bourbons, interrupted by the short-lived French Parthenopean Republic in 1799, the Bonapartes, and Joachim Murat. After 1815 the Bourbons were back with the restored Ferdinand IV, who proclaimed himself King Ferdinand I of the Two Sicilies at the Congress of Vienna. They called him *Il Re Lazzarone* (The Vagabond King) because he understood the *lazzaroni* and they understood him. It was this Ferdinand who loved to hunt and fish—often to the exclusion of everything else—and who served pizzas at the palace of Caserta and gave the fabulous Water Fete in 1824. He was succeeded by his son Francis I, who introduced new corruptions that even the Neapolitans had not heard of.
>
> Lillian Langseth-Christensen, "Naples"

The modifiers are few, and they mostly work well. "Eight" gives us the specific number, so much more vivid than the "many" which a lazier researcher might have written. "Short-lived" is a tired metaphor, but it is descriptive and unobtrusive. The "restored Ferdinand" is an excellent example of how the modifier—a past participle here—can save words; "restored" substitutes with clarity for "who had been restored to the throne" or some such clause. "Fabulous" is the one example of a flawed adjective here; it is a word that has lost its insides, for we do not think of "fable" when we hear it. It has become a vague word of praise like "marvelous." The author may well have intended "fabulous" as "known in fable," but her readers will not follow her. The end of the paragraph uses "new" nicely. "New" puts an accent on "corruptions," not specific, but suggestive enough. "New" in effect is a direction given to the "corruptions"; they are original, previously unknown, and therefore *gloriously* corrupt.

Take this passage:

> The November meeting at the Union League Club was widely reported in the press, which saw evidence of high enthusiasm and sober purpose in the proceedings. A period of feverish activity now ensued. Legal documents were drawn and redrawn (mostly by Choate), potential trustees were sounded out, and advice was solicited. On January 31, 1870, the first board of trustees was elected. The ingredients of this twenty-seven-man founding board were predictable—a pomposity of businessmen and financiers, a clutch of lawyers, a nod of city officials, and a scintillation of writers and architects; less predictable, perhaps, was the inclusion of four practicing artists—the painters John F. Kensett, Frederick E. Church, and Eastman Johnson, and the sculptor J. Q. A. Ward.
>
> Calvin Tomkins, *Merchants and Masterpieces*

Usually a careful writer, Tomkins sounds fatigued. Commonplace combinations of adverb and verb, or adjective and noun, make much of the prose tedious, wordy, and wasteful: "widely reported," "high enthusiasm," and "feverish activity." The clichés of color are there too: the "ingredients" of the "board" were "predictable." Other modifiers are decent qualifications, like "*November* meeting," and "legal documents." The author moves into color and vivacity through a series of nouns, "a clutch of lawyers, a nod of city officials, and a scintillation of writers and architects."

Revising Modifiers

When you revise your prose, question the need for every adjective and adverb. Can I do without these modifiers? Does the noun (like "postulate" in "basic postulate") or the verb (like "run" in "run quickly") do the job without the modifier? Or can I find another exact noun or verb to do the job in one word? Do I avoid a succession of adjective-noun combinations, the monotonous pairs? Do I fall into cliché by joining two words that are commonly used together? Do I, on the other hand, use the modifier when I need it, to make the discrimination, or to add the color, which makes the sentence expressive?

EXERCISES

1. Take an old theme, or a few pages from your daily writing, copy it out, and cross out all modifiers. See how many you really need, how many you can do without. If you see that some modifiers are imprecise, but leave a hole behind them, find new ones.

2. Write a description of a walk around the block without using adjectives and adverbs at all. Then describe the same walk using as many as you can. Overdo it. Then in a third version try to write the best you can, and use modifiers but only useful ones.

3. Analyze the use of adverbs and adjectives in these passages of prose.

   a. The essential problem of man in a computerized age remains the same as it has always been. The problem is not solely how to be more productive, more comfortable, more content, but how to be more sensitive, more sensible, more proportionate, more alive. The computer makes possible a phenomenal leap in human proficiency; it demolishes the fences around the practical and even the theoretical intelligence. But the question persists and indeed grows whether the computer will make it easier or harder for human beings to know who they really are, to identify their real problems, to respond more fully to beauty, to place adequate value on life, and to make their world safer than it now is.

   Norman Cousins, *Saturday Review*

   b. Far out along the autumn plain, beneath the sloping light, an immense drove of cattle moved eastward. They went at a walk, not very fast, but faster than they could imaginably enjoy. Those in front were compelled by those behind; those at the rear, with few exceptions, did their best to keep up; those who were locked within the herd could no more help moving than the particles inside a falling rock.

James Agee, "A Mother's Tale"

c. The face was black, smooth, impenetrable, the eyes had seen too much. The negroid hair had been treated so that it covered the skull like a cap, in a single neat-ridged sweep, with the appearance of having been lacquered, the part trimmed out with a razor, so that the head resembled a bronze head, imperishable and enduring.

William Faulkner, "Go Down Moses"

d. Nick looked at the burned-over stretch of hillside, where he had expected to find the scattered houses of the town and then walked down the railroad track to the bridge over the river. The river was there. It swirled against the log spiles of the bridge. Nick looked down into the clear, brown water, colored from the bubbly bottom, and watched the trout keeping themselves steady in the current with wavering fins. As he watched them they changed their positions by quick angles, only to hold steady in the fast water again. Nick watched them a long time.

Ernest Hemingway, "Big Two-Hearted River"

e. Personal consideration of various and sundry matters of considerable importance have led numerous observers to ultimately conclude that the final end of Western civilization is certainly closer to a realistic possibility than might earlier have been tentatively assumed.

f. Fishing is one of man's oldest occupations and fish stories entered folklore very early. Poets and nature fakers added their touches to marine superstitions that persist to our day. The popular press still cannot resist unsubstantiated stories of sea monsters.

When the helmet diver appeared a century ago, the saga gained the ultimate dramatic ingredient, a human hero to descend and give battle to the fiends. Their sanguinary engagements have been portrayed by dry writers ashore. The lonely, hardworking divers may be forgiven for their silent endorsement of the sagas. Indeed the helmet diver, imprisoned in his casque, and almost always working in filthy harbors and channels, is unable to determine whether an interference with his air pipe is caused by a giant squid or a rotted spar. Doubt leaves room for interpretation.

Jacques Cousteau, *The Silent World*

g. We were camping in the oasis. My companions were asleep. The tall, white figure of an Arab passed by; he had been seeing to the camels and was on his way to his own sleeping place.

I threw myself on my back in the grass; I tried to fall asleep; I could not; a jackal howled in the distance; I sat up again. And what had been so far away was all at once quite near. Jackals were swarming round me, eyes gleaming dull gold and vanishing again, lithe bodies moving nimbly and rhythmically, as if at the crack of a whip.

Franz Kafka, "Jackals and Arabs"

h. Braggioni sits heaped upon the edge of a straight-backed chair much too small for him, and sings to Laura in a furry, mournful voice. Laura has begun to find reasons for avoiding her own house until the latest possible moment, for Braggioni is there almost every night. No matter how late she is, he will be sitting there with a surly, waiting expression, pulling at his kinky yellow hair, thumbing the strings of his guitar, snarling a tune under his breath. Lupe the Indian maid meets Laura at the door, and says with a flicker of a glance towards the upper room, "He waits."

Katherine Anne Porter, "Flowering Judas"

4. You might enjoy making assignments out of the eight examples above. Here are some possibilities:

    a. Use each passage to review the usage of verbs and nouns.

    b. Take example d, and put an adjective with every noun that lacks one, and an adverb with every verb. Make the additions as good as you can, and see what you have done.

    c. Try to rewrite a or b, omitting adverbs and adjectives. How much, and what, do you lose?

5. Here are five simple nouns and five simple verbs. Make up ten sentences, using one of the words in each, in which you use an adverb or adjective that would not be a normal association. But let your context make the modifier work. If "snow" were the word, you might speak of "warm snow" as Updike does, and make it work by a word like "adhesively."

cut	sand
scramble	humility
search	concern
waver	hut
bask	scholar

6. In published prose, find five sentences in which an adjective or adverb is useless, either because it is redundant, like "white snow" or "basic postulate," or because it is a vague intensive, like "very cold out." Do not use "very" because it is too easy to find.

ORIGINAL WORDS: COMPARISONS

The Need for Originality

When we put words together—adjective with noun, noun with verb, verb with object—we start to talk to each other. We begin to show our original selves, or we show a dull copy of somebody else's original. Originality is clarity and vigor. A source of originality in language is forms of comparison—simile, metaphor, and analogy. In order to talk about metaphoric writing and originality, we must go over some old ground again.

Formulas or clichés or trite expressions substitute for the originality available to each of us. A girl who was mourning the death of her grandfather wrote, at the beginning of her first theme of the term, "A tragedy recently occurred at my ancestral home." In conference, the girl wept over the death, she was pale, her hands shook. Her body showed her wretchedness, but her prose showed her reading of a weekly country newspaper. No grief was in her phrasing, only the reminiscence of headlines or lead sentences in newspapers. Perhaps the formulas came to her pen so that she might avoid the pain of real feeling. Or perhaps they came because she did not know the difference, in words, between the formula that communicates nothing, and the originality that communicates feeling. "A tragedy occurred" is a formula that denies the tragic. Compare "a catastrophe was averted" and "a blessed event took place"; they all communicate the same source; but also, they all deny feeling, not *only* by being familiar (reminding us of the source) but by being passive or fancy.

A formula or a cliché comes into being not just because it is used so commonly, but because it prevents feeling. The phrase "rain fell" is more common than "a tragedy occurred," yet we do not think of it as a formula because we do not use it to prevent the expression of feeling. A psychiatrist once described clichés as "the lies we tell ourselves, that we *want* to hear." When the student wrote, "A tragedy recently occurred at my ancestral home," she was not lying overtly, or intending to lie. It was not like saying that she did not chop down a cherry tree when she really did. The lie was internal, the lie of using language to avoid difficult reality, the lie of euphemism.

Overhearing Your Original Self

Listen to yourself as you daydream, or think idly. Are you reciting the formulas of newspapers or of greeting card verse? If you overhear yourself, in your own head, thinking trite sentimentality about your love, something is wrong with your loving.

In general, trying to *overhear* yourself is a good idea. On some days, you can listen to the dreaming voice easily; on other days it seems mute; it is more likely that we are deaf. The dreaming language is clichés sometimes, sometimes puns or phrases of crazy originality. Sometimes the voice hums the tune of a song; when you remember the lyrics a coded message is there, like "Eleanor Rigby" when you are feeling lonely or abandoned, or when something inside you feels that you will be lonely soon. The puns and crazy phrases are codes too. Look at them closely. They have information for you. They are the speech of your original self, looking for attention from your conventional self, which is the self trained by parents and school and television to think like a train on a track. The crazier the phrase, the more devious the pun, the more deep the source in the self. When the dreaming voice talks in cliché, it is the train track getting in the way of the real voice, because the real voice would tell us the truth we would find painful.

Overhear yourself to know yourself. Then you can farm your daydreams for original verbal images that express feeling. The crazy image and the pun do not make good writing in themselves—though often they can be the leaping-off point in daily writing—but give clues to feelings that the conscious mind can follow. Here is an unrevised passage from a student's daily writing:

> I was taking out the garbage this morning and I heard (in my head) Fanny Davis's voice talking. She has a funny way of talking, Englishy but not really, and I knew it was her. She was saying, "I like to use the word 'to intimate' without any regard for its actual meaning." I kept stuffing the garbage bags into the cans, wondering why I made that up, and why I chose Fanny's voice. It's always sounded affected to me. But that wasn't the sort of thing she says. She talks about her family and the home on the lake up North and going skiing in Switzerland. I was feeling blue. Bob had gone to New York and I knew that Sally

was there, his old girl friend, and I worried about that. Then I started laughing, right at the garbage, because I saw that "to intimate" and "too intimate" are close, but "to intimate" is a long way from the meaning of "too intimate." I was blue because I was too close to Bob, and I could get hurt. I think I chose Fanny because she always seemed totally sexless.

The girl had uncovered something—which she almost knew already —by overhearing a daydream pun and by figuring it out. We may start dreaming; we end up thinking. Now she might be ready to examine her feelings about Bob, or her feelings about her feelings.

Looking for Original Images

We can try to activate the daydreaming part of our mind. We will not always succeed. The girl who wrote the paper beginning "A tragedy occurred" was never fully able to write about her grandfather. But her writing and her self-knowledge improved. In her daily writing she returned to the subject many times. The week after her initial theme, she wrote, "A month ago my grandfather died," and went on for a few rather dry sentences. Though the prose was colorless, it was much more honest than tragedies occurring at ancestral homes. Still, it had no images, no pieces of *sense*.

Later, thinking about things she could associate with her grandfather, she wrote about "farm implements," that were "unused," and "hanging on the wall of the barn." Then she changed "farm implements" to "rake and hoe." Then she revised the sentence again and added an image that could come only from the imagination extending itself into the unseen but the probable. "His hoes and rakes hang from pegs in the barn. Spiders will spin webs there while the iron turns red with rust." She had farmed the dreaming part of her head, which imagined the barn, with a selective intelligence, and wrote two sentences that, in their detail and their associations, began to embody her feelings of melancholy and loss.

Simile and Metaphor

Images are groups of words that give an impression to the senses. Most images are visual, but we can also make images of taste, touch, hearing, and smell. Images communicate feeling, and locate them firmly, really talking from writer to reader. Comparisons in simile and metaphor usually involve images, and become devices to communicate emotion.

Similes are comparisons that use "like" or "as," little words that announce a comparison. Metaphors omit the announcement. We write, "Her face bloomed with affection," and the word "bloomed" compares the girl to a flower; the face-flower is pretty, it is coming into its maturity, and it is associated with spring or summer. The writer may wish to go on talking about the girl in similes that use garden images. Perhaps her dress "rustles like leaves" and her skin is "as soft as petals." The difference between similes and metaphors is small—the presence or absence of a signal—but it is real; the simile, because it announces itself, is more reasonable, more conscious of what it is doing.

For the sake of clarity, we must distinguish this brief comparison from the word "comparison" as it is used later in this book, when we discuss comparison and contrast as structures of argument and exposition; also, we must distinguish it from the grammatical sense—the "comparison of adjectives." A comparison of the gross national products of Greece and Turkey, or of "less" and "least," is not like comparing an old cheese to an untidy hog.

The new, verbal comparison—simile, metaphor, and analogy—is our most original act of speech, and the originality comes from the dreaming part of the self. Although we cannot always manufacture metaphors at will, we can learn to be *alert* for comparisons, and we can stimulate their coming. The dead grandfather's funeral took place during a thunderstorm. When the girl tried to write about it, she encountered the problem of the trite associations of thunderstorms and death. She began simply:

> The funeral was 2 p.m. He was laid out in the front parlor, which was always closed except for weddings and funerals. Fifty people were there, some crowded into the parlor, others backed into the living room. The minister talked a little and read scripture. Then the sky turned dark.

The prose is simple and direct but it lacks energy. "The minister talked a little and read scripture" would probably be better if it included direct and indirect quotation. "Then the sky turned dark." *How* dark? How did you *feel* about the sky turning dark? We have the sense reading this prose that the feelings (formerly denied and lied about in journalistic clichés) are still restricted, held back, reserved.

Suppose the sky turned "as dark as" something. If it turned "as black as the ace of spaces," we would be nowhere. What does the ace of spades have to do with her grandfather or her feelings? Even if she had told us that the old man was a poker-playing farmer, the simile is so hackneyed that no one will see the black of the playing card when she says it. The useful comparison will be new and will relate to the context: to her memories of the man, to the scene of the funeral, to the idea of death. To say "the sky turned as dark as the soot from a factory chimney" would seem inappropriate; what would a factory have to do with a farm? "The sky turned black, like my grandmother's dress" would be a better direction; but maybe that's too black, or the texture is wrong. Or she might want to compare it to something she remembers and associates with the dead farmer: "The sky turned black, like inside the barn after milking." "The sky turned dark as a blueberry."

Sometimes one phrase will not be adequate. You want your comparison to go on longer than that. "The sky turned dark. I could see a black round storm cloud coming. I remembered leaning over the open well, staring down into the round black eye of the water." Here, we find a comparison within the comparison; the water is an "eye," and the reader alert to the insides of words will reconstruct the dead metaphor: "The eye of the storm"—and revive it—although (or because) the author has not stated it.

Originality and Memory

To find the right comparison, we must draw on memory and daydream; imagination is the new combination of old things remembered; it is always present, and often hard to discover. Memory is crucial to our writing, thinking, and feeling. By scrutiny of the retained past, we begin to understand and to express that understanding. In the floating world, we connect feelings in the present to feelings of the past. We express these connections mostly by comparisons. In the uniqueness in each of us, we can find something that the sky grew as dark as.

Analogy

We use this third term, besides simile and metaphor, for a comparison that makes or illustrates a point, and usually takes longer to say than a metaphor or a simile. An analogy can be extended into a whole essay; ministers' sermons are sometimes analogies—life is like the hundred-yard dash; birth is the starting gun, the tape is death,

God is the judge. A whole book, or system of thought, can be based on analogy. Oswald Spengler, in *The Decline of the West*, at the beginning states an analogy, that a civilization is an organism, is born, grows old, and dies; then he writes a long book to make a factual case for his analogy.

Analogy often works best within a unit no longer than the paragraph. Frequently, it illustrates the sense in which an abstraction is intended. Analogies may make points; they don't prove them; they show how you feel, or they clarify your use of an ambiguous or all-inclusive word; "love" and "hate" are two of the vaguest words going. Suppose we were tempted to support the stick-figure philosophical assertion, "Love is better than hate." We would not get far with such a proposition, because it is too vague for support, but we would at least put eyes and ears on our stick figures if we went on, "It is a meadow in the country compared to an alley of garbage and broken glass."

An analogy often runs through a paragraph like a thread in tweed, not separated into patches of assertion followed by comparison, but interwoven. James Thurber wrote this paragraph about working with the *New Yorker* editor, Harold Ross:

> Having a manuscript under Ross's scrutiny was like putting your car in the hands of a skilled mechanic, not an automotive engineer wtih a bachelor of science degree, but a guy who knows what makes a motor go, and sputter, and wheeze, and sometimes come to a dead stop; a man with an ear for the faintest body squeak as well as the loudest engine rattle. When you first gazed, appalled, upon an uncorrected proof of one of your stories and articles, each margin had a thicket of queries and complaints—one writer got a hundred and forty-four on one profile. It was as though you beheld the works of your car spread all over the garage floor, and the job of getting the thing together again and making it work seemed impossible. Then you realized that Ross was trying to make your Model T or old Stutz Bearcat into a Cadillac or Rolls-Royce. He was at work with the tools of his unflagging perfectionism, and, after an exchange of growls or snarls, you set to work to join him in his enterprise.

Thurber begins by announcing his subject, "Having a manuscript under Ross's scrutiny," departs from it for the rest of a long sentence, returns to the manuscript for a sentence, then in the final two sentences develops his analogy, makes it funnier, and makes his point about Ross as an editor. He makes points by contrasts: "mechanic" not "engineer"; not "bachelor of science" but "guy." And he makes it by developing his analogy into impossibility (repairing a Model T into a Cadillac), and developing it out of all relationship to reality; the customer joins with the mechanic to rebuild his torn-up machine. The analogy expresses feeling, it is witty, and it is a pleasure to read. Consider this alternative, omitting the garage and substituting abstraction and generality for analogy:

> Having a manuscript under Ross's scrutiny was an edifying if terrifying experience. He was a skilled editor, not an academic, but a practical man. When you first gazed, appalled, upon an uncorrected proof of one of your stories or articles, each margin had a thicket of queries and complaints—one writer got a hundred and forty-four on one profile. You beheld all your work torn apart, and it seemed impossible to put it together. Then you realized that Ross was trying to make ordinary prose into prose of the highest order. He was using his editorial skills with unflagging perfectionism, and, after an exchange of growls or snarls, you set to work to join him in his enterprise.

This eviscerated version is slightly shorter in words, but the cutting loses rather than gains: the paragraph diminishes in energy and expression.

The Unintended Comparison

With analogy as with other forms of comparison, you must be wary of the dead, the mixed, and the inadvertently comic. Often a writer will trap himself in an unconscious analogy expressing an attitude that he really feels but denies to himself. The comic disparity is as slapstick as a top-hatted man with his trousers missing. Here is an English critic, writing about American music in the London *Times Literary Supplement*. He writes in attempted praise of American energy and vitality, but other messages come through his bad prose:

> The American composer is neither enriched nor shackled. He had nothing to start from but old rags and bones of European culture that, imported to a new environment, soon lost their

savor. Then gradually, in the pulping machine of a polyglot
society, the rags and bones began to acquire a taste of their
own.

Look at the main analogy, rags and bones. When they were imported
here, they "soon lost their savor." Did the gentleman actually expect
rags and bones to taste good? His idea of the American stew
expresses his distaste by an analogy to eating the products of
something like a paper factory: ". . . in the pulping machine . . . the
rags and bones began to acquire a taste of their own." This writer
expressed his feelings, but he expressed feelings he didn't know he
had. He appears to believe that he *likes* American music, but
something unacknowledged inside him is holding its nose.

To express a feeling without examining it is worthless. Originality
combines opposites: we dream—with our eyes open; we are
inspired—then we scrutinize and revise. Scrutiny provides the motive
to revise. We need to look into words—to see the connection between
"rags and bones," "savor," and "taste"—and we will sometimes
discover feelings we had not wished to acknowledge. Then we can
revise ourselves or our prose or both. We must float on daydream and
memory for new words, and then put the new words under scrutiny
again. Only by developing all these mental abilities can we begin to
be honest. The paradox is that to be sincere we must struggle; we
must struggle to be spontaneous, and then struggle to revise, refine,
and order that spontaneity. To speak our most intimate selves we
must revise.

One way to cultivate our sensitivity to the insides of words is to
develop an ear for the unintended comparison. (The unintended
comparison is often an overt, and sometimes extended, version of the
dead metaphor.) In the fall of 1971, on a Monday night football
broadcast, Howard Cosell said of a new quarterback that he "walked
in the wake" of a great predecessor. Here, the unintended
comparison approaches blasphemy.

Looking for Analogies

An analogy can be thought out, on purpose, more easily than the
lone metaphor, which, to most writers, seems a gift from the god
within us, an inspiration. Suppose you are discussing what can make
a love affair succeed. Suppose you decide that it takes a lot of work.
The word "work," itself a metaphor nearly dead, can lead you into

analogy. What kind of work is it like? Is it like a nine-to-five job? You can make an analogy in the negative: "This work is no nine-to-five job." Is it like building a house? Rebuilding a destroyed city? Making the sets for a play? Being a skilled mechanic or an automotive engineer? What kinds of buildings, business, roads, cars?

The liveliest prose moves from analogy to analogy without strain. It takes practice to learn how to invent, and practice to learn when to stop inventing. When the area of analogy shifts abruptly, the effect is usually ridiculous, and comic writers can use these sudden shifts to their advantage; if in one sentence you compare tennis with big game hunting, do not compare it in the next sentence with knitting unless you want a laugh. Often a sentence or a paragraph of general summary or narrative separates passages of differing analogies, keeping them from clashing.

One more example of the varied use of comparisons brings imaginative combinations of words to the borough of Brooklyn, New York. The author is expressing complex feelings about its space.

> Manhattan is large, yet all its distances seem quick and available. Brooklyn is larger, seventy-one square miles as against twenty-two, but here you enter the paradoxes of the relative. You know, here: only a few miles from wherever I stand, Brooklyn ends; only a few miles away is Manhattan; Brooklyn is walled with world-travelled wetness on west and south and on north and east is the young beaver-board frontier of Queens; Brooklyn comes to an end: but actually, that is, in the conviction of the body, there seems almost no conceivable end to Brooklyn; it seems, on land as flat and huge as Kansas, horizon beyond horizon forever unfolded, as immeasurable proliferation of house on house and street by street; or seems as China does, infinite in time in patience and in population as in space.
>
> The collaborated creation of the insanely fungoid growth of fifteen or twenty villages, now sewn and quilted edge to edge, and lacking any center in remote proportion to its mass, it is perhaps the most amorphous of all modern cities; and at the same time, by virtue of its arterial streets, it has continuities so astronomically vast as Paris alone or the suburbs south of Chicago could match: on Flatbush Avenue, DeKalb, Atlantic, New Lots, Church, any number more, a vista of low buildings and side streets of glanded living sufficient to paralyze all conjecture; simply, far as the eye can strain, no end of Brooklyn,

and looking back, far as the eye can urge itself, no end, nor
imaginable shore; only, thrust upon the pride of heaven, the
monolith of the Empire State, or different mode of life, and
even this, seen here, has the smoky frailty of a half-remembered
dream.

from James Agee, "Southeast of the
Island: Travel Notes"

Though portions here may be overwritten—I have my doubts about
"is walled with world-travelled wetness" as a way to say "borders
the ocean"—there is imagination and order in the connected comparisons. Look at the order of sizes: Brooklyn, Kansas, China, then
from an abverbial peak, downward: "astronomically vast as Paris
alone or the suburbs south of Chicago." Look at the body-metaphors,
perhaps coming from the phrase "the conviction of the body": "ar-
terial," "glanded," "paralyze." Look at the brief analogy of a quilt at
the start of the second paragraph. The energy and import of this
prose derive from simile, metaphor, and analogy.

Revising for Comparison

First, check your sentences to make sure that you are in control of
the comparisons you make. Make sure that you do not inadvertently
turn a quarterback into a deity, or an art form into a bad smell.
Second, see that you have not made cliché comparisons that no
longer function, like "black as the ace of spades."

Then do the more difficult. *Add* simile, metaphor, and analogy.
Most of us in our first drafts lack energy and feeling. Our prose
resembles the pale version of Thurber, after the analogy was deleted.
The prose is too plain to reach the reader with excitement and
precision. Float on memory and daydream to invent; scrutinize with
critical intelligence to cut and to improve. Ask yourself if your
invention is new, if it is appropriate, if it does not clash with anything
else. In a paragraph of exposition, *think* if you can clarify by
analogy. What was it *like*, to have your prose edited by Ross? What
was it like, the day your grandfather died?

EXERCISES

1. Discuss, in a paper or in class, the style of the passage by
James Agee on pages 84–85. Discuss the comparisons, the use of
parts of speech, the attention to the insides of words, and whatever
else appeals to you; or appalls you.

2. Analyze the following formulas, trying to see what they might originally have been intended to say. Invent new phrases as alternatives. An alternative to "anchored to the spot" might be "fixed in orbit." Provide a context in which your alternative fits.

> toe the line
> an axe to grind
> chip on his shoulder
> pick a bone with you
> heart to heart talk

3. Looking through your old themes or daily writing, find examples of clichés that you consider "the lies we tell ourselves, that we *want* to hear."

4. In reading whatever you read, watch for unintended comparisons and for dead metaphors used with unconscious comedy. Write down any that you find, in a notebook, and bring them to class. Prizes for the longest list, and the funniest example.

5. In your daily writing, see what you can do by overhearing yourself daydream. Then scrutinize your prose for its originality and its banality.

6. Take any three comparatives, like "as long as" or "as bright as" or "as wet as," and write three sentences in which you make new similes.

7. Make a parody analogy, like "Life is like a hundred-yard dash." Be consistent and absurd.

8. Discuss forms of analogy, metaphor, and simile in the following passages. Criticize any illogic or error that you find.

a. But the thing that really tormented them was the thought of those two old-age pensioners living in their house, usurping floorspace, devouring food, and paying only ten shillings a week. I doubt whether they were really losing money over the old-age pensioners, though certainly the profit on ten shillings a week must have been very small. But in their eyes the two old men were a kind of dreadful parasite who had fastened on them and were living on their charity. Old Jack they could just tolerate, because he kept out-of-doors most of the day, but they really hated the bedridden one, Hooker by name. Mr. Brooker [the landlord] had a queer way of pronouncing his name, without the H and with a long U—"Uker." What tales I heard about old Hooker and his fractiousness, the nuisance of making his bed, the way he "wouldn't eat" this and "wouldn't eat" that, his endless ingratitude and, above all, the selfish obstinacy with which he refused to die! The Brookers were quite openly pining for him to die. When that happened they could at least draw the insurance money. They seemed to feel him there, eating their substance day after day, as though he had been a living worm in their bowels.

George Orwell, *The Road to Wigan Pier*

b. Even at the conventional level it is surely easy to see that knowing what is not so is often quite as important as knowing what is. Even when medicine can suggest no effective remedy for the common cold, there is some advantage in knowing the uselessness of certain popular nostrums. Furthermore, the function of negative knowledge is not unlike the uses of space—the empty page upon which words can be written, the empty jar into which liquid can be poured, the empty window through which light can be admitted, and the empty pipes through which water can flow. Obviously the value of emptiness lies in the movements it permits or in the substance which it mediates and contains. But the emptiness must come first. That is why Indian philosophy concentrates on negation, or liberating the mind from concepts of Truth. It proposes no *idea*, no description, of what is to fill the mind's void because the idea would exclude the fact—somewhat as a picture of the sun on the windowpane would shut out the true sun's light. . . .

from Alan W. Watts, *The Way of Zen*

c. The average American judge, as everyone knows, is a mere rabbinical automaton, with no more give and take in his mind than you will find in the mind of a terrier watching a rathole. He converts the law into a series of rubber-stamps, and brings them down upon the scalped skulls of the just and unjust alike. The alternative to him, as commonly conceived, is quite as bad—an uplifter in a black robe, eagerly gulping every new brand of Peruna that comes out, and converting his pulpit into a sort of soap-box.

from H. L. Mencken, "Mr. Justice Holmes"

d. Burroughs' domain is the interface of individual mind and social mind—*control*. When social conditions become demented, suicidal, the individual must break from them and find his own health. This book is a discussion of the control-busting techniques Burroughs has explored. Scientology's E-meter, word-subversion, violence, doing nothing, tape recorders, apomorphine, contradictory commands. All methods of seizing the social tools and turning them against themselves.

Its important research is a critical, invisible realm. My only carp would be Burroughs' assumption of crafty, subtle, efficient intellects behind society's controls . . . which describes Burroughs but hardly describes the tired men I've seen earnestly coping with the top jobs in the Pentagon and the Department of the Interior. Their main activity is trying not to fall over their own feet.

SB, in *The Last Whole Earth Catalogue*

e. Manson's greatest work of magic, however, was the transformation of Charles Denton Watson. When they met Watson in the spring of 1968 at Dennis Wilson's house, Watson was a swinger dating a stewardess from Chicago. The family was proud that it could create a change in Tex Watson, the holder to this day of a Texas high hurdles track and field record. Watson dressed mod. He looked mod. He had a wig shop. He was strictly now. But they erased the swinger from him. Years later, when he was down to 110 pounds, weeping in his cell, covered over with a blanket, just before they shipped him to the Atascadero nut hatch, he was truly now. No past—time burnt—books burnt—past burnt. All bridges melted with dope and fervor. All time factors in the now. The now of Charlie.

Ed Sanders, *The Family*

f. A gentleman is one who cultivates disadvantage. He will not positively pursue it. But he takes little prudential or evasive action when it comes. There is laziness in your true gentleman, a streak of recumbency. But also fastidiousness: the dividends of the world— honors, power, earned fortune—come greasy. A man may win the game but stay grimy to his elbows. There is something about defeat, material setback, even personal betrayal by those one trusted that leaves one clean. At its purest, gentility is dated. It goes, perhaps unfairly, with camel's-hair coats and shooting sticks, with talc and loyal setters. The entire code was a feature of England before 1914, when caste was firm and private incomes were adequate to the many small defeats, impracticalities, covert ostentations, and boneheadednesses that made up a gentleman's non-career. Both the men and the manner were largely wiped out in the muck of world war. This was indeed the supreme imposition, the disadvantage least to be flinched from. But now and again the sandy mustaches, the pale, astonished eyes of the true gents still haunt the imagination.

George Steiner, "Gent," *The New Yorker*, February 12, 1972

g. But his position was weak. Like a cougar, the army was constantly perched above him, ready to pounce.

John Gerassi, *The Great Fear in Latin America*

III

SENTENCES

STYLE AND THE SENTENCE

A sentence is a group of words with a period, exclamation point, or
question mark at the end. But no definition of the sentence is likely
to help us much in writing one. Sentences happened first; gram-
marians named them later. We learn sentence structure by speaking and listening, by reading and writing, more than we learn by
studying types of sentence. Still, after studying we can listen harder,
read more closely, speak more eloquently, and write more clearly; we
can learn to *vary* the style of our sentences to express our feelings
and ideas and, at the same time, we can learn to *control* the style
of our sentences so that they come together to make a satisfying
whole. To *vary*, and to *control*. A paradox of style: we must have
variety and sameness, combine unity and diversity, in the same
group of words.

Distinctions between simple, compound, and complex sentences
belong to the discussion of style and the sentence, and I see no virtue
in inventing new terms.

TYPES OF SENTENCES

Simple Sentences

A sentence is "simple" as long as it remains one clause, containing
one predicate. "John laughed" is a complete, two-word sentence,

89

simple and common in its structure: subject/verb. We could add modifiers, "Big John laughed loudly," or a preposition, "John laughed at her," and the sentence would remain simple.

A sentence can be quite long and yet still be simple. The following sentence is simple, but elaborates the predicate with prepositional phrases:

> Neal runs / with his wife / before classes / at Waterman Gymnasium./

A subject can be long, too:

> The ape-man in the gray loincloth, a wooden spear in his hand, attacked.

Or the verb can be elaborated:

> The ape-man attacked swiftly, with a sharp cry, from behind the rocks.

Or we can have a direct object, and the object can be elaborated:

> The ape-man attacked the sluggish warriors, those intruders tired from their lengthy searching.

Or the simple sentence can elaborate all its parts and remain simple:

> The ape-man in the gray loincloth, a wooden spear in his hand, attacked the sluggish warriors swiftly from behind the rocks, the boulders shining in the hot sun.

The basic sentence is still, "The ape-man attacked," though by this time we have more definition for each of the parts, more information, and too many adjectives.

Compound Sentences

A compound sentence has two or more main clauses, each containing a subject and a predicate, each describing an action complete in itself. The clauses of the compound sentence are joined by a connective—"and," "but," "or," or "nor"—or by a semicolon or colon.

> Shelley wanted to feed Ezra the beef stew, but Gayle thought he had eaten too much already.

These clauses are independent in the sense that they could become two sentences with minimal change of meaning and writing.

Shelley wanted to feed Ezra the beef stew. Gayle thought he had eaten too much already.

In the compound sentence, notice that the two complete clauses are nearly equal, or *coordinate*. The two parts are balanced. A compound sentence, of course, can have more than two or three parts. But a series of coordinate clauses is usually boring.

Complex Sentences

If, however, one part of the sentence depends on the other—if the one is the cause of the other, for instance—we have a complex rather than a compound sentence. We call the clause that depends upon the other, for explanation or completion, *the subordinate clause*. A complex sentence would be, "Since Gayle said that Ezra had eaten too much already, Shelley decided not to feed him the beef stew."

We can vary sentences even when we keep to simple clauses and compounds of equally complete clauses. The complex sentence provides further variety, and allows us additional conciseness and precision. Clauses introduced by relative pronouns, "that," "which," or "who"—sometimes called relative clauses—are subordinate to a main clause; they depend on it. In other sentences, we attribute cause or sequence, perhaps, and not just contiguity or juxtaposition, and we do it by a conjunction like "because" or "after." Then we have all the other conjunctions that can introduce subordinate clauses, each with its own precise meaning to be used by the careful writer—like "although," "after," "if," "since," and "when."

Compound-Complex Sentences

Frequently, we combine compound and complex sentences, using at least two main clauses and one subordinate clause.

I was late *because it was raining,* and I kept everybody waiting.

The clause in italics is subordinate. The clauses in roman are both main clauses.

Incomplete Sentences

Another type of sentence commonly used is the incomplete sentence, or fragment. The incompleteness is the lack of a subject or of a predicate. "John laughed" was our example for the briefest complete sentence. Neither "John" nor "laughed" would be complete by itself, but it would be possible to use either of them alone in context:

> She thought about whom she might ask to the picnic. Harry? Harry was too grubby. John? John.

> When she saw him she covered her mouth and, though she tried to suppress it, laughed. Laughed. He could not believe it.

But the more common incomplete sentence is a phrase or a clause of several words.

> The essay by Ellsberg shows great control of sentence variation. Like the variety in the first paragraph.

The incomplete sentence is informal. In a more formal prose, other ways could have been found to work "like the variety in the first paragraph" into a long sentence. We use the incomplete sentence also with many common phrases like "No comment," "Not at all," and "Of course." The incomplete sentence, if the diction is informal enough, provides yet another possible variation of rhythm and structure. It isolates a fragment in time, because the period creates a pause longer than the pause of a comma or a semicolon.

> We were going to be consumed by fire once more, and once more the world would let it happen. As usual. What was true yesterday will be true tomorrow.
>
> Elie Wiesel, *A Beggar in Jerusalem*

Only be careful to use incomplete sentences in an informal context, and deliberately, like Elie Wiesel, to establish pause and emphasis. A careless writer may make clauses into sentences (with periods and capital letters) without purpose, and with choppy results.

> He was a writer. Which is a difficult profession.

> She looked tall. Although she was really only 5'3".

Avoid this sort of thing. These sentences need to become complex, with commas.

There is another possible danger in incomplete sentences. They tend to avoid committing themselves. If we take notes on a history lecture, using fragments rather than sentences, we may look at them a month later and read something like, "Too many wars. Bad economy." Unless we remember the context, these phrases may leave us puzzled. They could imply that the number of wars, at sometime in history, destroyed the economy of nations. Or they could imply that bad economy created the wars. Or both. Lack of a verb, and lack of the order of subject and object to complete an action, leaves the meaning vague. For clarity, take notes in whole sentences. "A bad economy—unemployment—created the conditions for war." No puzzle here. So when you write prose, the rule is the rule of clarity. Scrutinize your incomplete sentences for ambiguity.

EXERCISES

1. Looking into your daily writing, or old themes, find and copy examples of the following:

    a. A simple, complete sentence.
    b. A compound sentence.
    c. Three complex sentences of two clauses, in which you use different conjunctions. If you do not have three examples, revise until you do.
    d. A compound-complex sentence.
    e. An incomplete sentence.

2. Identify each of these sentences as simple, compound, complex, compound-complex, or incomplete:

    a. Since Margaret had brought the elephant into the house, Sandy had to take her sculptures down to the basement.

    b. Lost in thought, she didn't hear the thunder begin in the mountains far off, or feel the wind starting to blow harder.

    c. Rose ordered an apricot sour despite the fact that she had been drinking daiquiris, and winked at her companion as she did.

    d. This sentence, for example.

    e. Rocking back and forth on his heels, Nick said, "Let's have a song."

    f. Larry went up for the jump-shot and Dave leaped to block it.

    g. The man in the Foster Grants strolled down the crowded street, a beret on his head, a cane in his hand.

    h. Always cheerful, Mr. Sputter the mailman smiled, although a German Shepherd hung by its teeth from his sleeve.

    i. Without hesitation, thinking only of the trapped ocelot, Branny dashed through the rising flames.

    j. He grabbed the chicken feathers and threw them off the cliff, screaming and dancing all the while, although the rites were not yet due to begin and he, a crazed poet, was forbidden to take part.

VARIETY OF SENTENCES

The Uses of Variety

By using different sentence types, we can vary the speed and style of our prose. Also, we can match the variety of sentences to the need for subtle expression, and use a knowledge of sentence-possibilities to increase the range and conciseness of expression.

Subordinating for Brevity: Complex Sentences

Subordinate phrases and clauses, used as modifiers, and without connectives, can save us words, and strengthen our sentences. These subordinates give our prose density and variety.

For instance, in the absolute construction, we omit the connective and the verb, or sometimes a preposition, and modify directly and clearly.

    Day done, he raised his pitchfork to his shoulder.

Here we have cut from "When day was done," or a longer construction.

    The desk ordered, pencils sharpened, paper blank, he was ready for a day of combat with the English language.

    The fullback twisted and plunged, his legs pistons, his head an iron wedge.

Closely related is the adjective with a prepositional or comparative phrase.

    Spring air, thick with odor of lilac, moved through the gardens of Montgomery.

Similar in effect is the appositive, a construction that identifies the word preceding it.

    Joe, the mailman, said hello.

The appositive is more simply adjectival than the adjective with prepositional phrase, and briefer than clausal versions: "Fred the horse thief walked in" is more concise than "Fred, who is the horse thief, walked in." In relative phrases not in apposition we can also omit words when the relationship is clear without them; when they can be omitted, they should be. Say, "The flowers she picked were lying on the newspaper," not "The flowers that she picked. . . ." This device is often useful in expository prose. "He had taken a position that was both unworthy and untenable" becomes more forceful when we say, "He had taken a position both unworthy and untenable."

We can frequently use participles in relative phrases in place of whole subordinate or independent clauses, and thereby use fewer words. Participles past or present:

> Tiring of the game, Hamilton took out his doughnut cutter.

> Tired of the game . . . etc.

These versions are briefer than the following alternatives:

> Hamilton was tired (tiring) of the game. He took out his dough-nut cutter.

> Hamilton was tiring (tired) of the game, and he took out his doughnut cutter.

> When he tired of the game, Hamilton took out his doughnut cutter.

Notice the insides of syntax. Each arrangement makes a gesture of meaning that differs from the others. The final example, with the subordinate clause beginning with "when," is an alternative to the participle many writers prefer. It is more precise. "Tired of the game, Hamilton . . ." doesn't make a definite connection between the tired-ness and Hamilton's act. It implies a connection, but it doesn't state it. "When he tired of the game, Hamilton . . ." states sequence. "At the moment when he tired, he. . . ." Although it is not logical to assume that, because one event follows another, the first was the cause of the second, we usually assume so unless we are told not to. But if we wanted to emphasize causation, we could use another conjunction, "Because he was tired of the game, Hamilton. . . ." In many contexts, the "because" might seem overinsistent, or bullying. We have no way of deciding, without context, what form of the sentence would be best. In relaxed, informal writing, the participle might feel right. But the participle leaves questions for the reader, questions that conjunctions like "when" or "because" would answer. The writer has to decide, with each sentence, how much, and with what precision, he wants to tell his reader.

For information on punctuating the complex sentence, see *Commas*, in the Glossary, pp. 270–271.

Long Sentences

In the most controlled prose, in the long sentences of writers being formal, clause follows clause, the sentence is compound as well as complex, and absolutes, participles, and appositives combine with prepositional phrases—a combination of combinations that includes, balances, and ultimately unifies.

If we took the sentence above and reduced it to its constituent parts, one complete clause for each idea, we might end with something like this:

> Some prose is highly controlled and the sentences are long. This happens when the writer is being formal. There are many clauses. The sentence can be compound and it can also be complex. The sentence can also include absolutes, participles, appositive and prepositional phrases. This combination makes the sentence inclusive. It gives it balance, and it gives it unity.

Seven sentences, in this version, and fifty-nine words. The earlier version was one sentence, and forty-three words. The gain in brevity is trivial, but the shorter version is more accurate. It is more accurate by its use of subordination, not only in the agreement of form and content, but by making direct syntactic connections instead of continually stopping the flow of sense and picking it up again with a pronoun.

But the example is made up for the occasion. Here are some sentences from writers at work. Auden is defining the sea as symbol in religion and in literature.

> The sea, in fact, is that state of barbaric vagueness and disorder out of which civilization has emerged and into which, unless saved by the effort of gods and men, it is always liable to relapse.
>
> W. H. Auden, *The Enchafed Flood*

This sentence starts slowly, with "in fact" and "state of," but ends with a flourish of periodic triumph. The parallelism of the prepositions and relatives "out of which" and "into which" finds its action in the exact verbs "emerged" and "relapse," interrupted, with a precision of syntactical sense, by the "unless" clause that separates the relative and the verb of the final clause. We might try once more to supply a version of the sentence as *we* might have written it:

> The sea literally depicts a state of being that is barbaric. Also, it is vague, and it does not have any order in it. Civilization is what has come out of the sea. Civilization is always liable to go back into the sea. But civilization is saved by the efforts of gods and men. Or it has been so far, anyway.

Let us find more examples of long sentences, graceful and agile.

> In the early morning the distant image of Cannes, the pink and cream of old fortifications, the purple Alps that bounded Italy, were cast across the water and lay quavering in the ripples and rings sent up by sea-plants through the clear shadows.
> F. Scott Fitzgerald, *Tender Is the Night*

The passage begins and ends with prepositional phrases, and in between there are more of them, and adjectives, and a varied use of verbs: "bounded, cast, lay quavering." The verbs, which follow each other in time, have as subject the three phrases and clauses before—an elaborated subject, which includes the verb "bounded" as well as nouns and adjectives. Then we move into more prepositions and nouns, another verb, preposition and noun, preposition, adjective, and noun. At the center stand the verbs that carry the sentence. The prose is ornate and well-ordered, but not so formal as the prose of some historians and essayists. Here is a whole paragraph, beginning with a simple sentence:

> Perhaps Philip had not made up his mind either. The English had given him provocation enough: Drake's impudent raid down the Spanish coast and across to the West Indies, Leicester's army in the Netherlands, the worsening fate of the English Catholics for whom, ever since his marriage in England, Philip had felt a special responsibility. The Pope exhorted him to act, the English exile begged him to hurry, and among his counsellors the war party was in the ascendant. It may be that

> Philip was only making haste slowly because, as he had once
> written, in so great a matter it was better to walk with leaden
> feet.
>
> Garrett Mattingly, *The Defeat of the Spanish Armada*

Here is classic prose that is vigorous and formal at the same time. Try to recast the second sentence into a series of simple sentences. Notice the use of the colon to imply that something follows which had been announced by the phrase before the colon. Notice how the list of provocations starts with a long compound subject, varies into a short subject, and then concludes with a long subject ending with a subordinate clause. After this long, complex sentence, the historian varies the pattern by writing a compound of three parts, and ends with a longer complex sentence.

The long, complex sentence lends itself to organizing things that are related to each other, like events in history, plots of stories, or arguments consisting of different parts.

Punctuation and Variety:
Compound Sentences

We use a comma, generally, when the two independent clauses of a compound sentence are long.

> The man wore a green bandana around his neck, but his wife
> wore a Brooks Brothers suit and a black silk tie.

Short compound sentences, however, need no commas. "He was fat and she was thin." The contradiction of "but" often suggests the pause of a comma, but it is a matter of ear, of judgment, rather than of rule. "He was thin, but he was tall" draws more attention to the speaker's insistence on an opposition of terms than does the same sentence without a comma, "He was thin but he was tall," which seems more matter-of-fact, more conversational. Context determines choice.

Compound sentences are loosely held together; a semicolon can substitute for the connective "and." The semicolon implies the close relationship between two clauses, which "and" also implies, but the semicolon makes a different rhythm, by substituting a pause for a connective word. It is a useful variation, and it feels more formal. Avoid a long series of loose compounds, correlative clauses all in a row. Prose that repeats the same loose structure comes to feel too lax. We are all familiar with the speaker who cannot pause:

> I saw her and she was carrying a kitten and it had a crooked tail and I think it was part Siamese and . . .

Some of the same boredom afflicts us when the writer multiplies compounds:

> I saw her and she was carrying a kitten. It had a crooked tail and it was part Siamese. The cat was making tiny squeaks and struggling in her arms. She smiled and then she let out a shriek. The cat had clawed her and jumped out of her arms and run away.

It is easy enough, without radical change, to introduce variety; we vary the type of sentence, using some subordination, and we vary the punctuation in the compound sentences:

> When I saw her she was carrying a kitten with a crooked tail. It was part Siamese. The cat struggled in her arms, making tiny squeaks. She smiled. Then she shrieked. The cat had dug its claws into her, jumped out of her arms, and run away.

Without variety we will be bored. But the variety we choose can be more or less expressive. In this small anecdote the action of the last sentence may be best expressed by the three loose clauses, which were there in the original version; however, the long compound has more effect when it follows the two short sentences—two periods make the rhythm choppy with pause—than it had when it followed other compounds. In a small way, the grammar and the rhythm add to the feeling, or the expression, which is the meaning.

When we join two or more clauses in a compound, we use a connective word or a semicolon, except on rare occasions when we join brief clauses by commas. The classic example is Caesar's "I came, I saw, I conquered," in which the commas make the pauses appropriately brief. Periods—"I came. I saw. I conquered."—make too much space between these clauses. Remember, however, that if the clauses are long, a comma will not hold them together by itself. We need a comma *and* a connective, or a semicolon. In:

> The hair fell to the floor of the barbershop, the man with the broom was dozing in the corner.

the comma is misleading. The sentence could be two sentences, with a period and a capital letter. Or a semicolon could take the place of the comma. Or we could insert the word "and" or "but" after the comma. The distinction between "long" and "short" in this advice is vague, and must remain so. It is clear that in clauses as brief as:

> John blushed, Sara wept, Linda shrieked, the whole class erupted at once.

the commas work. In the bad barbershop example above, the comma would not work. When you come to clauses of middling size, you must decide. It could be:

> I climbed the hill, Susan climbed with me.

or,

> I climbed the hill; Susan climbed with me.

or,

> I climbed the hill. Susan climbed with me.

or,

> I climbed the hill, and Susan climbed with me.

We might well prefer a subordinate phrase—"I climbed the hill, Susan with me." No rule will decide among these arrangements. Context and tone should decide. The writer should first be aware of the alternatives, and should refine his sensitivity to the differences.

The insides of syntax and punctuation show themselves in slight differences in meaning. Thus the first version above is rapid and idiomatic and informal. The semicolon of the second example increases the pause slightly, and increases the formality considerably. The period makes the longest pause, and creates a choppiness, perhaps even a Dick-and-Jane tone. (All comments on the implication of these forms are speculative; a context could make the choppiness rhythmically satisfying, for instance.) The final example is the loosest, the most lax; it is not so grammatically informal as the first, but it is closest to loose speech. The first example, by omitting the connection, is a tighter unit.

We have been talking as if "and," "but," or "or" either took a comma or didn't, depending on the length of the clauses, or whether the sense will benefit from a pause. Sometimes when the clauses on each (or either) side are long, we may want to use the semicolon, so that we can take a longer breath, yet still indicate a close relationship by keeping the two clauses in the same sentence.

> The block was dilapidated, gray, the houses raw and the sidewalks sprouting grass; but he knew he was home.

This use of the semicolon before the connective becomes more common with "yet" and "so." We can write:

> The lion was sleeping in the corner of the cage, yet his feeder approached him warily.

But we are more likely to use the greater pause:

> The lion was sleeping in the corner of the cage; yet his feeder approached him warily.

When we use adverbs as connectives—words like "however," "therefore," and "consequently"—we always use a semicolon.

> The lion stirred awake in the corner of the cage; consequently, his feeder threw down the pail of food and ran away.

Notice that the adverb-connective takes a semicolon in front of it and a comma after it. Or we can make the two clauses into separate sentences.

Much good style, for variety as well as for accuracy to feeling, mixes sentences that are complex and compound, simple and loose, short and long, and incomplete.

Mixing the Types

We can manipulate the types of sentence we use for variety, and to create an expressive effect, to establish a mood, or to emphasize a point. Here are some examples. Keep in mind that the effects of the passages are not achieved by the sentence structure alone, but by the whole apparatus of words and ideas. Sometimes, for the sake of sense or mood, we may manipulate our phrases to achieve more regularity than variety:

> In a little house on the mountain slopes above Delphi lived an old woman with her witless son. The house consisted of a single room; one wall was the mountainside itself, and always dripped with moisture. It was really not a house at all, but a ramshackle hut which herdsmen had built for themselves. It

stood quite alone away up in the wild mountain, high above
the buildings of the city and above the sacred precincts of the
temple.

                                    Pär Lagerkvist, *The Sybil*

The structure of sentences in this passage contributes to a feeling of
simplicity, calm, and stability. The construction is uncomplicated
and regular. All the sentences except the first are regular in word
order, beginning subject/verb and continuing evenly, without parenthetical expressions, or phrases set off by commas, or any other com-
plications of the syntax. The syntax is as undisturbed as the scene.
The sentences are medium in length, and similar in length, establishing a rhythm that reinforces the stability and simplicity in the scene
described. We participate in the rhythm of untroubled isolation.
That rhythm is established, even more, by the uniform length of the
main phrases within the sentences. If we listen to ourselves reading
the passage we will find that natural pauses divide the phrases in this
way:

> In a little house on the mountain slopes above Delphi/
> lived an old woman with her witless son./
> The house consisted of a single room;/
> one wall was the mountainside itself,/
> and always dripped with moisture./
> It was really not a house at all,/
> but a ramshackle hut which herdsmen had built for themselves./
> It stood quite alone away up in the wild mountain,/
> high above the buildings of the city/
> and above the sacred precincts of the temple./

It has enough variation to avoid monotony. But on the whole, the
evenness of length contributes not only to the stillness of the scene,
but to our sense of the narrator's calm, unemotional objectivity.

The following passage from Norman Mailer's *The Armies of the
Night* exhibits different sentence construction, with different effects:

> So it became a rite of passage for these tender drug-vitiated
> jargon-mired children, they endured through a night, a black
> dark night which began in joy, near foundered in terror, and
> dragged on through empty apathetic hours while glints of light
> came to each alone. Yet the rite of passage was invoked, the
> moral ladder was climbed, they were forever different in the

morning than they had been before the night, which is the
meaning of a rite of passage, one has voyaged through a chan-
nel of shipwreck and temptation, and so some of the vices
carried from another nether world into life itself (on the day of
one's birth) may have departed, or fled, or quit; some part of
the man has been born again, and is better, just as some hardly
so remarkable area of the soul may have been in some minuscule sweet fashion reborn on the crossing of the marchers over
Arlington Memorial Bridge, for the worst of them and the most
timid were moving nonetheless to a confrontation they could
only fear, they were going to the land of the warmakers.

In this passage the long, driving, complicated sentences, with many
clauses, give a sensation of high energy, of involvement and enthusiasm. The long sentences will not let the reader relax, but drive him
forward with the marchers. The syntax gives us the sense of struggle
in the rite of passage. It twists and turns, struggling forward, stopped
momentarily by parenthetical expressions ("on the day of one's
birth"); by repetitions ("a night, a black dark night"); and by subordinate clauses ("which is the meaning of a rite of passage").
The relentless speed is impressive; notice the reliance on commas; we
have no place to take a long breath except at the period, and perhaps
a medium-long one at the semicolon. Whereas Lagerkvist, in the
passage quoted earlier, used regular, short sentences to give fictional
events a dispassionate sense of objective reality, Mailer uses long
sentences and complex, forceful syntax to bring the strongest sub-
jectivity to real events.

Revising for Variety and Conciseness

Look over your writing for the construction of sentences. Ask yourself if you vary enough to avoid monotony, if your variations are as
expressive as they might be, and if your informal sentences are appropriate and sufficiently precise.

Also, see if you can be more concise. To revise for conciseness
often requires conjunctions and complex sentences. Conciseness and
precision go together. We ramble on, in our first drafts or in our daily
writing, assuming connections and causes but not stating them. If we
try to make our prose more concise, by writing complex sentences
with precise conjunctions, we often discover that what we wanted to
imply does not really derive from what we said. So this device of

revision—by adding the conjunction—becomes another way of testing, and achieving, the identity of expression and meaning. Precision of time and cause is a responsibility, a responsibility that the loose or compound sentence may evade. In an earlier example, a tiny revision illustrated a small gain in brevity and responsibility:

> I saw her and she was carrying a kitten. It had a crooked tail . . .

became:

> When I saw her she was carrying a kitten with a crooked tail.

Maybe the greatest change here is a change of tone; the writer seems to be controlling something, not merely rattling on.

Here is a passage from a theme in which the writer dumps things together without showing relationships. He wastes words by repetition, and he wastes the power of words by the lack of organization:

> The building was still burning and firemen couldn't put it out. An hour or so went by. The National Guard looked nervous and young. They drove around in their jeeps with their guns. They tried to look tough. We didn't know if their guns were loaded or not. They were scary just because they had guns but they looked scared themselves. They were about the same age as the students. Yet they were guarding them.

Because the relationship between remarks is often vague in this passage, we could not rewrite it with certainty without knowing the facts, or the feelings the author tried to express. Reading the passage, we may doubt that the student had arranged the facts in his mind with clarity, or had understood his feelings. Later, he revised the passage, and his sentence structure accounted for much of the improvement—though as with writing always, the *whole* is an assembly of everything we label as parts (punctuation and verbs; metaphors and participles) and of things that we cannot label:

> As we watched the building burn for hours, the firemen standing by helpless, we became aware of the patrolling jeeps of the National Guard, young men the same age as the students they were guarding, young men who tried to act tough but looked as frightened of their guns as we were.

The gain in economy and vividness is great. So is the gain in clarity of thought and feeling.

EXERCISES

1. Revise a suitable passage from your daily writing in order to introduce variety of sentence structure. Try to use your variations not just for their own sake, but to increase the precision of the writing. Remember that the comma, the semicolon, the colon, and the period are aids to rhythm, and therefore to meaning, expressiveness, and clarity.

2. Find and identify, in your sentences, a subordinate clause, an independent clause, an appositive, a participle, and an adjective with a preposition.

3. Revise the following passage into one complex sentence. You will have to make your own assumptions about causal and temporal relationships. Do more than one version if you can see the possibility of different meanings.

It was raining. It was about seven o'clock the next morning. The jeeps sloshed through the street outside the window. We couldn't sleep. We had breakfast. We all felt hungry. All there was was some beans and brown bread left over. We felt better. The sun came out about nine o'clock.

4. Rewrite the sentence by F. Scott Fitzgerald (p. 97) or the paragraph by Garrett Mattingly (pp. 97–98) as a bad example, with repetitive sentence structure, wordiness, pallor, and lethargy.

5. Write six complex sentences, three of them straight and three of them ridiculous, inappropriate, or melodramatic in their complexity.

6. Try to write one long, silly sentence using as many devices as possible; try to make it compound and complex, with an appositive, a participle, an adjective with a prepositional phrase, and whatever else you can get into it. Then dismantle it and change it into a short passage with a more reasonable sentence structure and more than one sentence.

7. Analyze the following passages for the structure of each sentence, and for the variety of sentences within the same paragraph. Praise or find fault, as you see fit.

a. Down the hall in Apartment 2 the reporter found a very "strong case." There were holes in both the floor and the ceiling, big enough for the biggest rats. Cockroaches crawled up the kitchen wall. A curtain divided off a section of the room for a bedroom, and out from it peeked an old woman. She smiled at the visitors and watched them with interest. Isabel Sánchez, the head of the house, was pointing out some more ratholes. A teen-age girl sat staring at a television set whose screen was filled with a constantly wavering, almost undistinguishable cowboy movie, spoken in Spanish. The reporter walked to the kitchen to watch the cockroaches, and observed that some dishes were sitting on the table that contained the remains of rice and beans.

Dan Wakefield, *Island in the City*

b. Just as the Scaliger fish-tails fret the battlements of North Italian buildings with the symbolic tooth-marks of one particular family biting magnificently at the Lombard sky, so in contemporary America a fish-tail of different shape has come to symbolize, in recent years, a particular and characteristic yearning. This American fish-tail is most readily seen in the shape of those great rudder fins, larger every year, which sprout from the sterns of Cadillacs to support ever more monstrous red rear-lamps. In London, you may study them in and around Grosvenor Square. In the United States they leap backwards from taxicabs and super-automobiles with impartial splendour. They are useless, absurd, vaguely attractive. Most Americans laugh at them. Every American finds them on his new car, whether he wants them or not.

Anonymous, "Jumbo Fish-tails" (1960)

c. The young officer, to whom this seemed a matter of routine, continued to give his orders, in accordance with the general directions of his Group Commander, in a calm, low monotone, and the three reinforcing squadrons were soon absorbed. I became conscious of the anxiety of the Commander, who now stood still behind his subordinate's chair. Hitherto I had watched in silence. I now asked: "What other reserves have we?" "There are none," said Air Vice-Marshal Park. In an account which he wrote about it afterwards he said that at this I "looked grave." Well I might. What losses should we not suffer if our refuelling planes were caught on the ground by further raids of "40 plus" or "50 plus"! The odds were great, our margins small; the stakes infinite.

Sir Winston Churchill, quoted in *The War in the Air*

d. The universe and everything in it constitutes God. The universe is a gigantic human organism and man is a tiny image of it, a toy replica of God. Because he is a miniature of the universe, by a process of spiritual expansion a man can mystically extend his own being to cover the entire world and subject it to his will. It is because all things are aspects of one thing that all things are grist to the magician's mill. The complete man, who has experienced and mastered all things, has vanquished Nature and mounted higher than the heavens. He has reached the centre where man becomes God. The achievement of this is the Great Work, the supreme magical operation, which may take a lifetime or many lifetimes to complete.

Richard Cavendish, *The Black Arts*

e. The voice of the turtle is heard in the land, heard in all the arts—in literature, painting, and music—and in the voices of men and women speaking to one another. It is not the voice of the dove, that sweet and melancholy sound which the translators of the Authorized Version presumably had in mind; it is the croak of isolation and alienation issuing from within a vault of defensive armor—the voice of the reptilian turtle. This armor we wear—the armor of technology separating us from the rest of the natural world—has created us lately in the condition of exiles. Nature exists within as well as without, and we are become, therefore, exiled from ourselves.

John N. Bleibtreu, *The Parable of the Beast*

f. When that did not work, and indeed the Viet Cong seemed to be growing stronger, the next solution was to bomb North Vietnam in order to bring that country to the conference table. North Vietnam did not come to the conference table, so the United States decided to bomb Haiphong and Hanoi.

Apparently that is still not the solution and the search for the roots of the trouble goes on. What will be next? The canals and dikes of North Vietnam, whose bombing will result in the deaths of tens of thousands more? Laos? Cambodia? The nuclear installations of the People's Republic of China? Peking? The escalation route of Washington is heading that way, and the survival of the human race itself is threatened. What Washington does not realize is that the root of the problem is not in the Ho Chi Minh trail, or Hanoi, Haiphong or Peking, but in the heart of the Vietnamese peasant. The war in Vietnam has already lost its meaning, and the longer it goes on, the deeper the hatred and frustration in the heart of the Vietnamese.

Thich Nhat Hanh, *Lotus in a Sea of Fire* (1967)

g. Lönnrot avoided Scarlach's eyes. He looked off at the trees and the sky broken into dark diamonds of red, green, and yellow. He felt a chill and an impersonal, almost anonymous sadness. It was night now; from down in the abandoned garden came the unavailing cry of a bird. Lönnrot, for one last time, reflected on the problem of the patterned, intermittent deaths.

Jorge Luis Borges, "Death and the Compass"

8. Examine the following passages to discover the way in which the sentence structure and variation express the content.

a. Shortly, everybody in Coach House Road was aware that Eli Peck, the nervous young attorney with the pretty wife, was having a breakdown. Everybody except Eli Peck. He knew what he did was not insane, though he felt every inch of its strangeness. He felt those black clothes as if they were the skin of his skin—the give and pull as they got used to where he bulged and buckled. And he felt eyes, every eye on Coach House Road. He saw headlights screech to within an inch of him, and stop. He saw mouths: first the bottom jaw slides forward, then the tongue hits the teeth, the lips explode, a little thunder in the throat, and they've said it: Eli Peck Eli Peck Eli Peck Eli Peck. He began to walk slowly, shifting his weight down and forward with each syllable: E-li-Peck-E-li-Peck-E-li-Peck. Heavily he trod, and as his neighbors uttered each syllable of his name, he felt each syllable shaking all his bones. He knew who he was down to his marrow—they were telling him. Eli Peck. He wanted them to say it a thousand times, a million times, he would walk forever in that black suit, as adults whispered of his strangeness and children made, "Shame . . . shame" with their fingers.

                                        Philip Roth, "Eli, the Fanatic"

b. And then the Arab drew his knife and held it up toward me, athwart the sunlight.
A shaft of light shot upward from the steel, and I felt as if a long, thin blade transfixed my forehead. At the same moment all the sweat that had accumulated in my eyebrows splashed down on my eyelids, covering them with a warm film of moisture. Beneath a veil of brine and tears my eyes were blinded; I was conscious only of the cymbals of the sun clashing on my skull, and, less distinctly, of the keen blade of light flashing up from the knife, scarring my eyelashes, and gouging into my eyeballs.

                                        Albert Camus, *The Stranger*

UNITY

The Need for Unity

W. B. Yeats, the poet, said that a finished poem made a noise like the click of the lid on a perfectly made box. Prose makes the noise too, only less loudly and clearly than poetry. A good passage of prose combines its variety into a final unity, a resolution of rhythm, emotion, and idea into a pleasing whole.

Unity and variety need each other. They are the two poles, and the world spins between them. Without variety, there is nothing to be unified. A series of identically constructed sentences has the unity of chicken wire. Dick-and-Jane has this unity, which is perhaps why we want to leave first grade for second. Paragraphs of sequent compound sentences are similarly boring. But variety without unity is dissatisfying, a disorder that partakes of the lack of focus discussed in the first chapter of this book. As the whole essay must include a sense of resolution, of summing up, of everything coming together—so must smaller units, down to the paragraph, the long sentence, or the sequence of varied sentences.

Grammatical Unity

The good prose already quoted has exemplified unity of agreement, consistency, and the coherence of conjunctions. I bring such terms together in this section because they are grammatical matters that unify and clarify our sentences.

Misplaced Modifiers. The proper placing of modifiers is essential to the unity of content and construction. We must always be careful that a clause does modify the word that its position makes it appear to modify. The dangling participle, with its often comic effect, destroys unity:

> Being six years old and rusted through, I was able to buy the car for a song.

Arranged in this way, the clause "Being six years old and rusted through" modifies "I"; it implies that "I" was six years old and rusted through. Here the best solution would have been a subordinate stating cause:

> Because it was six years old and rusted through, I was able to buy the car for a song.

A similar mistake is the dangling appositive noun phrase:

> A good teacher, his superiors saw to it that he was promoted.

Solutions:

> He was a good teacher; his superiors saw to it that he was promoted.

> Because he was a good teacher, his superiors saw to it that he was promoted.

Yet another kind of misplaced modifier is the dangling participle introduced by a preposition:

> On achieving the age of twenty-seven, his parents threw him out of the house.

(The author may have *intended* the parents to be twenty-seven, and expelling a small child; but we would know that much from the context.)

Or the dangling phrase can be adjectives:

> Tall and strong, the job was easy for him.

There is a prevalent dangling adverb:

> Hopefully, this book will be done by late July.

Does the book really hope? The simplest rewriting would be, "I hope the book will be done by late July."

In all such misreferences, ambiguity is possible. Worse is the frayed edge of misapplied order. There is a laxity that cannot be excused as informality. The *disunity* is unpleasant.

Conjunctions and Unity: Complex Sentences. When we make complex sentences using words that imply sequence or cause or other forms of subordination, our sentences will be whole and solid only if the context supports the idea implicit in the conjunction. This unity of the responsibility of conjunctions is frequently violated. Writers violate it often because they omit something, and their conjunction appears illogical, when, with all the information, the conjunction would make sense. If we read:

> The work was hard; however, John was an extraordinary worker.

the word "however" is illogical. The hardness of the work should not be a potential negative to John's ability. If we read:

> The work was hard; however, the pay was good.

the function of "however" is logical: pay as compensation for difficulty. The first sentence omits something like this:

> The work was so hard it was difficult to imagine anyone doing it; however, John was an extraordinary worker and therefore he could do it.

Here the protestations of the second half of the sentence ("how-ever . . . extraordinary") balance the extremity of the first half ("so hard it was difficult to imagine anyone doing it"). The two parts of the sentence go together, and the conjunction earns its place.

A beer commercial (the brand changed) has an interviewer ask a man,

> "As a lawyer, what do you think of Fitz's?"

The relationship of the two clauses is mysterious. The possibilities of sentences in this pattern are without limit. We could say, "As a re-tired major-league relief pitcher, would you tell me the median rain-fall in the Canary Islands?" Really, the beer commercial hides a meaning; it only appears to be as pointless as the parody of it. Its illogic conceals a social statement. Other beer commercials in the series include women who don't find beer drinking unfeminine, a black man who identifies himself as a professional artist, and several working-class males. The lawyer finds his way into the series to imply that beer-drinking is acceptable among rich chaps too. He likes beer best after sailing all afternoon in his catamaran. So beer is *not* just lower-class, white, and male, and the interviewer means something by his weird sentence. But what he means, he is not allowed to say: "We want to show that the upper-class, professional, chic sailing types drink Fitz's. You are a lawyer who sails. Do you like Fitz's?" Information is suppressed, and the result is, "As a lawyer, what do you think of Fitz's?"

Sometimes when we assert a cause we make our prose vague:

> Because it was raining she did not go to work.

A low pressure area of ambiguity spreads out from this sentence. Does it imply that whenever it was raining she did not work, perhaps because she was a house painter? Or does it imply that the rain keeps her home from work because she likes to garden in the rain? Or does it imply that on this day, when it was raining, she impulsively de-cided not to work? Information has been omitted. We are given a sentence that states causation but leaves us with a hundred ques-tions. The apparent tightness of the complex sentence dissolves be-cause, with information omitted, the parts do not fit logically. Two simple sentences, making fewer claims, would be more satisfying here:

> It was raining. She decided not to go to work.

Contiguity implies connection, but, without further information, the accurate dimness of contiguity is better than the specious clarity of "because."

When we first discover the intricacies of the complex sentence, we sometimes abuse our conjunctions in order to vary for variation's sake, and we can turn out some remarkable prose. Here is a passage someone wrote for an exercise in the complex sentence:

> While the sun was hot, the day was not warm, for the month was May, which, in the year that I am remembering, turned cold, because of a lowering of the temperature.

Except for a sag at the end, the sentence *sounds* all right; but if we examine it, it leaves us with so many questions that we become snagged on every fourth word. This example is extreme, but subtler misuses of conjunctions are common; they make disunity in the search for a complex unity. Or, as in the beer ad, they distort a meaning for a rhetorical purpose. Advertising men and politicians can misuse syntax, to deceive us, as much as they can deceive us by abstraction or euphemism. And so can we deceive ourselves.

Agreement. With errors of agreement, as with misplaced modifiers, ambiguity is possible. But the stylistic disunity is perhaps more distressing than the ambiguity. Agreement is grammatical consistency. Singular noun goes with singular verb, plural noun with plural verb:

> The *boy* with the purple cougar *was* bow-legged.

> The *boys* with the purple cougar *were* bow-legged.

Errors of agreement are common in the use of indefinite pronouns. "One," "none," and distributives like each, every, everybody, nobody, and everyone—all take singular verbs. Here are typical errors:

> Everyone says they had a good weekend.
> None of the machines work.
> Everybody had their tennis racket with them.

Common speech accepts most of these errors in agreement; but the most unified style rejects them. We should write:

> Everyone says he had a good weekend.
> None of the machines works.
> Everybody had his tennis racket with him.

Consistency of Tenses. Similarly, we should stick to one verb tense in describing one action. An account of something that happened to us usually sounds best in the past tense, but occasionally fits the present. A summary of a book takes either tense, often the present. But it is not the choice of past or present that matters most (context decides, as ever); it matters most that we stick to the tense we start with. In careless writing, we drift back and forth without noticing it:

> The maple turned red in September, a bright range of reds from near-gold to near-Chinese. The sky is blue, and the maples show fiercely against it, making the colors more deep. On October the first frost came, and. . . .

The second sentence should take the past tense, to agree with its neighboring sentences. On rare occasions, and usually at a paragraph break, we can change tenses. A leisurely description moves into sudden action, and a break from past to present signals this change. Be careful if you try this device; and know that you are doing it.

Structural Unity

Under this heading I will discuss attributes of stylistic finish and polish which come from the organization of the sentence, rather than from diction. Ranging from the definable *Parallelism* to the intangible *Rhythm*, these structural attributes are optional. Grammatical unity, on the other hand, is obligatory in good prose.

Parallelism. Parallelism is generally a feature of formal prose, and frequently appears in informal prose as well. Parallel constructions are phrases or clauses within the same sentence that repeat the same word forms (nouns, verbs, adjectives, and the like) in the same order to perform the same function.

> He quit the job because the boss was cruel, the pay was meager, and the work was dangerous.

> the boss was cruel / the pay was meager / the work was dangerous

After the conjunction, each subordinate clause follows the pattern of article/noun/past tense verb/predicate adjective. Parallelism is not a grammatical necessity, like agreement. It helps us to manage sentences, and to *clarify* grammar. It is a matter of clarity and symmetry, not of correctness.

We use parallelism most obviously when we use pairs of words to introduce the parallels: "both/and," "either/or," "neither/nor," "not/but," "not only/but also," "first/second/third." The sentence beginning with one of these pairs should pivot on the other; also, the parallel clauses should be syntactically parallel. Do not write:

> Not only did he run into the fire, but also wearing no shoes.

This nonparallel construction is comprehensible, but it feels stylistically lax. These clauses are not parallel because the second uses a participle instead of the active verb that operates in the first clause. We could rewrite it:

> Not only did he run into the fire, but also he wore no shoes.

In writing a long series of clauses, it is common to depart from parallelism and destroy unity.

> His reasons were: first, the overwhelming size of the debt; second, that the company was ill-managed; third, having so little leisure in such a job.

The sentence can be rewritten in numerous ways; for instance:

> His reasons were: first, that the debt had grown huge; second, that the firm was ill-managed; third, that the job afforded little leisure.

The parallelism would remain the same—and we would still want parallelism—if the sentence dropped its enumerations:

> His reasons were that the debt had grown huge, that the firm was ill-managed, and that the job afforded little leisure.

The briefest way to write the sentence would be to make parallels in the predicate subordinate to one "that," by using the verb "to be" once and then understanding it elsewhere in its absence:

> His reasons were that the debt was big, the firm ill-managed, and the job onerous.

The more concise the sentence becomes, the more formal the prose.

With "either/or," "not only/but also," and similar correlative expressions, be sure that by position in the sentence you make the words correlate the same parts of speech in each clause. We frequently misplace our "eithers" and "onlys." We say:

> Either she committed the crime or someone else did.

and we are right. This "either" and this "or" correctly refer to "she" and "someone else." But too often we say:

> Either she ironed all morning, or she watched television.

Because the verbs are being related, the sentence should read:

> She either ironed all morning or watched television.

Here are other ambiguous uses followed by clear ones:

> Either the Professor was asleep or drunk.

> The Professor was either asleep or drunk.

and:

> They not only ran to the grocer, but also to the florist.

> They ran not only to the grocer, but also to the florist.

In making a list, either use an article or a preposition once, at the beginning of the list, or use it throughout:

> The soup, spaghetti, lamb, and salad,

or

> The soup, the spaghetti, the lamb, and the salad,

but not a mixture:

> The soup, spaghetti, the lamb, and salad.

Use:

> Through wind, sleet, and snow,

or

> Through wind, through sleet, and through snow,

but not:

> Through wind, sleet, and through snow.

Not for formal prose, at any rate. For rhythm and emphasis, in informal prose, or in a poem, one might depart from parallelism and profit by the departure.

When one or more prepositional phrases contain several words, parallelism always repeats the preposition. It says

> Through wind, through sleet that stung his cheeks, and through snow.

not,

> Through wind, sleet that stung his cheeks, and snow.

When you use long clauses, introduced by parallel conjunctions, repeat the conjunction. With long clauses, we need the repetition for clarity. In short clauses, we can omit them after the first:

> Although day was done, and night approaching, he kept on ploughing.

But:

> Although the sun had gone down more than twenty minutes ago, and although shadows thickened in the field, he kept on ploughing.

Also, use parallel parts of speech. Verbs go with verbs in a parallel, nouns with nouns, and adjectives with adjectives. This parallelism begins with lists:

> From a distance, he looked tall, gray, well-dressed, and a foreigner.

Instead of "a foreigner," which is a noun, the sentence should fulfill its unity by using the adjective "foreign." A common departure from parallelism is to pair a participle and an infinitive:

> He talked to prove he was intelligent and showing off his cultural background.

This writing is stylistically inconsistent, and it jars the ear like an untuned piano. We should say:

> He talked to prove he was intelligent and to show off his cultural background.

Two participles would be stylistically acceptable, but the infinitives make a more vigorous sentence.

Another frequent lapse of parallelism is to omit a "to" in a series of infinitives. In formal prose, we preserve the infinitive "to" even in a series of simple verbs. We do not say,

> To see, want, and buy is the essence of the American consumer.

We say:

> To see, to want, and to buy is the essence of the American consumer.

The longer the clause, the more upsetting the omission of a "to":

> His desires were few: to live on the ocean, to spend at least a portion of each day sketching the sea-birds, to sleep alone, and cook for himself only.

The unity of the sentence departs when the "to" is omitted before "cook." Yet in informal prose, and speech, we sometimes use an elliptical structure that resembles our practice with articles and prepositions; the "to" remains with the first infinitive, and is understood with the rest:

> He wanted to move back, get a job, buy a convertible, and drive through town in style.

As with the rule on prepositions and articles, the word "to," once omitted after the first use, may not slip back again.

Constructions on two sides of coordinates should agree. If we find ourselves writing:

> Either he was rotten or a badly misunderstood young man.

we should improve it by keeping the parts of speech parallel:

> He was either rotten or badly misunderstood.

Sometimes we make sentences like this one:

> He hoped that she would come and she would wear the blue dress.

The first clause uses "that" and the second violates unity by omitting it. The sentence should read:

> He hoped that she would come and that she would wear the blue dress.

The word "that" can safely be omitted entirely, when no parallel clause is used. "He hoped she would come" by itself is fine, but when "He hoped" more than one clause, we need parallel "thats." In the single clause, follow your ear.

Emphasis. Since emphasis works to construct a sentence firmly, emphasis promotes unity.

Parallelism makes emphasis; so does repetition in general. Where the politician's speech as a whole gathers speed by repeating a phrase, like "And what is your answer to *this*, Mr. President?" so the sentence gathers firmness by repeating parts:

> We must agree that the present administration is bankrupt, that it has no cash reserves of the spirit, that its morale is a total liability.

Balance, the subject of the next section, also contributes to emphasis.

The variety of sentence types can also become emphatic (and thus variety can lend its power to unity) when we shift suddenly from one sort of sentence to another. Most commonly, we see a short sentence provide emphasis after a series of long sentences:

> We cannot agree that the Cabinet has been ineffective, because as far as we can tell the Cabinet does not exist. If it exists, will someone please tell us if it has met? For we have been unable to discover when it meets, or where, or with whom in attendance, or if the President knows his own Secretaries by name. We think he doesn't.

The emphasis developed by a contrast of sentence types is an emphasis within the development of the paragraph.

Development within the sentence itself is the contribution of emphasis to the unity of the sentence. For emphasis, we put the most important words of the sentence at the beginning or at the end—and mostly at the end. (See *Concluding the Sentence*, pp. 122–123.) If a sentence has three parts, which we could score from one to three from least to most interesting, the emphatic sentence probably would be 2, 1, 3; it could be 3, 1, 2, and it could be 1, 2, 3; it could not end with 1 and remain emphatic.

When the sentence saves the best for last, we call it a periodic sentence.

> That the spring was late this year, that the dogwood never bloomed and that the flowers struggled wanly out of the garden, all of these failures must have contributed to the moment when Frederick, suddenly and without warning, shot his wife.

This order, reduced to a skeleton of itself, is surely 2, 1, 3.

When we have a series of details or ideas to present in a sentence, the emphatic order is the crescendo. If one of the details is a surprise—something that may seem out of place, and paradoxically belongs there—it should come last. Otherwise the order is simply the order of intensity:

> After the flood, we saw great willows uprooted, houses ripped from their foundations and drifted against canyon walls, and the swollen bodies of the dead.

> The President has tricked the workers, ignored the poor, soaked the rich, and murdered the military.

Departures from an emphatic order destroy unity by appearing fortuitous. A periodic sentence feels constructed and planned, as opposed to a loose sentence, which trails off into "many other instances of this kind." An emphatic order creates a sense of control opposite to the sense of randomness. It is one more device contributing to the click of the box.

Balance. Balance and parallelism are related; both have to do with repetition. Both can create emphasis. But parallel construction is a matter of maintaining equal grammatical structure, and balance has to do with the weight of sentence parts. Balance is style, it is not grammar, nor can it be described grammatically. A balanced sentence is one in which the main parts of the sentence are of approximately the same rhythm and importance. It is important to remember that a balanced sentence need not have *two* parts in balance; it may have three or four or more. Balance is a less precise matter than parallel construction.

> In his day, Frank built model airplanes of balsa wood and went to the movies on Saturday; / now, at the same age, Jim cruises around in his own car and flies to New York for the weekend.

> Fred said it was dangerous, / but Bill insisted on going.

These sentences have balance but do not have precisely parallel construction. For accurate expression, and without ambiguity, they depart from exact parallelism. Of course balance and parallelism are not necessarily exclusive. Not only are they similar in the unity they create, but both can work in the same sentence:

> The Grogs wanted only to share and be reconciled; they wanted only to kill or be killed.

Balance and parallelism give emphasis to a sentence, and help us to remember it. Many proverbs and epigrams employ them for these reasons.

Here is parallelism without balance:

> We are to have what we have as if it were loaned to us and not given; to be without proprietary rights to body or soul, mind or faculties, worldly goods or honors, friends, relations, houses, castles, or anything else.
>
> Meister Eckhart

Balance without parallelism:

> People possess four things
> that are no good at sea: /
> anchor, rudder, oars,
> and the fear of going down.
>
> Antonio Machado

Balance and parallelism:

> The foxes have their holes and the birds have their nests; but the Son of Man has no place to lay his head and to rest.

Extreme balance and parallelism, as in wise sayings:

> The old pine-tree speaks divine wisdom; the secret bird manifests eternal truth.
>
> Zen proverb

Rhythm. Rhythm and resolution, which we name together because they seem related, are more difficult to define or exemplify than any other words used in this book. By rhythm we mean the pleasing arrangement of sounds, the sort of emphatic arrangement we might gesture to accompany, or want to tap our feet to. The Hemingway passage quoted on page 16–17 succeeds by means of its rhythm. Here is another example of superb rhythm, quite different from Hemingway's, more lush and energetic:

> Witches, werewolves, imps, demons and hobgoblins plummetted from the sky, some on brooms, others on hoops, still others on spiders. Osnath, the daughter of Machlath, her fiery hair loosened in the wind, her breasts bare and thighs exposed, leaped from chimney to chimney, and skated along the eaves. Namah, Hurmizah the daughter of Aff, and many other she-devils did all sorts of somersaults. Satan himself gave away the bride, while four evil spirits held the poles of the canopy, which had turned into writhing pythons. Four dogs escorted the groom.
>
> Isaac Bashevis Singer, "The Gentleman from Cracow"

Rhythmic pleasure is essential to the resolutions of good style, but rhythmic effects cannot be separated from the meaning of the words embodying the rhythm. Look at the examples elsewhere in this book of carelessly constructed sentences, for instance pp. 77, 99, and 104. In these examples we can feel the difference between prose that is strong in rhythm and resolution, and prose that is weak in rhythm and resolution.

I suspect that a writer's ear is his most subtle, and possibly his most valuable, piece of equipment. We acquire a good ear by reading the great masters until their cadences become part of our minds. The stored memory of a hundred thousand sentences becomes the standard of the writer's own ear.

Resolution. Resolution is the art of ending a thing so that the reader feels satisfied. So resolution partakes of sound, sense, feeling, and emphasis. The periodic sentence, holding back its emphasis until the end, is an obvious method of achieving resolution. Here is another periodic sentence:

> Without schooling, without friends, without money, without the accent that is necessary for success in Britain, he arrived in London.

This device is so pointed that we cannot do it often, and must usually rely on more subtle resolutions. There can be no rules for resolution or rhythm, only example and exhortation, because each click of the box is improvised. The more we know the materials of style, the more extensive our ability to improvise. Look back at F. Scott Fitzgerald (p. 97) and see the slow, rising beginning, the calm plateau of the verbal center, and the slow peaceful descent at the end. Then contrast it with the quicker-moving, informative prose of Garrett Mattingly (pp. 97–98). Each sentence is its own little dance, in which variety arrives at unity by way of improvisation; and each sentence relates to each other sentence as part relates to part, so that the paragraph is a sequence of dances that become one dance.

In talking about rhythm and resolution, we are not so much covering new material as looking at old material from another point of view. Asking you to practice rhythm and resolution is asking you to write well.

Concluding the Sentence. I have been speaking—in *Emphasis*, and in *Resolution*—about ending the sentence well. No sentence can have resolution if it trails off in flatness or emptiness. Let us look at some common failures in the endings of sentences. In conversation, and in unedited writing, we frequently start a sentence with high energy and then collapse when we try to conclude it: We have a subject, but we haven't the faintest notion of a predicate. We say:

> The increase in heroin consumption in the early seventies

because we are worried. But we don't know exactly what to say about it, so we reach around for a predicate-filler, to end our sentence:

> is a matter of the utmost importance,

or

> requires our immediate attention,

or

> is an aspect of contemporary life that must concern us all.

Sometimes a writer will string together a series of such sentences—all strong subjects with weak predicates:

> The increase in heroin consumption in the early seventies is of paramount concern to us all. Firm international controls are of the utmost necessity. The identity of heroin-producing nations is a matter of public knowledge. The destruction of crops at their source is one way of dealing with the problem.

Each sentence achieves the art of falling. These dancers trip on their skirts. The writer has a partial idea—like a sentence fragment—but makes it into a pseudo-complete sentence with trite predicates. The mind that writes such sentences seems to be disorganized, or lazy about organizing. The series of unresolved, trailing-off sentences communicates a vacuum. Yet with a little attention, the writer could have talked plainly, with the decency of whole ideas, and an attendant fullness:

> The increase in heroin consumption in the early seventies requires international controls to destroy the crops at their source in the heroin-producing countries.

We used only a third of the words, in this version, and the sentence is unified.

Formulas for ending sentences are like other verbal formulas. All formulas are to be avoided, but some are more destructive than others. The filler-predicate is certain to destroy any possibility of a satisfactory coda, the ending that satisfies us by its rhythm and resolution.

Unity of Diction

Earlier, we called some words "fancy," and we have alluded to formal and informal styles. Now, in a chapter on the sentence, it will be wise to consider the levels of diction, the tones of voice our prose can aim for. We think of them now, under the general subject of the unity of the sentence, because consistency of tone is another means of holding our writing together, another means to unity.

Formality and Informality. Choosing a level of diction, as I mentioned in *Words*, is a matter of tact. You do not use the same vocabulary, sentence structure, or organization of thought on contrasting occasions. The doctor delivering a paper to his colleagues writes a formal and scientifically exact prose; the same man, writing an alumni newsletter, writes a relaxed and conversational prose. If one style wandered for a moment into the opposite prose, we would have disunity:

> The amino acids were observed to disappear from the patient's urine which was a helluva note.

or:

> "Pa" Barker writes that he and his child bride have settled into suburbia where they are expecting obstetric surgery.

The alumni note could be an attempt at humor. Much humor depends upon disunity. More examples will follow presently.

Of course "formal" and "informal" are relative, and many points fall between the extremes. We must think about three things: first, what distinguishes formal from informal; second, the occasions requiring or suggesting different tones; third, the degree of unity of tone appropriate to an essay or a story, and the degree of variety it will tolerate, accept, or enjoy.

It will be good to start with examples of formal and informal prose, as touchstones, or concrete reference points for our abstractions. For formal prose, look at this passage from Ecclesiastes in the King James translation of the Bible. The King James Bible always combines vigor and formality:

> I returned and saw under the sun, that the race is not to the swift, nor the battle to the strong, neither yet bread to the wise, nor yet riches to men of understanding, nor yet favour to men of skill; but time and chance happeneth to them all.

Or look at this contemporary passage of literary criticism:

> But to make the modern world possible in art is not the same, as Lawrence would have insisted, as making life possible in the modern world. The myths that Mr. Eliot is at such pains to parallel are, almost without exception, not acceptable to Lawrence. They were, indeed, the very things that made living his life all but impossible. He chose, both as an artist and as a man, not to manipulate myths but life itself. It is this that stigmatizes him as a dangerous heretic. He was, in fact, anarchy compounded, which may explain, if not justify, the element of panic in Mr. Eliot's attack that leads him into such unwarranted abuse.
>
> Wright Morris, *The Territory Ahead*

For informal prose, here is a passage from James Thurber's *The Years with Ross*:

> Ross began as a dice shooter in the AEF, and ended up with a gambling compulsion. Nobody knows how many thousands of dollars he lost in his time at poker, backgammon and gin rummy, but it ran way up into five figures. He finally gave up sky's-the-limit poker, but would often play all night in Reno or Colorado, on his trips West, in games where the stakes were

only a dollar or so. He must have won at poker sometimes, but I don't think he ever really got the hang of the game; certainly he didn't bring to it the intuitive sense he brought to proofs and manuscripts. He once told me about what he called the two goddamdest poker hands he had ever seen laid down on a table. "One guy held a royal flush, and the other had four aces," he said. When I asked, "Who got shot?" he looked puzzled for a moment and then said, "All right, all right, then, it was a straight flush, king high, but I've been telling it the other way for ten years." His greatest gambling loss occurred in New York, in 1926, when he plunged into a poker game with a tableful of wealthy men. He got off to a lucky start, and was two thousand dollars ahead and going to drop out when one of the players said, "Winners quitters, eh?" Ross, who was drinking in those days, stayed in the game, kept on drinking, and lost thirty thousand dollars.

The more formal the prose, as a rule, the more complicated the sentence structure, and the more pronounced the parallelism.

In the choice of words, formal prose avoids the slangy, the colloquial, or the novel. A writer attempting a formal style sometimes falls into temporary informality because he cannot think of the appropriate word; because his vocabulary is inadequate, or because he is too lazy to look for the word. Writing a research paper on the exports of a small nation, we want to imply that the Minister of the Treasury lacked financial integrity; but "lacked financial integrity" is a pompous formula. What do we say of him? If we call him "a crook," we will intrude an alien vocabulary upon this paper. The slang is like an error in tact. The best solution is to say something particular, and avoid the generality. Perhaps we can say that he was convicted of taking bribes.

In a more informal context, "crook" might be just the right word, bringing in a touch of the roughness of slang, a little asperity. Tact is all. And it is like social tact, which is often called hypocrisy. When you see an old friend for the first time in six months, you may call him all sorts of names that you would not use in front of your priest's sister. When you are introduced to the Rumanian ambassador between the acts of the visiting ballet, you do not use the same epithets you would use with your old friend; you are more apt to say something original, like, "How do you do, Mr. Ceascu?" If you called him "you old son of a bitch" (which is no more original, of course), you would have a social problem.

Formality Gone Bad. We can help to define our terms by looking at what they are not. The virtue of informality can slide into the vice of obscurity, wasted words, or vague terms. The virtue of formality can wiggle in a hundred directions into the many vices of pomposity, fanciness, pretense, jargon, and meaningless abstraction. George Orwell turned a good formality into a horrid one by rewriting the passage from Ecclesiastes that I quoted earlier. In this parody, his modern version is the High Abstraction of sociology in particular. He takes:

> I returned and saw under the sun, that the race is not to the swift, nor the battle to the strong, neither yet bread to the wise, nor yet riches to men of understanding, nor yet favour to men of skill; but time and chance happeneth to them all.

and turns it into:

> Objective consideration of contemporary phenomena compels the conclusion that success or failure in competitive activities exhibits no tendency to be commensurate with innate capacity, but that a considerable element of the unpredictable must invariably be taken into account.

Orwell's parody, which would pass for good prose with many people, sounds untouched by human hands, like a monstrous frozen dinner fabricated from sawdust and boiled crayons.

Some years earlier, Sir Arthur Quiller-Couch did a parody of part of Hamlet's "To be or not to be . . ." soliloquy. Quiller-Couch's parody is not sociological jargon in particular. His parody collects a little anthology of typical modern faults in formal writing, formal attempts ending in pomposity and verbosity. As in Orwell's parody, the result is the abstract and the general rather than the metaphorical and the particular. Here is the Shakespeare, and then the Quiller-Couch:

> To be, or not to be: that is the question:
> Whether 'tis nobler in the mind to suffer
> The slings and arrows of outrageous fortune,
> Or to take arms against a sea of troubles,
> And by opposing end them? To die: to sleep;
> No more; and by a sleep to say we end
> The heart-ache and the thousand natural shocks
> That flesh is heir to, 'tis a consummation
> Devoutly to be wish'd.

To be, or the contrary? Whether the former or the latter be preferable would seem to admit of some difference of opinion; the answer in the present case being of an affirmative or of a negative character according as to whether one elects on the one hand to mentally suffer the disfavour of fortune, albeit in an extreme degree, or on the other to boldly envisage adverse conditions in the prospect of eventually bringing them to a conclusion. The condition of sleep is similar to, if not indistinguishable from that of death; and with the addition of finality the former might be considered identical with the latter: so that in this connection it might be argued with regard to sleep that, could the addition be effected, a termination would be put to the endurance of a multiplicity of inconveniences, not to mention a number of down-right evils incidental to our fallen humanity, and thus a consummation achieved of a most gratifying nature.

Neither the Orwell nor the Quiller-Couch parodies are examples of formality. Because of their imprecision, they could be called sloppy, though never informal; imprecision is a quality of most bad prose, whether it is formal or informal in its intent. These parodies are examples of a stiff prose style that *passes for* formality among many writers.

Pompous Language. We use pompous language to paint over a reality we wish to evade. Earlier, I mentioned euphemisms; sometimes, whole sentences are euphemistic. The airline has the stewardess say, "Would you care to purchase a cocktail?" instead of, "Do you want to buy a drink?" because the second sentence sounds crass, plain, and barmaidish. For the same reasons, "beverage" is often substituted for "drink." These words are fancy substitutes for plain talk, and we use them (or they are used on us by commerce) for deceit. They are a vice to which formality is put. But they are not genuinely "more formal." "Wealthy" is not more formal than "rich," it is just more fancy. "Rich" is not slang; it belongs in the most formal discourse. It is plain, and formality can include plainness without disunity, as it cannot include slang without upsetting its wholeness of tone. Think of the difference between "crook" and "rich." And think of the difference between "tool" and "implement." Like "rich," "tool" is plain, and perfectly suited to formal discourse; "implement" is polysyllabic and general, and often a pompous alternative to "tool."

Formal and Informal Sentence Structure. The question "Do you want to buy a drink?" is neither formal nor informal in itself. "Would you care to purchase a cocktail?" is pompous. "Want to get sloshed?" is slangy, which is not the same as informal. We could use "Do you want to buy a drink?" in a context that was either formal or informal, because its words are plain. Informally:

> The girl came down the aisle looking tidy and cheerful. In back of the makeup and the hair, which looked as if it would break off in chunks if you touched it, perhaps there was a living girl, somebody with a name like Eileen or Carol. She wanted to say, "Do you want to buy a drink?" But the airline had enamelled her talk along with her hair. "Would you care to purchase a cocktail?"

Or, more formally:

> When you arrive at the age of fifty, your ability to choose has narrowed, and you find yourself at the narrow end of the funnel, blocked from expanding or wandering, focused instead on one bleak point at the bottom of the page. When you were young, you questioned: Do you want to be an actor, or a poet? Will you live in London, New York, or Paris? Now you are no longer young: Will you eat lobster for dinner? Do you want to buy a drink?

The difference here is *more* a matter of sentence (and paragraph) structure than it is of vocabulary. It includes words also, but except that fancy euphemisms are excluded from both camps, the difference in vocabulary is relative. "Tidy" and "cheerful" could go in either passage. The idiomatic gesture of "along with," in the first passage, is relatively informal; perhaps "as well as" would be the formal equivalent. "Chunks" has an informal sound. But the sentence structure of the second passage—complex, pointed, controlled—mainly accounts for its greater formality.

Informality Gone Bad. The fault typical of informal prose, when it goes bad, is incoherence. It does not hang together. (Pompous-formal prose, or jargon, at least *seems* to hang together.) Here is a journalist's parody of what the Gettysburg Address would have sounded like, if President Eisenhower had delivered it:

> I haven't checked these figures but 87 years ago, I think it was, a number of individuals organized a governmental set-up here in this country, I believe it covered certain Eastern areas,

with this idea they were following up based on a sort of national independence arrangement and the program that every individual is just as good as every other individual. Well, now, of course, we are dealing with this big difference of opinion, civil disturbance you might say, although I don't like to appear to take sides or name any individuals, and the point is naturally to check up, by actual experience in the field, to see whether any governmental set-up with a basis like the one I was mentioning has any validity and find out whether that dedication by those early individuals will pay off in lasting values and things of that kind.

Well, here we are, at the scene where one of these disturbances between different sides got going. We want to pay our tribute to those loved ones, those departed individuals who made the supreme sacrifice here on the basis of their opinions about how this thing ought to be handled. And I would say this. It is absolutely in order to do this.

But if you look at the over-all picture of this, we can't pay any tribute—we can't sanctify this area, you might say—we can't hallow according to whatever individual creeds or faiths or sort of religious outlooks are involved like I said about this particular area. It was those individuals themselves, including the enlisted men, very brave individuals, who have given this religious character to the area. The way I see it, the rest of the world will not remember any statements issued here but it will never forget how these men put their shoulders to the wheel and carried this idea down the fairway.

Now frankly, our job, the living individuals' job here, is to pick up the burden and sink the putt they made these big efforts here for. It is our job to get on with the assignment—and from these deceased fine individuals to take extra inspiration, you could call it, for the same theories about the set-up for which they made such a big contribution. We have to make up our minds right here and now, as I see it, that they didn't put out all that blood, perspiration and—well—that they didn't just make a dry run here, and that all of us here, under God, that is, the God of our choice, shall beef up this idea about freedom and liberty and those kind of arrangements, and that government of all individuals, by all individuals and for all individuals, shall not pass out of the world-picture.

Oliver Jensen, "The Gettysburg Address in Eisenhowese."

And here, in case you do not remember it, is Lincoln's formal original:

> Fourscore and seven years ago our fathers brought forth on this continent a new nation, conceived in liberty, and dedicated to the proposition that all men are created equal.
>
> Now we are engaged in a great civil war, testing whether that nation, or any nation so conceived and so dedicated, can long endure. We are met on a great battlefield of that war. We have come to dedicate a portion of that field as a final resting-place for those who here gave their lives that that nation might live. It is altogether fitting and proper that we should do this.
>
> But in a larger sense, we cannot dedicate—we cannot consecrate—we cannot hallow—this ground. The brave men, living and dead, who struggled here, have consecrated it far above our poor power to add or detract. The world will little note nor long remember what we say here, but it can never forget what they did here. It is for us, the living, rather, to be dedicated here to the unfinished work which they who fought here have thus far so nobly advanced. It is rather for us to be here dedicated to the great task remaining before us—that from these honored dead we take increased devotion to that cause for which they gave the last full measure of devotion; that we here highly resolve that these dead shall not have died in vain; that this nation, under God, shall have a new birth of freedom; and that government of the people, by the people, for the people, shall not perish from the earth.

The parody is twice the length of the original, yet doesn't convey any more information. In fact, it is much less specific—substituting nebulous phrases like "this big difference of opinion, civil disturbance you might say" for clear and simple ones like "a great civil war." The sentences wander and repeat themselves ("It was those individuals themselves, including the enlisted men, very brave individuals . . .").

It would be easy to continue the list of faults, because they were planted deliberately. But it is more important here to notice how they change the effect of the statement. The writing is so diluted and drifting that we don't feel that the speaker cares for the subject itself; we don't believe that he is genuinely moved. One common fault that helps to create this impression is the repeated use of pointless qualifications like "I think," "I believe," and "I would say." Many people mistakenly think that such qualifications make writing more informal and natural. But these personalisms are understood without being said, and they make one feel that if the speaker (or writer) is so hesitant and tentative about speaking his mind then he is probably not certain of it.

Be wary of becoming careless in the effort to be informal. Carelessness is partly a matter of vagueness of words: "individual," which is jargon for "person," is vaguer than "person" or "people." But it is also a matter of lacking sentence and paragraph structure, of trailing off at the ends of sentences, of a lack of resolution and emphasis. Series of simple and compound sentences that bore us are usually careless; parts do not mesh into a whole; there is no consistency. If you write with some respect for variety and unity—if you write with a sense of shape and finish—you will avoid such failings, and inhabit some point along the line that stretches from formality to informality.

Subject and Audience. The choice of a level of diction comes from subject and audience. We know, before we think it over, that a recollection of family reunions will be more informal than an essay advocating the abolition of the post office. Content and circumstance determine permissible areas on the line from formal to informal, and will determine whether we choose "crook" or "criminal" before we come to it. In a recollection of junior high school, if a student writes:

> After a month of missing wallets and empty purses, we decided that somebody in the classroom was a crook.

we read along easily, and the slangy word is vigorous at the end of the sentence. If the student had written:

> After a month of missing wallets and empty purses, we came to the conclusion that someone in the classroom was a criminal.

we would find the style ponderous—"come to the conclusion that"— and serious to the point of comedy. "Criminal" is a heavy word for petty thievery in the junior high.

On the other hand, if the student was writing an essay on the traffic in heroin, and wrote:

> In 1969, an investigation organized by Interpol showed that high officials in three Mediterranean countries, in which opium grew, in which opium was refined into heroin, and from which

> illegal shipments started for the United States, were crooks
> making vast profits by virtue of their public positions.

the word "crooks" would be inappropriately informal, in a sentence
so formal in diction and structure. "Criminals" would be the better
word.

We must learn to look for errors in tact when we revise; we must
look for the low word in the high place, and for the high word in the
low place. When we have used the wrong word or construction, we
can revise it out. If we write "crook" because we cannot think of
"criminal" we can consult the dictionary. If we fall into repeated
compound sentences in a formal context, we can complicate some of
them. If in the middle of a modest piece of prose, we find that we
have slipped unwittingly into polysyllables and long, complex sentences, we can simplify. But in order to learn to revise we must learn
what to look for.

Mixing Formal and Informal Diction. We would write more easily
if we could think of prose as either informal or formal, as if nothing
existed between the poles. But most good prose lives in the temper-
ate regions on either side of the equator. The informal essay enjoys
an occasional periodic sentence, or unusual word. The formally deft
argument uses a sudden colloquialism with charm and wit.

A sentence by E. B. White exemplifies the mixture a witty man can
make. White has been talking with appropriate disdain about a pam-
phlet on writing that, among other things, admonishes us, "Whenever possible, personalize your writing by directing it to the reader."
"Personalize" is a slimy word. As White says, "A man who likes the
word 'personalize' is entitled to his choice, but we wonder whether
he should be in the business of giving advice to writers." The word is
used commercially to mean an imprinted name, "personalized stationery" for instance, and does not mean "to make personal" or "to
direct toward another person." White's comment, after he quotes the
advice, is the sentence:

> As for us, we would as lief Simonize our grandmother as per-
> sonalize our writing.

The mini-analogy expresses White's feeling: it would be monstrous
to "personalize our writing." He compares the offensive diction to an
unnatural act. At the same time, he uses a cunning and *personal*
oddity of diction. The plain way to say the sentence is, "we would as

soon Simonize our grandmother," but White uses the old-fashioned "as lief." And "lief" nudges against "Simonize," the old-fashioned word against the trademark. The bizarre mixture of dictions—the *dis*unity—makes its point.

So the mixture of dictions can be expressive as well as comic. Often it is chiefly comic. W. C. Fields' polysyllables are comic because he uses high words in low matters—or for low purposes, like conning people.

Revising for Unity. Unity brings us much to consider in revision. Go over your prose, thinking of it as something that ought to be as whole and as shapely as a clay pot or an automobile fender. Maybe a little less shiny and symmetrical than an automobile fender.

Look for rhythm and resolution, paying special attention to the ends of your sentences. Look for parallelism, emphasis, and balance. Repair any grammatical disunity that may have crept in. Look for places in which your tone shifts for no good reason, and make repairs.

EXERCISES

1. Rewrite the phrases that follow, to give them emphatic unity, or to remove errors or ambiguities.

a. Without knowing which one was best, the chocolate-covered one appealed to me most.

b. Having arrived at the airport fifteen minutes ahead of schedule, my friends were nowhere to be seen.

c. A genius at seven, his parents were worried about his relationships with second-grade classmates.

d. Hopefully, some of these exercises are simple.

e. Everyone wore levi jackets with their names printed on them.

f. While the sunset was beautiful, the aroma of the garden was more beautiful still.

g. In Zambia, Russia, Poland, and in Venezuela . . .

h. When the game was over, when the stands emptied, when the pop-corn was swept up, and the lights were extinguished, a vast silence overtook the stadium.

i. Intelligent, pretty, sympathetic, a good friend, Jane was known to everyone in the dormitory.

j. She danced to prove she didn't care, and implying she did.

k. He answered that he didn't care what she did, that he was furious with her, and he would never speak to her again.

l. Either you come inside, or get a spanking.

2. Analyze the grammatical unity in the following passages:

a. Byron never left the world, nor could he ever abandon any of the existing conceptions of it. His is therefore the most social of Romantic imaginations and so the least Romantic. Few poets had less trust in their own consciousness, and no great English poet had less faith in the validity of his own powers than Byron. The powers were exuberant, but Byron's Devourer was very nearly as strong as the Prolific portion of his being, and this conflict of contraries could rarely be accepted by the poet as a value in itself, which in Don Juan it finally proved to be. Byron's imagination found its escape from self-consciousness in the social ideal of "mobility," but "mobility" did not always find a way back to an identity with Imagination, as the heightened awareness of both actuality and human possibility.

Harold Bloom, *The Visionary Company*

b. Whenever a word appears in a radically new context it has a radically new sense: the expression in which it so figures is a poetic figment, a fresh literary creation. Such invention is sometimes perverse, sometimes humourous, sometimes sublime; that is, it may either buffet old associations without enlarging them, or give them a plausible but impossible twist, or enlarge them to cover, with unexpected propriety, a much wider or more momentous experience. The force of experience in any moment—if we abstract from represented values—is emotional; so that for sublime poetry what is required is to tap some reservoir of feeling. If a phrase opens the flood-gates of emotion, it has made itself most deeply significant. Its discursive range and clearness may not be remarkable; its emotional power will quite suffice. For this reason again primitive poetry may be sublime: in its inchoate phrases there is affinity to raw passion and their very blindness may serve to bring that passion back. Poetry has body; it represents the volume of experience as well as its form, and to express volume a primitive poet will rely rather on rhythm, sound, and condensed suggestion than on discursive fulness or scope.

George Santayana, "Poetry and Prose"

c. If our comparison of the imaginative writer with the day-dreamer, and of poetic production with the daydream, is to be of any value, it must show itself fruitful in some way or other. . . . Let us try, for instance, to examine the works of writers in reference to the idea propounded above, the relation of the fantasy to the wish that runs through it and to the three periods of time; and with its help let us study the connection between the life of the writer and his productions.

Sigmund Freud, "The Relation of the Poet to Daydreaming"

d. I have shared that monster's fate more than once in my sleep, have feared him and been him in the same dream, and I suspect that perhaps even you have lived through a similar night. Or was it in the Carpathians as Count Dracula welcomed you to his webbed castle where you were to feel the light touch of teeth on your throat and were to rise at night yourself, undead and hot with a thirst for living blood? Or did you seek freedom from the wolf's curse that drove you, all shaggy hair and sharp fangs, through moonlit streets, hungry for death and life? Or did you linger, scarred and mad, in the catacombs of the Paris Opera, or stalk the night protecting the mummified remains of a princess you loved 3,700 years ago? These dreams are as much a part of us now as the doubts of Hamlet or the frenzy of Lear. They come to us from a variety of sources—perhaps even, as Robert Eisler suggested in *Man into Wolf*, from "the subhuman strata of the 'collective unconscious.'" But certainly they have come most clearly to us today from the films of our youth, the horror movies we sat through eagerly, showing after showing, and dreamed of during those hectic nights that found us shivering under covers even in a hot and sultry summer.

R. H. W. Dillard, "Even a Man Who Is Pure at Heart: Poetry and Danger in the Horror Film"

3. Decide whether each of the following sentences has balance, parallel construction, both, or neither.

a. Let him who seeks cease not in his seeking until he finds; and when he finds, he will be troubled, and if he is troubled, he will marvel, and will be a king over the All.

Jesus Christ

b. Only when you have no thing in your mind and no mind in things are you vacant and spiritual, empty and marvelous.

Zen Buddhist saying

c. He who knows does not say; he who says does not know.

Lao-Tzu

d. But logic does not always win popularity, and a man who points out the gloomy end of things can hardly expect to gain popular esteem.

Robert L. Heilbroner, *The Worldly Philosophers*

e. A common opinion prevails that the juice has ages ago been pressed out of the free-will controversy, and that no new champion can do more than warm up stale arguments which everyone has heard.

William James, "The Dilemma of Determinism"

f. Another odd feature of the human landscape in these climactic years is that both sides claim to be moved by the purest impulses of human brotherhood.

I. F. Stone, *The Haunted Fifties*

g. Let the actor for the time being keep to himself, store up his emotions, his spiritual materials, his reflections about his part, until his feelings and a definite, concrete, creative sense of the image of his part have become crystallized.

Constantin Stanislavski, *Creating a Role*

h. I think a nation such as ours, with its high moral traditions and commitments, has a further responsibility to know how we became drawn into this conflict, and to learn the lessons it has to teach us for the future.

Alfred Hassler, *Saigon, U.S.A.*

i. A self that consisted of conventional lies, shams, self-deceptions, memory images, a self just like that of other people, grew in me again but behind and above it stood a greater and more comprehensive self which impressed me with something of what is eternal, unchanging, immortal and inviolable and which ever since that time has been my protector and refuge.

Karl Jaspers, *General Psychopathology*

j. My father and mother were certainly of vital importance, not only in themselves but because they created a world for me to revolt against.

Ingmar Bergman, *Four Screenplays of Ingmar Bergman*

4. Write three balanced sentences without parallel construction, three with parallel construction but without balance, and three with balance and parallel construction.

5. Revise a page or two from your daily writing, keeping in mind unity, emphasis, parallelism, balance, rhythm, and resolution. Not only avoid disunity, but employ unity for the sake of expression.

6. Revise the following passage so that it has a more satisfying rhythm.

The old man lived in the gloomiest part of the forest. He had a house there. It was made of crude bricks. All kinds of trees grew around the house. There were oaks, fir trees, and kinds that had no name. They shut out the sun. Only scattered patches and changing shapes of sunlight showed on the ground. The old man didn't mind. He had lived in the city for many long years. He had grown to hate the neurotic scurrying about. And the hypocritic smiles and cement-block faces.

He loved the peaceful and sensuous darkness. He felt at home in it. He loved the freedom that the darkness gave to his imagination. He spent hours sometimes filling the darkness with memories, with images, and with fantasies. He filled it with the bodies of beautiful women. He filled it with the faces of kindly young men. He filled it with seas that held treasures and monsters. His demons terrified him sometimes. But it was exciting at the same time. And after a while he couldn't tell if he was telling stories to the darkness; sometimes he thought the darkness was telling the stories to him.

7. Revise the following sentences so that they are resolved more meaningfully, more specifically.

a. The Vietnam War is a conflict which is a matter of the utmost importance.

b. *Moby-Dick,* a masterpiece of the nineteenth century, is a great piece of writing.

c. The dark-haired girl that he had only glimpsed before was very attractive.

d. If David and Susan don't manage to compromise somewhat they'll have trouble.

e. The dog was strangely reserved, almost sinister; Dan didn't like it much.

f. The two of them were excited and pleased with their new car; it performed well.

g. The murder of the senator was a senseless and tragic act.

h. In the face of the increasing violence in our city drastic measures must be taken.

i. We must try to write better.

j. Racial hatred in this country affects all of us.

8. Looking into sources available to you (textbooks, magazines, newspapers, college catalogs) find five sentences in which the writer uses a pompous or fancy construction in place of a possible plainer one. Rewrite for plainness, and speculate on the reasons behind the pomposity.

9. Rewrite these sentences as simply as possible. Cut out all the pretentiousness.

a. He couldn't comprehend how the thermostat mechanism was to be operated.

b. The general voiced the personal opinion the defoliation was a reasonable measure in a police action such as this.

c. Your utilization of the word "sensuality" is improper.

d. That wedge is merely a portion of the circle's entirety.

e. We subscribe to the belief that negligence on your part was responsible for the damage incurred by our apartment's furnishings.

f. My lower appendage does not have a great deal of mobility, confined as it is by the plaster cast.

g. She doesn't minister to my emotional requirements for affection with a great deal of conscientiousness.

h. His investment in the emotional complex of their relationship, which had been ongoing for somewhat over five years, was minuscule.

i. Due to private considerations the precise nature of which I cannot reveal I will not be adopting the course of action you proposed as a substitute for my own.

j. The culinary offerings of this establishment are not of a very high quality.

10. Rewrite this passage as clear informal prose, without wasted words:

I was walking on down by the Forum and I saw this guy I know whose name is Caius Marcellus. He looks all shaken up and I wondered why, so I asked him. He could hardly talk he was so upset. He said, "Caesar's been murdered!" I was so shocked I couldn't believe it. He told me how it happened, that Brutus, Cassius, and some other guys tricked him and got him when he wasn't looking. They stabbed him all over, shouting that he was a tyrant and that it was for the good of the people.

As he was telling me this stuff, we saw a big crowd and we heard a lot of noise from the direction of the steps of the Senate. And we saw Marc Antony getting up on the steps and making motions like he wanted the people to be quiet.

11. Write ten sentences, five formal and five informal, in which one word stands out as being inappropriate to the diction of the sentence. For instance, "The senator, having risen to the platform with difficulty, stated that he believed the measures the Senate had taken in the recent crisis, despite their intentions, were crummy."

12. Does the word "wealthy" belong in the passage quoted from Thurber on pages 124–125? Why?

13. Take this passage from *Ecclesiastes*, or this Shakespearean speech, and make a parody like the parodies by George Orwell and Sir Arthur Quiller-Couch.

And I hated all my labour wherein I laboured under the sun, seeing that I must leave it unto the man that shall be after me. And who knoweth whether he will be a wise man or a fool? Yet will he have rule over all my labour wherein I have laboured, and wherein I have shown myself wise under the sun. This also is vanity.

Now my co-mates and brothers in exile,
Hath not old custom made this life more sweet
Than that of painted pomp? Are not these woods
More free from peril than the envious court?
Here feel we not the penalty of Adam,
The season's indifference, as the icy fang
And churlish chiding of the winter's wind,
Which when it bites and blows upon my body
Even till I shrink with cold, I smile, and say
This is no flattery; these are counsellors
That feelingly persuade me what I am.
Sweet are the uses of adversity,
Which, like the toad ugly and venomous,
Wears yet a precious jewel in his head.
And this our life, exempt from public haunt,
Finds tongues in trees, books in the running brooks,
Sermons in stones, and good in everything.

As You Like It, II, 1

14. Use the clause or sentence, "he never wanted to write again," in two paragraphs, one formal and the other informal.

15. Make two paragraphs, one using the word "phoney," and one the word "insincere." Keep a unity of tone in each paragraph.

16. Examine this passage for faults. Then rewrite it by replacing words and phrases with inappropriately formal ones.

But I'd watch them rambling around the fields all day looking for something to do, so their wives would think they were real busy hard-working men, and they weren't fooling me either. I knew they secretly wanted to go sleep in the woods, or just sit and do nothing in the woods, like I wasn't too ashamed to do. They never bothered me. How could I tell them that my knowing was the knowing that the substance of my bones and their bones and the bones of dead men in the earth of rain at night is the common individual substance that is everlastingly tranquil and blissful? Whether they believed it or not makes no difference, too.

Jack Kerouac, *The Dharma Bums*

17. Rewrite this passage by replacing words and phrases with inappropriately informal ones. See if you can find fault with the passage itself.

The illustrative materials used in this study are of mixed status; some are taken from respectable researches where qualified generalizations are given concerning reliably recorded regularities; some are taken from informal memoirs written by colorful people; many fall in between. In addition, frequent use is made of a study of my own of a Shetland Island crofting (subsistence farming) community. The justification for this approach (as I take to be the justification for Simmel's also) is that the illustrations together fit into a coherent framework that ties together bits of experience the reader has already had and provides the student with a guide worth testing in case-studies of institutional social life.

Erving Goffman, *The Presentation of Self in Everyday Life*

18. In the following passages, analyze diction and structure for formality and informality. Be prepared to find some mixture.

a. With the passing of the last natural frontier—that series of horizons dissolving westward—the raw-material myth, based, as it is, on the myth of inexhaustible resources, no longer supplies the artisan with lumps of raw life. All of it has been handled. He now inhabits a world of raw-material clichés. His homemade provincial wares no longer startle and amaze the world. As a writer he must meet, and beat, the old world masters at their own game. In his "Monologue to the Maestro," Hemingway states the problem in his characteristic manner:

> "There is no use writing anything that has been written better before unless you can beat it. What a writer in our time has to do is write what hasn't been written before or beat dead men at what they have done. The only way he can tell how he is going is to compete with dead men . . . the only people for a serious writer to compete with are the dead that he knows are good. . . ."

With this credo the Portrait of the Artist as a Young American is permanently revised. The provincial is out. The dyed-in-the-wool professional is in. Not only do we have to meet the champ, we have to beat him.

Wright Morris, The Territory Ahead

b. A dramatic necessity goes deep into the nature of the sentence. Sentences are not different enough to hold the attention unless they are dramatic. No ingenuity of varying structure will do. All that can save them is the speaking tone of voice somehow entangled in the words and fastened to the page for the ear of the imagination. That is all that can save poetry from sing-song, all that can save poetry from itself.

Robert Frost, Selected Prose of Robert Frost

c. "Omit needless words!" cries the author on page 17, and into that imperative Will Strunk really put his heart and soul. In the days when I was sitting in his class, he omitted so many needless words, and omitted them so forcibly and with such eagerness and obvious relish, that he often seemed in the position of having short-changed himself, a man left with nothing more to say yet with time to fill, a radio prophet who had outdistanced the clock. Will Strunk got out of this predicament by a simple trick: he uttered every sentence three times. When he delivered his oration on brevity to the class, he leaned forward over his desk, grasped his coat lapels in his hands, and in a husky, conspiratorial voice said, "Rule Thirteen. Omit needless words! Omit needless words! Omit needless words!"

E. B. White, The Elements of Style

d. So Elvis Presley came, strumming a weird guitar and wagging his tail across the continent, ripping off fame and fortune as he scrunched his way, and, like a latter-day Johnny Appleseed, sowing seeds of a new rhythm and style in the white souls of the white youth of America, whose inner hunger and need was no longer satisfied with the antiseptic white shoes and whiter songs of Pat Boone. "You can do anything," sang Elvis to Pat Boone's white shoes, "but don't you step on my Blue Suede Shoes!"

Eldridge Cleaver, *Soul on Ice*

e. Every adult, whether he is a follower or a leader, a member of a mass or of an elite, was once a child. He was once small. A sense of smallness forms a substratum in his mind, ineradicably. His triumphs will be measured against this smallness, his defeats will substantiate it. The questions as to who is bigger and who can do or not do this or that, and to whom—these questions fill the adult's inner life far beyond the necessities and the desirabilities which he understands and for which he plans.

Erik Erikson, *Childhood and Society*

f. This is a society which has little use for anything except gain. All is hacked down in its service, whether people, ideas, or ideals. The writer, say, who achieves some entrance into the mainstream of American letters is almost immediately in jeopardy of being stripped of his insight by the ruffians of "success." A man who writes plays and poems, for instance, is asked to be a civil rights reporter, or write a dopey musical—if he is talked about widely enough—if not, there is no mention of him, and perhaps he is left to rot in some pitiful mistake of a college out in Idaho. A man who writes or makes beautiful music will be asked to immortalize a soap, or make sounds behind the hero while that blond worthy seduces the virgins of our nation's guilt. Even a man who is a great center fielder will still be asked to kick up his heels at Las Vegas.

Leroi Jones, *Home*

IV

PARAGRAPHS

THE USES OF PARAGRAPHS

The paragraph is the next-to-largest unit we deal with. We move from words, to sentences, to paragraphs, and finally to the whole essay or story. The paragraph is a small box of sentences, making a whole shape that is at the same time part of another whole. It is a miniature essay itself, with its own variable structure.

In that Bible for stylists, *Modern English Usage*, H. W. Fowler writes, "The purpose of the paragraph is to give the reader a rest." I called the paragraph a mini-essay; it is also a maxi-sentence: the blank space at the end of the paragraph, before we indent and begin a new one, is like a period at the end of the sentence, only longer. Paragraphs punctuate, not by a mark but by arrangement on the page. Paragraphs, like sentences, tell us that something completes itself. The paragraph tells us that we have come to the end of a series of statements composing a larger statement; now the reader must pause a moment, and see what the paragraph was doing.

Look at the preceding paragraph. Its organization is only one of many possible, but it is a common one. It begins with a quotation from Fowler, which announces the purpose of the paragraph. Then the paragraph and the sentence are compared. Fowler does not make this comparison, but in the paragraph the comparison is picked up

143

from Fowler's word "rest." In the last sentence I attempted to argue the function of the "rest." The paragraph elaborates and supports the first sentence, and the pause at the end should fulfill the function ascribed to it in the paragraph itself.

Paragraphs rest the eye as well as the brain. Unbroken print leaves no landmarks for the eye that wanders and returns; we sometimes find ourselves using a finger to keep to the correct line. Though context gives us other reasons for longer or shorter paragraphs, paragraphs are useful as visual aids to comfort in reading. Those little indentations are hand- and footholds in the cliff-face of the essay.

FOCUSING WITH PARAGRAPHS

Paragraphs represent our units of thought and feeling. The content makes the paragraph, and paragraphs become ways of organizing our complexity (for ourselves and for others) into units we can comprehend. When we set out to write an essay, one breakthrough comes when we see which part belongs with which part. We take tiny pieces, and assemble them into larger units, and assemble the larger units into the focused paper. The middle stage is often the paragraph. It associates detail into order; it concentrates; it begins to narrow our focus. We may start with notes like this (from an autobiographical essay):

> summer I was ten
> Robert Kennedy's assassination
> Martin Luther King
> going hunting with my uncle
> gun laws
> the bounty on hedgehogs
> Oswald's mail-order rifle
> my .22
> killing the baby hedgehogs
> how I felt afterward
> my uncle and World War II
> 4th of July parade
> Vietnam

The order of the whole essay is in question, but first, we must associate smaller units with each other. If these notes are on file cards, we can simply make different piles of them. Each pile would be a potential paragraph. If the notes are listed on a piece of paper or in a notebook, the writer can try associating one with the other by numbering each item, linking like to like with the same number. The most obvious order might start with the summer, the assassination, and the gun laws; then move for contrast to hunting with the uncle, with the anecdote; then end by contrasting attitudes of World War II veterans with those of young men now brought up on wars in Southeast Asia. Or a different order might start with this generalization, and end more dramatically with the anecdote. Any order is arbitrary, but some orders are better than others. I wish to show here not so much a *best* ordering of the whole, as a useful, preliminary sorting of material into units, small collections of notes, which may turn out to be paragraphs. For instance:

B_2 summer I was ten
B_3 Robert Kennedy's assassination
B_1 Martin Luther King
D_2 going hunting with my uncle
C_2 gun laws
E_1 the bounty on hedgehogs
C_1 Oswald's mail-order rifle
D_1 my .22
E_2 killing the baby hedgehogs
F_3 how I felt afterward
A_2 my uncle and World War II
A_1 4th of July parade
A_3 Vietnam

This way is only one of many. It is the second ordering suggested earlier, A through E. The units represented by the capital letters are not necessarily single paragraphs. Maybe A would be two paragraphs—first a description of the American Legion parading, the uncle puffing along in step, and then an ironic comparison of the attitudes of veterans and youths, or even possibly a comparison of the wars themselves. The items grouped under E—the anecdote of killing baby hedgehogs and the consequent feelings—might take several paragraphs. But the *order* would be:

4th of July parade
my uncle and World War II
Vietnam
— — —

Martin Luther King
summer I was ten
Robert Kennedy's assassination

— — —

Oswald's mail-order rifle
gun laws

— — —

my .22
going hunting with my uncle

— — —

the bounty in hedgehogs
killing the baby hedgehogs
how I felt afterward

Many a beginning writer, or a writer who has not learned to paragraph, might write the essay in the order in which the notes originally appeared. The result would be chaos, moving back and forth in time by random association. That is the way we talk, thinking of points afterward and crying, "Oh, I forgot to say . . . !" But writing is harder, and takes better organization. The paragraph is our middle unit of organization between sentences that incorporate raw data and the finished, shapely essay. In the development of explanation or narration, the rest or the hand-hold signals the reader that a limited subject has been dealt with, finished or put on hold, and that we now move to another topic—perhaps arising from the last one, perhaps in contrast to it, different in any case. The paragraph becomes a semantic unit. It carries meaning. The look of it on the page makes a statement; it tells us that a topic, or a detachable unit of an argument, or that an event, or a detachable unit of an event, is complete here. As even commas and sentence structure create meaning in our prose, the paragraph, well-used, makes a statement to the reader.

LENGTH OF PARAGRAPHS

Paragraphs are short and long, and we may construct them in various orders. In subsequent sections we will talk about order within paragraphs, and about transitions. We need to talk here about length in connection with style, and in connection with unity and variety.

The more formal the writing, usually the more lengthy the paragraphing. In narrative and fiction, we use paragraphs with more variety of length, and in informal writing our paragraphs shorten. Newspaper writing breaks up the solid column of print by making a paragraph out of every sentence or two.

In exposition, or in writing up research, we may move from topic to topic by long paragraphs that introduce a subject—a step in the presentation—elaborate it, enumerate it, explain it, or conclude it. We may frequently write paragraphs as long as a typewritten page. If the paragraphs get much longer, we should cut them down. There is always some point at which we can make a break that is not wholly arbitrary, and give the reader a rest. One argument could make a six-page paragraph, but it would be tiring to read. If we look back at it, we can find the steps of the argument. We can break between one step and another, even though the pause in reasoning is small. In a long description, we can break between one part of the subject and another. Talking of a barn, we can break between remarks about the colors of things and about the shapes of things and about the uses of things. Talking about a block we grew up in, suppose we want to write equally about ten houses. Ten tiny paragraphs would be too choppy; one paragraph would be two pages of solid print. Here, we can subdivide our houses by talking about one side of the block and then the other, or by making a division of three architectural styles, or different shades of paint, or lengths of time they had been occupied by their tenants.

Some paragraphs must be short. When we write dialogue, we show a change of speaker by indenting a new paragraph:

> "Did you go downtown after lunch?" He was tapping the arm of his chair with his index finger. Behind his glasses his eyes wandered.
> "Yes," she said. "I suppose I did."
> "Why?"

But that use of paragraphing is mechanical. In descriptive or expository or narrative writing—the usual ingredients of essay or autobiography, and frequently of story—a series of short paragraphs is choppy, a rash of blurts, like someone who talks in the manner of a machine gun. When we move from dialogue to description or narration, we should provide a change of pace by keeping the paragraphs relatively long. The long paragraph is a rest or relief after several short ones: here is a bed big enough to lie down on. We do not want:

> The room was large, the chairs comfortable. He sat down on the overstuffed sofa.
> All around him the ticking of clocks wove a mesh of sound.
> There was dust on the windowpane, and the rugs were shabby.

> Dark pictures hung on the walls, and the woodwork was dark.

It is too much like standing up and sitting down all the time. We want to relax and read the description straight:

> The room was large, the chairs comfortable. He sat down on the overstuffed sofa. All around him the ticking of clocks wove a mesh of sound. There was dust on the windowpane, and the rugs were shabby. Dark pictures hung on the walls, and the woodwork was dark.

And the paragraph should continue for another five or six lines. Sometimes when we chop our prose into too short paragraphs we may be deceiving ourselves with handwriting, which can make a few words into full-sized paragraphs, and think that we are writing a long paper when we are not. Or perhaps we find it difficult to move from one thing to another within the paragraph, and so we break the paragraph to indicate a switch to another topic. Often this break need not be made. And at times, short paragraphs reveal our laziness. We fail to collect and to develop our thoughts, and so write paragraphs that are little more than a sentence announcing a topic, paragraphs lacking detail, elaboration, and support. We need to think of further ideas to support arguments; details to make description carry feeling.

In narrative, the paragraph break is rather arbitrary. We could justify one after every sentence, we could justify none at all; but neither of these solutions would be tolerable. So we break for a rest when it is most nearly logical, as when the character turns a corner, or sees something new, or understands what is happening.

It is tempting to be dogmatic, and to say, "Outside of dialogue, keep your paragraphs between 200 and 250 words." Life would be more comfortable, and writing easier, if simple prescriptions solved our problems. Although a highly formal essay might follow some such rule, most good modern writing has much more variety to it. As it is hard to type the best contemporary stylists as formal or informal, so it is hard to put limits on the size of paragraphs. Although formal writing tends toward a more uniform length of paragraph, sometimes it uses something as short as a one-line paragraph. A skillful writer may make a long statement in periodic sentences, a 350-word paragraph that concludes with a flourish, and follow it by a paragraph that reads, in its entirety:

> On the other hand, maybe this reasoning is haphazard.

Then he may write another long paragraph. The one-liner has been a change of pace—at the same time restful, offhand, and revivifying: it keeps us on our toes. We don't know what might come next, we are perpetually a little off-balance. Look at this example from an essay by C. S. Lewis called "At the Fringe of Language":

> This, which is eminently true of poetry, is true of all imaginative writing. One of the first things we have to say to a beginner who has brought us his MS. is, "Avoid all epithets which are merely emotional. It is no use *telling* us that something was 'mysterious' or 'loathsome' or 'awe-inspiring' or 'voluptuous.' Do you think your readers will believe you just because you say so? You must go quite a different way to work. By direct description, by metaphor and simile, by secretly evoking powerful associations, by offering the right stimuli to our nerves (in the right degree and the right order), and by the very beat and vowel-melody and length and brevity of your sentences, you must bring it about that we, we readers, not you, exclaim 'how mysterious!' or 'loathsome' or whatever it is. Let me taste for myself, and you'll have no need to *tell* me how I should react to the flavour."

> In Donne's couplet
>> Your gown going off, such beautious state
>>> reveals
>> As when from flowery meads th'hills shadow
>>> steales
> *beautious* is the only word of the whole seventeen which is doing no work.

The style is quite formal, and the variety in length and structure of paragraph is functional—for the expression of meaning, and for the reader's comfort.

On the other hand, look at the paragraphing in the polemical style of Ivan Illich.

> I will use the words "opportunity web" for "network" to designate specific ways to provide access to each of four sets of resources. "Network" is often used, unfortunately, to designate the channels reserved to material selected by others for indoctrination, instruction, and entertainment. But it can also be used for the telephone or the postal service, which are pri-

marily accessible to individuals who want to send messages to one another. I wish we had another word to designate such reticular structures for mutual access, a word less evocative of entrapment, less degraded by current usage and more suggestive of the fact that any such arrangement includes legal, organizational, and technical aspects. Not having found such a term, I will try to redeem the one which is available, using it as a synonym of "educational web."

What are needed are new networks, readily available to the public and designed to spread equal opportunity for learning and teaching.

To give an example: the same level of technology is used in TV and in tape recorders. All Latin-American countries now have introduced TV: in Bolivia the government has financed a TV station, which was built six years ago, and there are no more than seven thousand TV sets for four million citizens. The money now tied up in TV installations throughout Latin America could have provided every fifth adult with a tape recorder. In addition, the money would have sufficed to provide an almost unlimited library of prerecorded tapes, with outlets even in remote villages, as well as an ample supply of empty tapes.

Ivan Illich, *Deschooling Society*

Here the short paragraph is an emphatic device; not elegant but forceful, and the paragraphs on either side of it elaborate classic devices of argument, definition in the one and detail in the other.

The variety and unity of the paragraph resemble the variety and unity of the sentence. The effectiveness of contrast, when the one-line paragraph follows the complex one, resembles the pleasure of a short, simple sentence after a long, complex sentence. One can mix a stew of variety without violating a unity that holds the essay together. The paragraph is one more ingredient of prose that the beginning writer can learn to use.

UNITY, SEQUENCE, AND COHERENCE

Always keep three things in mind when you make paragraphs.

One is the *unity* of the whole: the paragraph should contain nothing extraneous. The odd fact which happens to be true, but which is irrelevant to the topic, must be omitted from the paragraph. It is a violation of unity, and therefore distracting.

> We never had enough time to eat lunch in high school: half of the time I'd get a stomachache from hurriedly wolfing down the food. The food was lousy, anyway. We complained to the administration, but it didn't do any good. We were often held up in getting into the cafeteria because the lunchroom helpers were slow in getting the tables and the food ready. Then, if you were one of the people who got in toward the end, you would have to wait a long time in line. Sometimes the jocks, who acted as lunchroom police, would hold you up, too, trying to bully you into buying a football schedule.

The sentence about the food being lousy doesn't fit here; it is a digression from the topic, "We never had enough time to eat lunch in high school." We must be alert to maintain a unity of subject matter in our paragraphs, because the associations of our thought constantly lead us into irrelevance.

Second is *sequence*; the information or argument must be sequential. We cannot say, "Oh, I forgot to say . . . ," or leave out steps in our progress. We must move in an orderly way, for instance from earlier to later, or from less to more important, or from periphery to center, or from smaller to larger, or from larger to smaller. Sometimes we will want to move from center to periphery, from present to past. But we must not scatter our sequence—from larger to smaller to larger to larger to smaller to largest to larger to smallest to large. We may want A B C D E F. On occasion we may want Z Y X W V, but not A Q I X L D.

The order of the following paragraph is fine; we move from generality in the topic sentence to particulars that describe and substantiate it:

> Winter is a catastrophe. Life on skid row is lived out of doors, and the cold and the snow bring with them intense suffering. The men often get drunk enough to lie in the streets in the midst of a storm. The first time one sees a body covered with a light blanket of snow, stretched out on the sidewalk, the sight comes as a shock and a dilemma. Is the man dead or just drunk? Or worse, the habitues are so obsessed and driven that

stealing goes on in the dead of winter, and a man who needs a drink will take the shoes of a fellow alcoholic in the middle of January.

Michael Harrington, *The Other America:*
Poverty in the United States

The following paragraph, organized in a different way, moving from pieces of information to a general conclusion, is also well constructed.

Last January as he was about to leave office, Lyndon Johnson sent his last report on the economic prospect to the Congress. It was assumed that, in one way or another, the Vietnam War, by which he and his Administration had been destroyed, would come gradually to an end. The question considered by his economists was whether this would bring an increase or a decrease in military spending. The military budget for fiscal 1969 was 78.4 billions; for the year following, including pay increases, it was scheduled to be about three billions higher. Thereafter, assuming peace and a general withdrawal from Asia, there would be a reduction of some six or seven billions. But this was only on the assumption that the Pentagon did not get any major new weapons—that it was content with what had already been authorized. No one really thought this possible. The President's economists noted that plans already existed for "a package" consisting of new aircraft, modern naval vessels, defense installations, and "advanced strategic and general purpose weapons systems" which would cost many billions. This would wipe out any savings from getting out of Vietnam. Peace would now be far more expensive than war.

John Kenneth Galbraith, *How to Control the Military*

The organization of this paragraph, however, is not satisfactory:

The birds often flock in huge numbers on trees, sometimes breaking limbs off. They may bury a car parked below them in white dung. Starlings can be a terrible nuisance. The dark purplish-black pests may tear up a whole lawn in the process of searching for worms and insects, particularly as winter approaches and live food gets scarce. Their antics can drive a homeowner out of *his* tree. In large enough numbers, they can create a din of voices that blocks out all other sounds in the area. Their cries are strident and irritating.

In this paragraph we move from specific to specific to general to specific to general to specific to specific, without meaningful progression. It would make much better organizational sense to begin "Starlings can be a terrible nuisance" and to end "Their antics can drive a homeowner out of *his* tree."

The third consideration is *coherence*. Frequently, in unfinished writing, a sentence seems extraneous or irrelevant when it should not be; the author has a use for the information, but he has been unable to build it smoothly into his thought. The writer must learn how to blend his information so that it coheres in a meaningful whole: the relationship between the sentences must be clear, and the paragraph must seem a *whole*, not just a collection of individual sentences. Here is a paragraph, from some daily writing, which has little coherence:

> I had been having severe headaches and frequent dizzy spells. I was terrified of doctors. I went to the health clinic. I waited three days. It was the time of finals and I was very busy. I saw a doctor. He prescribed some pills. The problems continued.

It is impossible to tell what the relationships are between the bits of information related here. Did the speaker wait three days before or after going to the health clinic? Did he wait because of his fear of doctors or because he was busy? Was he busy studying for finals, or did he happen to be busy with other things during that time? Added to these confusions of sense, the rhythm is choppy. Here is a revised and more coherent version of the passage:

> I had been having severe headaches and frequent dizzy spells, but I hesitated to go to the health clinic because I was terrified of doctors. It was the time of finals and I was busy studying for them, so I made the excuse to myself that I didn't have time and that there was nothing the matter with me, just fatigue. Finally, I went, although I waited three days before making an appointment. I saw a doctor, and after he examined me he prescribed some pills. But despite the medication, the problems continued, even after I'd been taking the pills for two weeks.

Notice that the writer has achieved much of his coherence, in this revision, by using conjunctions and subordinate clauses.

NARRATIVE PARAGRAPHS

In narration, chronology (the natural order in which things happen in time) will usually provide the order of a paragraph:

> He looked down the street as far as he could see. A tiny figure walked in his direction, so far away he could not tell whether it was man or woman, much less the woman he had come to find. He hunkered beside the shed and sucked on a piece of grass. In ten minutes he could see that it was a girl. Gradually, it became a girl he did not know, barefooted, adolescent, dressed in a sack, dirty, with long and careless hair.
> "Come here," he said.

In this example, the spoken phrase could logically have ended the narrative paragraph, but the pause of a new paragraph provides a silent transition, taking the place of an unspoken final sentence, "He decided to speak to her."

At times, in narration and exposition, we want to leap ahead and then catch up. However, we must use this device fully aware of what we are doing.

> In December, 1941, Congress declared war on Japan, Germany, and Italy. The declaration was an immediate result of the Japanese attack on Pearl Harbor, but earlier events had made such a move inevitable. Perhaps the Treaty of Versailles. . . .

Here, the opening sentence states an ultimate topic, an event to be reached by way of causation, and the paragraph develops by reverse chronology. Presumably, the writer will turn around and advance through the twenties and thirties in a conventional forward direction. If we had begun this essay with reference to the earliest event mentioned—that is, if we had followed regular chronology—the reader might have expected, for a moment, that the Treaty of Versailles was the subject of the essay.

TOPIC SENTENCES

Paragraphs in argument or exposition are mini-essays. They deal with one topic, or closely related data, or an integral subsegment of a topic. The paragraph is homogeneous. It is orderly, but there are many varieties of order. Probably the most common order has the paragraph beginning with a sentence that announces the topic and an attitude toward it. A series of sentences follow to explain, elaborate, or enumerate examples or analogy in support of the topic sentence. Then a final sentence draws the elaboration to a conclusion, in a way that leads to the next paragraph. Topic sentences are frequently useful in establishing unity and sequence. Here is an example:

> At the end of the Second World War, the university moved from the periphery to the center. The university would unlock all the secrets of nature and train all the people needed to turn discoveries into weapons and money. It would lead the way to national power and prosperity and would see to it that we got there before the Russians. From a hotbed of radicalism the university became overnight the central factory of the knowledge industry, which was to be the foundation of our future. At the same time, the educational system, with the university at the top, became the national screening device through which individuals were to be put in the proper productive relationship to the national program of power and prosperity.
>
> Robert M. Hutchins, "How Should a University Administrator Respond to Radical Action?"

Many variations upon this order are possible. Variations are also desirable, because a long essay composed of paragraphs equal in length and identical in construction would be boring. Sometimes a topic sentence is not present, or is understood, in much the same way as a transition can sometimes be understood. For instance, a writer may just have mentioned that he spent a day in the town of Omaha. He might follow it with a paragraph:

> The visitor can enjoy the aroma of the stockyards. He can watch the rich sit at their clubs, drinking gin next to pools of chlorine, beside flat golf courses. The visitor can walk up the sides of ugly buildings on dry Sundays. He can watch grass grow, at least in early spring and early fall. He can listen to the medley of transistor radios in several parks. He can try sleeping for a week or so, until he is able to leave.

He needs no topic sentence. Or the position of the topic sentence can vary. Sometimes it can occur in the middle of a paragraph, preceded by introduction and followed by support. Sometimes we find the topic sentence at the end of the previous paragraph. The paragraph break serves almost as a colon.

> In general, chronology is the most satisfactory organization. However, we must not rely on it alone.
> We would reduce our psychological world to the order of the clock. We would become slaves of "then" and "afterwards." . . .

The first two sentences of the second paragraph are elaborations of the negative topic sentence which ends the first paragraph, but which could have introduced the second paragraph just as well. Sometimes, a topic sentence can come at the end of the paragraph, as a summary.

Topic sentences in narration often change the scene, introduce signposts in complicated country. Here are some examples of sentences that could be lead-ins:

> Finally, he thought it was time to return.

> The weather turned fine.

> When they turned the corner, the street changed abruptly.

> Election night began with a bad omen.

> When he heard footsteps outside in the darkness, he turned off the oil lamps and reached for his gun.

> The final chapters seem pointless.

In argument, or exposition, the topic sentences have more of the flavor of philosophical propositions. For instance:

> When a man needs help, he must know where to turn.

> The Biblical oratory of nineteenth-century politicians is no longer effective.

> The paragraph is a unit of sense, a discrete idea or topic.

When we revise our prose, it is useful to look into our paragraphs for topic sentences. We do not demand that every paragraph have one—but the *idea* of a topic sentence is an *idea* of focus and unity, and therefore essential to clear and forceful prose. We consider the topic sentence of a paragraph—overt or implicit, at beginning, middle, or end—to consider if the paragraph is sufficiently unified.

SOME WAYS OF DEVELOPING PARAGRAPHS

One can develop a paragraph in countless ways. No list can be comprehensive. But examples of some of the basic methods of paragraph development help us to see the range of possibilities. The choice of a type of development—the *how* of the paragraph—depends on the material we are using—the *what* of the paragraph. If we are listing the annual imports of Paraguay, we develop by listing, and not by comparison and contrast. *The shape of the container derives from the shape of what is contained.* One of our tasks in organizing a paper is to find the means of development that is *most appropriate to our material.* We may organize a paragraph to describe:

> At Rajghat, a few hundred feet from the river, a fresh pyre had been built of stone, brick, and earth. It was eight feet square and about two feet high. Long, thin sandalwood logs sprinkled with incense were stacked on it. Mahatma Gandhi's body lay on the pyre with his head to the north. In that position Buddha met his end.
>
> Louis Fischer, *Gandhi: His Life and Message for the World*

Or to list:

> Now the leadership elements of the Democratic Party began to filter through the suite of the nominee in a parade that was to last the rest of the day, to assist him in making up their mind. First of the big-city leaders to arrive was David Lawrence of Pennsylvania. Following him came the New York crowd Wagner, Harriman, DeSapio and Prendergast; then William Green of Philadelphia; then DiSalle of Ohio; then Bailey and Ribicoff of Connecticut; then all the others.
>
> Theodore H. White, *The Making of the President 1960*

Or to compare or contrast:

> In other respects, the film follows Hearst's career with mixed fidelity. The plot adjustments are significant. Both Hearst and Kane were only children, born in 1863, and both were expelled from Harvard. Hearst's father and mother were not, like Kane's, poverty-stricken boardinghouse keepers. George Hearst was a

well-to-do farmer's son, whose silver strike at the Comstock lode made him a millionaire, and whose later interest in the Homestake Mine still further increased his massive fortune; he became a senator and earned a respected place in the American Dictionary of Biography. In the film these parents are left a deed to the Colorado Lode by a defaulting boarder, Fred Grange, and the Kane fortune is thus founded not by the acumen and push of a paternal figure but by blind chance.

Charles Higham, *The Films of Orson Welles*

Or to define and elucidate:

The "duende," then, is a power and not a construct, is a struggle and not a concept. I have heard an old guitarist, a true virtuoso, remark, "The 'duende' is not in the throat, the 'duende' comes up from inside, up from the very soles of the feet." That is to say, it is not a question of aptitude, but of a true and viable style—of blood, in other words; of what is oldest in culture; of creation made act.

Federico García Lorca, "The Duende:
Theory and Divertissement"

Or to make clear by elaboration or rephrasing:

To seek out the "duende," however, neither map nor discipline is required. Enough to know that he kindles the blood like an irritant, that he exhausts, that he repulses, all the bland, geometrical assurances, that he smashes the styles; that he makes of a Goya, master of the grays, the silvers, the roses of the great English painters, a man painting with his knees and his fists in bituminous blacks; that he bares a Mosen Cinto Verdaguer to the cold of the Pyrenees or induces a Jorge Manrique to sweat out his death on the crags of Ocaña, or invests the delicate body of Rimbaud in the green domino of the saltimbanque, or fixes dead fish-eyes on the Comte de Lautréamont in the early hours of the boulevard.

Federico García Lorca, "The Duende:
Theory and Divertissement"

Or to analyze:

In his handling of the narrative parts of the film—most noticeably the opening and closing passages—Welles's command of visual effect is altogether striking. In his poetic images, such as the recurrent allusions to the snow scene, and the wonderful use of dissolves throughout, he is the complete master. He is weakest when he handles the important dialogue scenes involving Leland and Kane either in a mode of heavy comedy or in showy cadenzas with the camera seemingly lying on the floor. Too often he lets his technique draw attention to itself, permitting us to look at a muslin ceiling (not always convincing anyway) when we would be better engaged in looking into the characters' faces as they emphasize points in a phrase. It is, no doubt, a mark against his technique that one often notes things while listening to the sound track that were altogether lost while watching the film unfold.

Charles Higham, *The Films of Orson Welles*

Or to make an assertion and give reasons:

If conventions epitomize the mythology and legendry of American national politics, then Chicago epitomizes the convention city. For one hundred years, ever since the nomination of Abraham Lincoln at the Wigwam, it has been the favorite city of political convention-goers. Counting notches for fourteen Republican and nine Democratic national conventions in the last twenty-five quadrennials, Chicago can boast that here were first named all the following Presidents of the United States: Lincoln, Grant, Garfield, Cleveland, Harrison, Theodore Roosevelt, Harding, Coolidge, Franklin D. Roosevelt, Truman and Eisenhower.

Theodore H. White, *The Making of the President 1960*

Or to make a statement and then give relevant facts:

Gandhi recognized that the whites in South Africa thought they needed protection against a majority consisting of Negroes and Indians. The province of Natal, in 1896, had 400,000 Negro inhabitants, 51,000 Indians, and 50,000 whites. The Cape of Good Hope Colony had 900,000 Negroes, 10,000 Indians, and 400,000 Europeans; the Transvaal Republic 650,000 Negroes, 5,000 Indians, and 120,000 whites. In 1914, the five million Negroes hopelessly outnumbered the million and a quarter whites.

Louis Fischer, *Gandhi: His Life and Message for the World*

You will notice that, even in the examples above, these methods are not exclusive, but that one paragraph may use more than one method, or that one method may even involve using another. You can see, for instance, that in its final sentence the paragraph for "to make an assertion and give reasons," uses the listing of the second example.

Notice that in these quoted paragraphs the progress within the paragraph is the motion of thought. The exact detail, the example that locates the general in the particular, the comparison, the steps of logic—these motions develop the thought and unify the paragraph at the same time. Paragraph development makes coherence.

TRANSITIONS

This topic could belong with Sentences, or with The Essay, but I put it here because transitions happen *within* the paragraph as a way to move from one sentence to another, or *between* paragraphs, as a way of moving from topic to topic while keeping the essay whole. *And transitions are essential to the coherence of paragraph and paper.* A prose insufficient in transitions is nervous and obscure. It leaps from subject to subject, without stated or implied connection. The connection remains in the writer's mind.

Overt Transitions

Often a transition needs to be obvious, to carry the reader along our passage of thought; to make sure we don't lose him. Perhaps we are making an overt contrast. To draw attention to the contrast, we say, "On the one hand/on the other hand"—which is trite but hard to avoid. Or we use the context of our discussion: "Although most transitions are best left implicit, some are properly overt." Overt transitions are often ideas or actions in conflict, when the meaning of the essay depends upon full exploitation of the reality of the conflict. Or if we are piling detail upon detail, we might want to use a transition that calls attention to our multiplicity: "Not only . . . but also." In prose that reasons or argues, we need such overt transitions frequently. In prose that describes or narrates or summarizes, our transitions are more often internal (chronology, small to large) or subtle, turning on a word that we can repeat with a difference, or elaborating a hint from an earlier sentence. In any paper—even within a paragraph—a writer will use many devices for transition, all working ultimately to lead the reader from one moment to another.

Repeated Words or Phrases

One way to achieve a continuity of thought within a paragraph (or paragraphs), to make transitions between sentences and between statements, is to repeat words or phrases. One of the simplest of these devices, so simple that we might not think of it as one, is repeating pronouns. We use it for both economy and continuity.

> But towards Aumeister the paths were solitary and still, and *Aschenbach* strolled thither, stopping awhile to watch the lively crowds in the restaurant garden with its fringe of carriages and cabs. Thence *he* took *his* homeward way outside the park and across the sunset fields. By the time *he* reached the North Cemetery, however, *he* felt tired, and a storm was brewing above Föhring; so *he* waited at the stopping-place for a tram to carry *him* back to the city.
>
> Thomas Mann, "Death in Venice"
> (italics added)

But you should be careful when using a repeated pronoun, because if it is repeated too often it can become monotonous. You can get variety by occasionally using the name the pronoun refers to; Mann, in the story from which I've just quoted, uses "Aschenbach" every now and then instead of "he" or "him." You can also use constructions like "His nose itched" rather than "He felt his nose itching" in order to avoid using "he" too much. A writer also has to make sure that the reader knows what each pronoun refers to. If we say "Mr. Cortazar saw that the man was following him closely; he stared at him" it is not clear who is doing the staring. Here we may need to be more explicit: "Mr. Cortazar saw that the man was following him closely; Mr. Cortazar stared at him."

Any word or phrase, not just pronouns, can be repeated to make effective transitions if it is important to the meaning or the emotional tenor of the passage.

> If we once accept the premise that we can build a better world by using the different gifts of each *sex*, we shall have two kinds of freedom, freedom to use untapped gifts of each *sex*, and freedom to admit freely and cultivate in each *sex* their special superiorities. We may well find that there are certain fields, such as the physical sciences, mathematics, and instru-

mental music, in which men by virtue of their *sex*, as well as by virtue of their qualities as specially gifted human beings, will always have that razor-edge of extra gift which makes all the difference.

.   .   .

This has meant that men had to be willing to choose, win, and keep women as *lovers*, protect and provide for them as *hus-bands*, and protect and provide for their children as *fathers*. It has meant that women have had to be willing to accept men as lovers, live with them as wives, and conceive, bear, feed, and cherish their children. Any society disappears which fails to make these demands on its members and to receive this much from them.

But from men, society has also asked and received some-thing more than this. For thousands of generations men have been asked to do something more than be good *lovers* and *husbands* and *fathers*, even with all that that involved of hus-bandry and organization and protection against attack. . . .

Margaret Mead, *Male and Female* (italics added)

If we want to avoid the monotony of exact repetition, we can use variations (near-synonyms) for the key words in some places.

His *sculptures* seem like men and women stripped naked. They are *works of art* that seem to lack all artifice, *plastic creations* which, in their emotional if not in their physical presence, have the feeling of natural, organic creations.

These methods are commonly used for transition *between* para-graphs as well.

and the importance of spatial form in *modern* literature.
Modern thought, as well, has used the metaphor of dimen-sionality. . . .

Parallel Constructions

We can repeat structures as well as words. Parallel constructions can fulfill a need for transition that is not only structural and logical, but emotional; passages with parallel sentences can work like sentences with parallel phrases, to produce a dramatic effect, or to maintain emotional tension.

> Today, now that he is no longer among us, who can replace my old friend at the gates of this kingdom? Who will look after the garden until we can get back to it? . . .
>
> Albert Camus, "Encounters with André Gide"

> We describe how the poor are plundered by the rich. We live among the rich. Live on the plunder and pander ideas to the rich. We have described the torture and we have put our names under appeals against torture, but we did not stop it. (And we ourselves became torturers when the higher interests demanded torture and we became the ideologists of torture.) Now we once more can analyze the world situation and describe the wars and explain why the many are poor and hungry. But we do no more.
>
> We are not the bearers of consciousness. We are the whores of reason.
>
> Jan Myrdal, *Confessions of a Disloyal European*

Parallel constructions that respect a portion of a phrase are common and useful transitions, especially in exposition and in argument.

> and they never decided whether they were Bulgarians or Americans, rich or poor, artists or dilettantes.
>
> And we, on our part, could not decide whether they were heroes or frauds. . . .

Transitional Words and Phrases

We use many different transitional phrases to establish the relationship between sentences and between paragraphs, and to prepare the reader for shifts in subject or meaning. The most common are words like "and," "but," "or," and "for." Some are words of sequence and time—"meanwhile," "afterward," "before"; of qualification—"again," "also," "nonetheless"; and of reasoning—"for example," "because," "therefore." Although we often try to avoid phrases like these in fiction or narrative, they are useful and often essential to exposition or argument. Their very commonness and simplicity make them valuable to clarify a sequence of thought. The following paragraph openings use common phrases to accomplish transitions; they are taken from *The Naked Ape* by Desmond Morris:

> *Up to this point* I have been concentrating on the social aspects of comfort behaviour in our species . . .

> *In addition* to problems of keeping clean, the general category of comfort behaviour also includes . . .

> *Because* of his exploratory and opportunist nature, the naked ape's list of prey species is immense . . .

> *For the next major category,* that of parasites . . .

> *In order to* find the answer to this question we must first assemble some facts . . .

We commonly use comparison and contrast for transitions, especially in criticism and analysis. The means of transition are relatively simple. We can describe one of the objects for examination in one paragraph and then, in a following paragraph, compare/contrast traits of the other. The second term often begins with one of the transitional phrases that make for comparison or contrast, like "similarly," "in the same vein," or "however," "on the other hand," "in contrast," or "contrary to."

> Freud gave a picture of the unconscious mind as containing primarily memories and the remnants of suppressed desires. He saw the sexual drives as being the foundation of the unconscious.
> Jung, *on the other hand,* claimed that Freud's depth psychology wasn't deep enough, that there was another aspect of the unconscious which contained spiritual drives as important as the sexual drives. . . .

Remember that even in expository prose it is better to leave out well-worn phrases *if the sense is just as clear without them.* Many times, we can cut out the obvious direction-signals, and rely on implicit transition.

Implicit Transitions

Some of the most obvious clues to transition—within the paragraph or between paragraphs—are words of sequence, like "therefore," "later," "so," "then," and "next." They are so obvious that it is pleasant to do without them, if we can.

The order within the paragraph can itself be a means of transition. It gives the paragraph motion; it gives a reason for one sentence following another: left to right, down to up, smaller to larger; or other sorts of order: color to shape, spring to summer to fall to winter; or orders of ideas: from more obvious to less obvious; from less complex to more complex. These motions are clear enough in themselves to allow the movement from subject to subject without explicit directions. We need not say, "After spring came summer," within a paragraph, unless we are writing for people we can presume unaware of the order of the seasons. We would be more likely to move from rain and early flowers to the longest day of the year, to hot sun and to swimming and to no school.

Between paragraphs, sometimes the rest itself acts as transition. We take a breath, and we pivot on the pause. It shows that we are moving from one grouping to another. We don't always have to be reminded that we are moving. Sometimes we do, and sometimes we do not. Develop *tact* for transitions. Develop also a sense of the *multiple means* of transition. A good writer uses implicit, overt, parallel, repetitive—and many other forms of transition, and uses them in rapid sequence as he moves through his paragraphs, and from paragraph to paragraph.

Suppose we catalogue the contents of a boy's pockets. The next paragraph could begin, "Therefore, his pockets bulged as he walked, and he bumped into tables when he passed them. In fact, he bumped into almost everything. . . ." The paragraph could go on to discuss his clumsiness. But the "therefore" at the beginning is unnecessary. It is obvious, if I have made a catalogue of twenty items, that these items bulge out his pockets. Transition can be found in image. No reader need be led by the hand so carefully. The paragraph-break could read like this:

> He had on his person two rubber bands, a golf tee, two notes from a teacher, a bottle cap, and a gray-brown handkerchief.
>
> His pockets bulged as he walked, and he bumped into tables when he passed them. In fact, he bumped into almost everything.

The word "his," referring back to an antecedent in the previous paragraph, holds the two paragraphs together.

Transitions are a glue that holds parts together. You need enough, or the parts will fall apart. But if you have too much, you will see the glue instead of the parts. The space between the catalogue and the bulging pockets is a sort of invisible glue—but it holds, because we have sense enough to know that the objects listed cause the bulging. The next transition, from pockets to clumsiness, is less obvious and more necessary. It takes more doing. The only thing that bulging pockets share with clumsiness is that the little boy possesses both of them. Of course we could use some generalization as a transition:

> a bottle cap, and a gray-brown handkerchief.
>   In fact, he was generally rather gross and clumsy. He bumped into everything.

This transition would work, but it is not elegant. It is obvious and general. Suppose in the next paragraph we want to talk about his table manners, do we say again that he was "gross and clumsy"? No, we have used these words up. The stylish transition happens without drawing attention to itself. So we move from pockets to bumping into things by the image of the boy bumping into doorways with his fat pockets, and then we do a turn on the word "bumping" and we are off into a new subject before the reader knows it. He has been led from one subject to another by the elbow, as a kindly person helps a blind man across the street. But if we have done the job well, the reader does not feel the guiding touch of fingers on his arm.

Revising Paragraphs

Make sure that your paragraphing is useful, to the mind that understands and to the eye that reads. Consider your paragraphs for their length, their unity and variety, their sequence, their coherence, their internal organization, and for their transitions both internal and between paragraphs, both overt and implicit.

EXERCISES

1. The following phrases might be notes for the paragraphs of an essay. Arrange them in a possible order of paragraphs.

> the advent of the 747
> the modern airport
> ground transportation to and from airports
> the handling of baggage

the start of commercial aviation
the outlook for the future
the SST
the aerospace industry and the airlines
competitive routes
faster airlines
the DC-3
the 707
the CAB
midair collisions
VTOL
the decline of the railroads
the trouble with buses
youth fares
charter flights

2. Here is a short essay by Hermann von Kreicke, a chapter from a book recounting his adventures and travels as an émigré. Analyze this essay for its use of the paragraph. Apply the standards of this chapter.

It is time, perhaps, to withdraw for the moment from this picaresque account of our wanderings, in order to examine the question of exile as a psychological condition forced upon vast numbers of Europeans in the 20th century. My own generation was victim of the demented Austrian posing as a German. White Russians formed the bulk of the emigrant population in Paris when Hermione and I, all unwitting what awaited us in a subsequent decade, wintered there in the 20's. Transfer of populations between Turkey and Greece had earlier exiled thousands under the cruel guise of repatriation. The Irish question repeatedly forced Irish and Anglo-Irish to France and to England. During and after the war in Spain, Spaniards fled their country, hoping to return, but all too often to die in squalid exile—in France, in Puerto Rico, in New York, and of course in Latin America.

But I need not multiply examples further.

In our travels, Hermione and I made acquaintance with exiles from every corner of the globe. I have spoken of the Bulgarian F——— S———, of the Nigerian tribal chieftain whom I have called Okomo, and the South African socialist R——— Mc A———, and of others. I have not yet attempted to name the common thread that wove through all our conversations. This universal fabric, we have come to understand, is a profound and extreme ambivalence relative to the homeland, a love-and-hate so thoroughly intertwined that its dual structure can be discerned in the slightest utterance.

That ambivalence is the nature of human emotion, I have never doubted. One remembers the joke about elephants and national character. The American writes, "The Elephant and the Profit Motive." The Frenchman writes, "*Les Amours des Eléphants.*" The Englishman writes, "The Imperial Elephant." The Pole writes, "The Elephant and the Polish Question. All exiles are Poles, and if they drink wine they think of the wines of their youth; if they watch a magnificent sunset over the Pacific, they remember sunset over the Urals or the Austrian Alps or on the deserts of Africa. An item in a newspaper about a cabinet shift in Stockholm brings to mind the politics of change in their own country, and since they (I should say we) are all participants of loss, they remember with tenderness and rage the hopes and despairs of long ago.

We live in the twilight country of the remote past, and in a present country and present circumstance which is lit by dim light. We bump into the walls of the present, expecting to find an older wall, a window that is not there, and that looks over remembered landscape.

But the internal landscape is loud with the alternation of laughter and of tears. Klaus K——— walks through the railway station in New Haven, Connecticut, returning from Manhattan to his position as curator of the art museum at a large university. But he is not there; he is walking through a railway station in a small Bavarian town in 1936. He hears an aggregation of local musicians, in the December cold outside, and smiles to hear the energetic tuba trying and failing to keep the correct time. For a moment he has forgotten the purpose of his journey, which is to revisit the family estate in the forlorn attempt to settle his affairs before he must flee his fatherland. He emerges from the station. On the arm of the tuba player a cloth band proclaims by its swastika the vicious omnipresence of National Socialism. He must not show his feelings. He ducks his head into the wind and snow, grinding his teeth. And now, although it is May in Connecticut, twenty years later, Klaus ducks his head into the wind and snow that surround him still. He grinds his teeth in the light breeze of Connecticut spring.

Hermann von Kreicke, *The Migrant Swan*

3. Here is a parody essay of a literary critic introducing to American readers new translations by a modern Serbian poet. I have mixed up the order of the paragraphs and numbered them. See if you can reorder them in the most logical way. See if you can find more than one order that works well. Also, try to see if some paragraphs, because of transitional phrases or matters of logic, *must* follow each other.

(1) At the same time, strange metaphors creep into Radke's poems from another place. These strange metaphors have erupted from the ancient Serbian land, from dark caves, and from the mysterious mountain unconscious possed by the memory of witches and wise men with magical powers.

(2) In Serbian literature there is a much stronger division between "peasant" and "educated" writing than there is in England or America. There have been a considerable number of Serbian authors who have clearly fallen into one group or the other. Radke, with his German background, clearly falls into the second group, middle-European, learned, and allusive. He shows the level of excellence this tradition at its best can achieve.

(3) His poems wander like ghosts along the edge that divides Catholicism and Paganism.

(4) Radke's poems are like a hummingbird darting from the one blossom to the other.

(5) Scholars now concede Radke is the best twentieth-century poet of the Balkans. Early in his career, he was influenced by twin sources alien to the Serbian poetic tradition: to the imagist poetry of China in particular, and of Japan also, and to Spanish poetry, especially the Gongoresque tradition revived by the poets of *modernismo*. His best work also exemplifies the influence of ballad singers.

(6) Many of Radke's poems assume a method of associational discourse which make them hard to follow. His observations occur in a lively and unusual diction. Probably he is the most obscure poet of Serbia; yet his readers are many. His collections of poetry appear in editions which, if we adjust for the size of the potential audience, would make 150,000 copies in the United States. Yet he is a poet who accuses his readers, and himself, of emotional dishonesty, of pervasive falsity, and of moral cowardice.

(7) We read in his poems the exhortation to transcend the ego, much as we read in the Spaniards that we must admit the *duende*. Or as in certain Oriental poets we enter "the floating world." Radke knows well the spirits he speaks of. His poetry insists that his readers must learn to float, and to admit the dark power within them.

4. Do a stylistic analysis of paragraph length in the following passages. (You might also apply this analysis to one or two passages read earlier and discussed for other purposes.) Do the au-

thors provide variety? Are there moments when you would prefer that a long paragraph be broken up? Do any paragraphs seem choppy?

What, in our human world, is this power to live? It is the ancient, lost reverence and passion for human personality, joined with the ancient, lost reverence and passion for the earth and its web of life.

This indivisible reverence and passion is what the American Indians almost universally had; and representative groups of them have it still.

They had and have this power for living which our modern world has lost—as world-view and self-view, as tradition and institution, as practical philosophy dominating their societies and as an art supreme among all the arts.

By virtue of this power, the densely populated Inca state, by universal agreement among its people, made the conservation and increase of the earth's resources its foundational national policy. Never before, never since has a nation done what the Inca state did.

By virtue of this same power, the little pueblo of Tesuque, in New Mexico, when threatened by the implacable destroying action of government some twenty-five years ago, starved and let no white friend know it was starving. It asked no help, determined only to defend its spiritual values and institutions and its remnant of land which was holy land.

If our modern world should be able to recapture this power, the earth's natural resources and web of life would not be irrevocably wasted within the twentieth century, which is the prospect now. True democracy, founded in neighborhoods and reaching over the world, would become the realized heaven on earth. And living peace—not just an interlude between wars—would be born and would last through ages.

John Collier, *Indians of the Americas*

When it comes to the so-called obscene words, I should say that hardly one person in a million escapes mob-reaction. The first reaction is almost sure to be mob-reaction, mob-indignation, mob-condemnation. And the mob gets no further. But the real individual has second thoughts and says: Am I really shocked? Do I *really* feel outraged and indignant? And the answer of any individual is bound to be: No, I am not shocked, not outraged, nor indignant. I know the word, and take it for what it is, and I am not going to be jockeyed into making a mountain out of a mole-hill, not for all the law in the world.

Now if the use of a few so-called obscene words will startle man or woman out of a mob-habit into an individual state, well and good. And word-prudery is so universal a mob-habit that it is time we were startled out of it.

But still we have only tackled obscenity, and the problem of pornography goes even deeper. When a man is startled into his individual self, he still may not be able to know, inside himself, whether Rabelais is or is not pornographic; and over Aretino or even Boccaccio he may perhaps puzzle in vain, torn between different emotions.

One essay on pornography, I remember, comes to the conclusion that pornography in art is that which is calculated to arouse sexual desire, or sexual excitement. And stress is laid on the fact, whether the author or artist intended to arouse sexual feelings. It is the old vexed question of intention, become so dull today, when we know how strong and influential our unconscious intentions are. And why a man should be held guilty of his conscious intentions, and innocent of his unconscious intentions, I don't know, since every man is more made up of unconscious intentions than of conscious ones. I am what I am, not merely what I think I am.

However! We take it, I assume, that *pornography* is something base, something unpleasant. In short, we don't like it. And why don't we like it? Because it arouses sexual feelings?

I think not. No matter how hard we may pretend otherwise, most of us rather like a moderate rousing of our sex. It warms us, stimulates us like sunshine on a gray day. After a century or two of Puritanism, this is still true of most people. Only the mob-habit of condemning any form of sex is too strong to let us admit it naturally. And there are, of course, many people who are genuinely repelled by the simplest and most natural stirrings of sexual feeling. But these people are perverts who have fallen into hatred of their fellow men: thwarted, disappointed, unfulfilled people, of whom, alas, our civilization contains so many. And they nearly always enjoy some unsimple and unnatural form of sexual excitement, secretly.

D. H. Lawrence, "Pornography and Obscenity"

5. Take these excerpts from the *Detroit Free Press*, tiny newspaper paragraphs, and copy them out into longer paragraphs, as you would organize paragraphs in a theme. Break the paragraphs logically and usefully.

He may have been the greatest golfer who ever lived—or so the legend says, and legends are hard to dispute.

"The Phantom of the Links," he was called, and "The Garbo of Golf." Some called him one of the world's strongest men. Others called him a con man. Police records called him an extortionist, and there was talk of robbery and smuggling.

Some knew him as John M. Montague, the man Grantland Rice called "the greatest golfer on earth," and Walter Hagen termed "the most amazing golfer in the world."

A few may have even known him, all 300 pounds of him, as Laverne Moore. Because that was his real name—or so the legend says.

The man known as Laverne Moore and John M. Montague—golfer, millionaire, mystery man—has died at the age of 67.

He palled around with famous names—Bing Crosby, Spencer Tracy, Bob Hope—but his own rang no bells outside his own circle and was rarely emblazoned in headlines with Palmer, Nicklaus, Snead and Hogan.

He might have beaten those famous golfers with a baseball bat. Or a tennis racket and a dead mackerel. A truck axle. Anything he could lay one of his big hands on and swing at a golf ball.   (UPI)

Here's what the historic arms limitation agreements signed here Friday night in the Kremlin mean.

What they do, essentially, is to freeze a "balance of terror" between the world's two nuclear superpowers.

Each side, in these agreements, retains the ability to kill millions of defenseless civilians on the other side.

Washington and Moscow will be defended from nuclear attack with anti-ballistic missile systems (ABMs).

But Detroit and every other major city in the U.S. will remain undefended. So will Leningrad and Kiev, and other major cities in the Soviet Union.

Thus each side, in a sense, will hold the civilian population of the other side hostage—as a means of discouraging the other side from launching nuclear war.

The fact is, as Henry Kissinger, White House national security adviser, has put it: "Both sides are now vulnerable to each other . . . this has been a fact now for five or six years."

The new SALT agreements seek to freeze the 25-year-old nuclear arms race at that point—on the theory that a "balance of terror" is the best guarantee either side has, in this terrifying age, of preventing war.

But what of other major questions?

How important are the agreements? Can they work? Can they be monitored? Don't the agreements give the Soviets a numerical advantage? What will they mean to the average citizen?

James McCartney

6. In this passage from Ezra Pound's *Patria Mia*, I have changed the paragraph breaks, but not the order of the sentences. Try to decide where the original breaks were, and rearrange my version in the most sensible way you can. See if you can find several ways that are satisfactory.

It is well-known that in the year of grace 1870 Jehovah appeared to Messrs Harper and Co. and to the editors of *The Century, The Atlantic*, and certain others, and spake thus: "The style of 1870 is the final and divine revelation. Keep things always just as they are now." And they, being earnest, God-fearing men, did abide by the words of the Almighty, and great credit and honor accrued unto them, for had they not divine warrant?

And if you do not believe me, open a number of *Harpers* for 1888 and one for 1908.

And I defy you to find any difference, save on the page where the date is. Hence, when I say openly that there is more artistic impulse in America than in any country in Europe, I am in no peril of being believed.

The documents are against me. And when I add that there is no man now living in America whose art in letters is of the slightest interest to me, I am held for paradoxical. And the answer to that is, that there is practically no one in America who knows good work from bad—no such person, I mean, who is part of the system for circulation. It is cheering to reflect that America accepted Whitman when he was properly introduced by William Michael Rossetti, and not before then. When a young man in America, having the instincts and interiors of a poet, begins to write, he finds no one to say to him·

"Put down exactly what you feel and mean! Say it as briefly as possible and avoid all sham of ornament.

"Learn what technical excellence you can from a direct study of the masters, and pay no attention to the suggestions of anyone who has not himself produced notable work in poetry. Think occasionally (as Longinus has aforetime advised), what such or such a master would think if he heard your verses." On the contrary, he receives from editors such missives as this:—"Dear Mr. — — — —, Your work, etc., is very interesting, etc., but you will have to pay more attention to conventional form if you want to make a commercial success of it." This comes from Mr. Tiddlekins, who has a kindly feeling toward you.

It is sent in good faith. And nothing terrene or supernal can get Mr. T. to see it in any light but his own. He has been brought up to respect eighteenth-century fashions. He has never once considered any fundamental issue of art or of aesthetics.

He has been taught that one fashion is good.   (1913)

7. Look at old themes or daily writing. See what you can change in paragraphing. Rewrite to improve, or, if you are satisfied with your old paragraphing, to see if you can paragraph in a different way and still make the paragraphing work.

8. List topics for a possible essay. Then decide which items belong together in substructures that might be individual paragraphs.

9. Make up a paragraph of narration, the subject historical or personal or fictional, and then experiment with revising the chronological order, while you maintain clarity.

10. Make up ten sentences to introduce paragraphs of narration, summary, description, argument, or exposition.

11. Analyze the construction of the following two paragraphs, which are in sequence, from the essay in which E. B. White speaks of Simonizing his grandmother:

Communication by the written word is a subtler (and more beautiful) thing than Dr. Flesch or General Motors imagines. They contend that the "average reader" is capable of reading only what tests Easy, and that the writer should write at or below this level. This is a presumptuous and degrading idea. There is no average reader, and to reach down toward this mythical character is to deny that each of us is on the way up, is ascending. ("Ascending," by the way, is a word Dr. Flesch advises writers to stay away from. Too unusual.)

It is our belief that no writer can improve his work until he discards the dulcet notion that the reader is feeble-minded, for writing is an act of faith, not a trick of grammar. Ascent is at the heart of the matter. A country whose writers are following a calculating machine downstairs is not ascending—if you will pardon the expression—and a writer who questions the capacity of the person at the other end of the line is not a writer at all, merely a schemer. The movies long ago decided that a wider communication could be achieved by a deliberate descent to a lower level, and they walked proudly down until they reached the cellar. Now they are groping for the light switch, hoping to find the way out.

E. B. White, *The Second Tree from the Corner*

12. Rewrite these paragraphs to correct their incoherence. Check for irrelevant material, incorrect or obscure sequence, or inept beginnings or endings.

a. The heavy wooden door was painted red, but the wood showed through in many places where the paint was flaking off.

Dandelions covered the lawn, but there were few weeds in the dark grass. A white and black cat lay curled by the door. Three huge oaks threw their shadows across the wide lawn. Far off, a deer was watching from the edge of the woods. There was no knob on the door.

b. The days were unusually hot and humid, even for that part of the state. Joe didn't want to go to the beach. His girlfriend, Linda, did. She wasn't a good swimmer. She loved to swim. Joe was working on his car. He was a fanatical sports enthusiast.

c. He had found that the wolves subsisted mainly on a diet of mice. Farley had been dropped in the middle of the Canadian tundra. He discovered that the hunters were lying, and that they themselves were the insane murderers. Hunters had been complaining that the wolves were slaughtering thousands of caribou for the sheer pleasure of killing. He had made an astonishing discovery. He had been assigned to investigate the killing of caribou by timber wolves.

d. *Delivery* by Paul Jamesy is a story of the adventures of a group of department store delivery boys sent on a mission into the suburbs of a large metropolis. The journey is a revelation of the inner world of modern man—the wanton violence of five-year-old footballers, the vast boredom of the swinging teens, the horrors of afternoon romance in respectable families. The author himself is a former cheerleader and national frog-jumping champion. All but one of the young men become trapped in a labyrinthine and nightmarish Kresge's store. Only one, who wins the voluptuous blonde named Shirley, succeeds in making his big—*Delivery*.

13. How do the following paragraphs work? Can you find topic sentences? Do they define, analyze, compare, assert? What *is* their means of development? How do they manage transition?

a. The sea, autumn mildness, islands bathed in light, fine rain spreading a diaphanous veil over the immortal nakedness of Greece. Happy is the man, I thought, who, before dying, has the good fortune to sail the Aegean Sea.

Many are the joys of this world—women, fruit, ideas. But to cleave that sea in the gentle, autumnal season, murmuring the name of each islet, is to my mind the joy most apt to transport the heart of man into paradise. Nowhere else can one pass so easily and serenely from reality to dream. The frontiers dwindle, and from the masts of the most ancient ships spring branches and fruits. It is as if here in Greece necessity is the mother of miracles.

Towards noon the rain stopped. The sun parted the clouds and appeared gentle, tender, washed and fresh, and it caressed with its rays the beloved waters and lands. I stood at the prow and let myself be intoxicated with the miracle which was revealed as far as the eye could see.

Nikos Kazantzakis, Zorba the Greek

b. In Munch, the thinker, the poet and the painter are in equilibrium. He is no mere formalist. Art, as the realm of human imagination and creativity, found again in Munch that unity peculiar to the great artists of past ages: Georgione, Rembrandt, Tintoretto, Goya. No one can draw a distinction between the technique of their work and its content, between the content and the man. They are one.

Munch strove for the expression of new humanity. When he started out on his wanderings through Europe, he found the ground was already prepared by the conflict of ideas to receive his message. His personal fate, the sorrow he had experienced, the doubts with which he had wrestled, his attitude towards life gave a universal validity to what he had to impart to the world of his time.

J. P. Hodin, Edvard Munch

c. A philosopher—is a human being who constantly experiences, sees, hears, suspects, hopes, and dreams extraordinary things; who is struck by his own thoughts as from outside, as from above and below, as by *his* type of experiences and lightning bolts; who is perhaps himself a storm pregnant with new lightnings; a fatal human being around whom there are constant rumblings and growlings, crevices, and uncanny doings. A philosopher—alas, a being that often runs away from itself, often is afraid of itself—but too inquisitive not to "come to" again—always back to himself.

Friedrich Nietzsche, Beyond Good and Evil

d. Franco's reestablishment of the Catholic Church as a dominant force in Spanish life, through the restoration of religious education, of state financial support for the Church, and by the repeal of Republican anti-clerical laws, led in 1941 to a working arrangement with the Vatican that was finally formalized by a treaty in 1953.

These measures, however, did not serve to protect the Franco regime from the severe censure of the Allies after the Second World War. In July 1945, Spain found herself branded by the Potsdam Declaration as unfit to associate with the United Nations. In December 1946 the United Nations formally ostracized the Spanish government and recommended that all its member nations withdraw their ambassadors from Madrid. Thus Spain found itself practically friendless in the postwar world, with only the dictatorships of Portugal and Argentina still lending the Nationalist regime their support.

Robert Goldston, The Civil War in Spain

14. Invent ten examples of transitions from the end of one paragraph to the beginning of the next—five subtle, five necessarily obvious.

15. Write two paragraphs in which you use parallel sentences for transition. Write two paragraphs in which you use comparison and contrast for transition.

16. In the following paragraph the pronoun "he" is used in a monotonous and confusing way. Rewrite it so that we do not have the word "he" used so many times, and so that we are always sure who or what the pronouns refer to.

Robert and Daniel crouched in the cave, listening for the sound of approaching footsteps. He thought the troops must have left the area by now. For the moment he was reassured by the silence, but he worried about the sharp pain in his knee, and he wondered if he would be able to walk on it if he had to. He was glad to have his old friend with him. He looked at him. Their gazes meeting, he felt tears come to his eyes from straining to see in the half-darkness, and from thinking where he and his friend had been just yesterday.

17. Analyze the paragraphs by C. S. Lewis and by Ivan Illich, on pp. 149–150, for their movement, paying particular attention to the transitions within and between paragraphs. Do the same with the following passages:

Once again I had found myself in the presence of a truth and had failed to recognize it. Consider what had happened to me: I had thought myself lost, had touched the very bottom of despair; and then, when the spirit of renunciation had filled me, I had known peace. I know now what I was not conscious of at the time—that in such an hour a man feels that he has finally found himself and has become his own friend. An essential inner need has been satisfied, and against that satisfaction, that self-fulfillment, no external power can prevail. Bonnafous, I imagine, he who spent his life racing before the wind, was acquainted with this serenity of spirit. Guillaumet, too, in his snows. Never shall I forget that, lying buried to the chin in sand, strangled slowly to death by thirst, my heart was infinitely warm beneath the desert stars.

What can men do to make known to themselves this sense of deliverance? Everything about mankind is paradox. He who strives and conquers grows soft. The magnanimous man grown rich becomes mean. The creative artist for whom everything is made easy nods. Every doctrine swears that it can breed men, but none can tell us in advance what sort of men it will breed. Men are not cattle to be fattened for market. In the scales of life an indigent Newton weighs more than a parcel of prosperous nonentities. All of us have had the experience of a sudden joy that came when nothing in the world had forewarned us of its coming—a joy so thrilling that if it was born of misery we remembered even the misery with tenderness. All of us, on seeing old friends again, have remembered with happiness the trials we lived through with those friends. Of what can we be certain except this—that we are fertilized by mysterious circumstances? Where is man's truth to be found?

Truth is not that which can be demonstrated by the aid of logic. If orange-trees are hardy and rich in fruit in this bit of soil and not that, then this bit of soil is what is truth for orange-trees. If a particular religion, or culture, or scale of values, if one form of activity rather than another, brings self-fulfillment to a man, releases the prince asleep within him unknown to himself, then that scale of values, that culture, that form of activity, constitute his truth. Logic, you say? Let logic wangle its own explanation of life.

Because it is man and not flying that concerns me most, I shall close this book with the story of man's gropings towards self-fulfillment as I witnessed them in the early months of the civil war in Spain. One year after crashing in the desert I made a tour of the Catalan front in order to learn what happens to man when the scaffolding of his traditions suddenly collapses. To Madrid I went for an answer to another question: How does it happen that men are sometimes willing to die?

Antoine de Saint Exupéry, *Wind, Sand and Stars*

The mass of men serve the State thus, not as men mainly, but as machines, with their bodies. They are the standing army, and the militia, jailers, constables, "posse comitatus," &c. In most cases there is no free exercise whatever of the judgment or of the moral sense; but they put themselves on a level with wood and earth and stones; and wooden men can perhaps be manufactured that will serve the purpose as well. Such command no more respect than men of straw; or a lump of dirt. They have the same sort of worth only as horses and dogs. Yet such as these even are commonly esteemed good citizens. Others, as most legislators, politicians, lawyers, ministers, and office-holders, serve the State chiefly with their heads; and, as they rarely make any moral distinctions, they are as likely to serve the devil, without intending it, as God. A very few, as heroes, patriots, martyrs, reformers in the great sense, and *men,* serve the State with their consciences also, and so necessarily resist it for the most part; and they are commonly treated by it as enemies. A wise man will only be useful as a man, and will not submit to be "clay," and "stop a hole to keep the wind away," but leave that office to his dust at least:—

> "I am too high-born to be propertied,
> To be a secondary at control,
> Or useful serving-man and instrument
> To any sovereign state throughout the world."

He who gives himself entirely to his fellow-men appears to them useless and selfish; but he who gives himself partially to them is pronounced a benefactor and philanthropist.

How does it become a man to behave toward this American government to-day? I answer that he cannot without disgrace be associated with it. I cannot for an instant recognize the political organization as *my* government which is the *slave's* government also.

All men recognize the right of revolution; that is, the right to refuse allegiance to and to resist the government, when its tyranny or its inefficiency are great and unendurable. But almost all say that such is not the case now. But such was the case, they think, in the Revolution of '75. If one were to tell me that this was a bad government because it taxed certain foreign commodities brought to its ports, it is most probable that I should not make an ado about it, for I can do without them: all machines have their friction; and possibly this does enough good to counterbalance the evil. At any rate, it is a great evil to make a stir about it. But when the friction comes to have its machine, and oppression and robbery are organized, I say, let us not have such a machine any longer. In other words, when a sixth of the population of a nation which has undertaken to be the refuge of liberty are slaves, and a whole country is unjustly overrun and conquered by a foreign army, and subjected to military law, I think that it is not too soon for honest men to rebel and revolutionize. What makes this duty the more urgent is the fact, that the country so overrun is not our own, but ours is the invading army.

Henry David Thoreau, "On the Duty of Civil Disobedience"

V

THE PAPER

GETTING IDEAS

Many beginning writers find that getting started is the hardest part of writing. How do you find a starting point for a paper?

It depends on what you are doing. It also depends on the agility of your mind. But however spry or stiff you feel, you can learn to become *more* agile, *more* open, *more* prolific with ideas. If you have been doing daily writing, you have a warehouse of possibilities on the pages that you have accumulated. If you are writing a free theme, you can consult your daily writing for a thought or an anecdote that is apt for expansion. If you are assigned a theme to demonstrate a technique—a type of argument, for instance—you can find a starting point in your daily writing to develop and use.

If you are assigned to write a paper on Sino-Soviet relations, or on why you want to go to law school, or on a Kurt Vonnegut novel, your daily writing will not help you to find an idea. You must accumulate detail, allow ideas to grow from other ideas, and then shape the whole. I will speak more of this shaping later.

If you have no daily writing, and you are assigned a free theme, you have numerous ways of looking for subject matter. Topics come from your own life. For some papers, you can write anecdotal reminiscence. But even when you write exposition, or argument, the sub-

180

ject can come from your own life. If you wish to write an argument, think of recent conversations. Almost everyone involves himself in controversy from time to time. Choose a position to attack or defend, out of something in your own experience. Newspaper articles leave us feeling angry or approving—and are another source of topics for argument. Lacking ideas, look over letters from home, or remember your last visit there.

But argument or advocacy is not a necessary part of an essay. You may want simply to investigate something. Hearing about the increasing incidence of state lotteries, you may want to do research on them and set forth the information in a paper. You may want to write exposition on the safest way to ride a motorcycle, or how to organize a rent strike. Books, television, talk shows, and everything we see in our daily lives—from movies to the behavior of customers and shop clerks—can provide the topic for exposition. We must keep our eyes open. When we need to get an idea, we must let our inward eyes move freely over our experiences recent and past. A million topics wait for us.

ACCUMULATING DETAIL

Normally, an idea comes to us with a few bits of detail attached. For safety, the motorcyclist must wear a helmet and keep his equipment in good repair. During the Easter vacation when we went to Washington, the buses broke down and the cherry trees failed to bloom, Alice Notley had hepatitis, and Mrs. Reade disappeared for two days. A state lottery must distribute N per cent of its earnings or people will not support it.

We must do two contrary things with detail. We must accumulate a great deal of it; and we must cut it down to what is essential and useful. First, let us look at ways of accumulating detail; if the next section of this chapter tells us to cut and to shape, this section should tell us how to gather the material for shaping and cutting.

Paper-writing for most of us goes through many stages. First, we take notes at random, not trying to think in an orderly way, but simply to gather as much possibly useful material as we can. We should *brainstorm*, letting our minds float freely and writing down the memories and associations that swim around us. We should take notes even if we think we will probably never use them. Writing about lotteries, we might associate them with Bingo at the church, or with dog racing. Writing about motorcycle safety, we might think of the air bags proposed for automobiles. Probably both ideas will be cut in the third stage of composition, in shaping the paper. But when we are brainstorming, we censor nothing; at this stage, it is impossible to be certain what will fit our paper's shape, because we do not have the shape.

So write notes freely and loosely, secure in the knowledge that no one but you need ever *read* your notes. Training in daily writing is useful at this stage. Write down what may be silly and what may be pompous; just write. Follow the train of thought even when you have no idea of its destination. Stop, put the notes away, and come back to it later. When you return, you will usually discover that some secret part of your head has been doing homework in the meantime; you will discover a fresh flow of details.

I have been describing the kind of paper that comes from your memory, your thought, and your imagination. Some papers properly take you to the library, or to an interview. You will need facts and figures to talk about state lotteries. You will be doing research, which is another matter. But before you begin research, before you look at your first index, you should brainstorm; you can accumulate speculative notes about what to look for and where to look.

When you have accumulated detail by floating freely, you may find that you can create more detail by scrutinizing what you have written down. Perhaps this scrutiny could be called another stage in writing the paper. Looking over your brief notes, *think* about each one, asking yourself if the one bit of information implies any other. If Mrs. Reade was missing for two days, what were the other teachers on the trip up to? The cherry trees did not bloom; was there any other vegetation? color? smell? By scrutiny and self-questioning—apparently opposite mental acts from the dreamy note-taking of the first stage—you can acquire more detail.

SHAPING THE PAPER

But to write a good paper, you have to organize details in the best order, and you must leave out any details, however attractive, which do not contribute to the whole. I talked about order when I discussed organizing materials into paragraphs, pages 144–146. In the same chapter, I talked about extraneous detail, pages 146–150. At the beginning of the book I talked about focus and unity, pages 10–14. It might be a good idea, now, to look back at these pages to refresh your memory. The idea of focus in the first chapter is perhaps the most important *formal* idea in making a paper.

For focus we need *order*. A different order of ideas can make a different statement, even when the ideas or details remain the same. In a reminiscence, if we begin with pleasant associations and move to horrid ones, we leave the reader with a negative impression; if we move from horrid to pleasant, we are liable to leave the reader feeling positive. We could accumulate identical details for each paper, but make a different impression by our organization. There are "insides" to the order of details, as well as to words and syntax. One student wrote, in a history paper,

> The rainfall in the Southern provinces is approximately two inches a year. On the average. What this means is that most years the country people starve in a drought; one year in five, they drown in a flood. However, the combination of a surviving Indian ritual, and a local brand of Roman Catholicism, keeps the people remarkably cheerful and content.

For the same assignment, writing from the same source, another wrote:

> Indian rituals which still survive, combined with a peculiar indigenous Catholicism, keep the natives of the South apparently contented. However, the climatic conditions are deplorable. The rainfall averages two inches a year. This means that the peasants parch for several years in drought, and are drowned in floods the next one.

Both students' notes for this passage were, approximately:

> Catholicism and Indian stuff
> happy
> infant mortality
> rainfall
> floods
> starvation, drought

The two students were heading in different directions—the first toward an expository essay on daily life in the tribe, the second toward an argument for public works such as irrigation and flood control—but they started from the same information, which they organized or pointed in different ways.

Notice that neither student used the detail about infant mortality in this sequence of details. It was not directly related to religion, or

to the economy of water. Because it was not a part of the movement
of the passage, it was irrelevant to it. When we shape into our paper
the details we have accumulated, we will find that we have to cut
many of them.

Cutting Detail

Professional writers often find that they do most of their revision by
cutting. They cut details that are irrelevant to their point, they cut
details that repeat the same feelings or information that other details
have already carried, and they cut explanations of the obvious. Revision is more than omission, but learning what to omit is a good part
of the art of *finishing* a piece of writing. Ezra Pound talks about his
experience in writing a poem, and what he says of poetry is also a
strong example of what we must do continually in prose:

> Three years ago in Paris I got out of a "metro" train at La
> Concorde, and saw suddenly a beautiful face, and then another
> and another, and then a beautiful child's face, and then another
> beautiful woman, and I tried all that day to find words for what
> this had meant to me, and I could not find any words that
> seemed to me worthy, or as lovely as that sudden emotion.
> . . . I wrote a thirty-line poem, and destroyed it because it was
> what we call work "of second intensity." Six months later I
> made a poem half that length; a year later I made the following
> *hokku*-like sentence:—

> "The apparition of these faces in the crowd;
> Petals on a wet, black bough."

Writing is acquiring material (the floating on memory, the rapid
daily writing) and it is ordering and cutting that material. The writer
must be a paradoxical combination of opposites; the big spender
and the miser, the nymphomaniac and the virgin, the all-acceptor
and the all-rejector. Probably we are more troubled with irrelevant
detail when we write out of our own lives than when we write from
any other source. Cutting can take place when we try to organize our
notes before writing, or it can come later; probably we cut at both
stages. When we start to write, it is often hard to know which details
are going to prove relevant. Many writers consciously write too
much in their first drafts, knowing they do not yet know what will be
useful, and knowing that they will later cut for focus and form.

Suppose you describe a particular day. At the end of a vacation, you had a perfect (or perfectly horrible) day. On that Thursday, when you woke up, it was 8:35. You ate scrambled eggs with catsup. These details could be relevant, or they could be mere padding. Cut what does not contribute to the whole. But first, you must have a whole. The point of your paper could be the triviality of your day; a dog barked, the mail was junk, nobody was home when you telephoned your friends. The point is to have a point. Find one—or even make one up. Truth-to-feeling is the point; we are not under oath in a court. If we are remembering a sequence of events—A, B, C, and D—we can rearrange the sequence to make a piece of writing more true to the feeling of the whole. If event B happened second, but in retrospect was the emotional climax, we can *lie* a little, in order to tell the emotional truth. We can use C, A, and D in that order, and save B for last. We are still writing out of our own life. We are telling the truth in the serious sense. Within the limits of credibility, we can even combine different events into one, or different people into the same character. Suppose in a family anecdote two uncles were moving in and out of a story, doing approximately the same things. In an anecdote, it might well be more shapely and pointed—and just as "true"—to turn them into one person.

To make a point, and to give our writing a shape, we must limit our material. Here we are back to unity again, a notion brought up in numerous forms in this book. If we try to write about a whole summer, we are most likely to write a series of disjointed paragraphs, and be boring and superficial. We should find one event, or one unifying device (a place, a person, an automobile, a time of day, a kind of food) to tie together different details. Contrast can make a glue as adhesive as similarity. We must find the combination of detail and form that will embody the spirit of the summer.

Beginnings: Narrowing the Topic

Beginnings of papers, in the work of inexperienced writers, are often shapeless. Experienced writers learn to pay special attention to beginnings. One professional says that if he can "find" the first sentence—as if a piece of paper were lying around on a dark shelf of the brain, with the right words on it—the rest of the essay is simple; the door opens, and he finds it easy to construct the house of the essay. But, he says, sometimes it takes him months to find the key.

Most of the time, we lack the months. Some hints about beginnings may help.

We usually overexplain, at the beginning of a paper, and begin too far back. Trying to talk about something that we did last weekend, we may realize that it resembled something we did last summer; then we may realize that the feelings of last summer were like the feelings we had at five when we started kindergarten; or at three, when we moved to a new town. All these details may be valid, but to include all of them would destroy the shape of our paper. The bridge into the country of last weekend would be longer than the country itself. With enough self-questioning, we could begin every autobiographical paper with "I was born," or, "My grandparents emigrated from Lithuania in 1905," or, "Life for my peasant ancestors in Medieval Turkey must have been difficult." This malady of origins and causes might be called the house-that-Jack-built syndrome.

Long bridges curse not only autobiography; the same malady can afflict all writing. In discussing the origins of World War II, we can begin with the fall of the Roman Empire. In making up a short story, we can supply causes from our imagination as prolifically as we can supply them from memory in writing autobiography. In assembling a research paper, we can go backward in time, or laterally in comparisons. Wanting to write about ecology, we may pick the declining population of whales as our topic; we can begin with the general topic of man's destruction of his environment, narrow it to his destruction of animal species, narrow it to whales, and then narrow it to one type of whale. The last category is the focus of the paper, but if we are not careful we can spend three-quarters of our paper walking the bridge to our topic.

The good, sharp beginning narrows the topic. Begin with something that arrests the reader, and points to the main topic. Reference back (or laterally) can follow if it is necessary, and it can be brief:

> Last weekend I broke up with Ed. I have not felt so lonesome since I moved to a new town when I was four, leaving the friends of my whole life behind me, and knowing no one at all.
> I know other people besides Ed, but I feel as if I didn't. The break-up had been coming for weeks. . . .

Or we can begin *without* an immediate lateral glance:

> Humpbacks are mammals, as all whales are; they breathe into huge lungs, bear live young, which they nurse for the better part of a year, and have vestiges of hair. . . .

In this research paper, the author catches our attention immediately with facts that will interest almost anyone, probably because they interested her and she shows it: "huge lungs," "for the better part of a year."

Editors of magazines sometimes refer to "zingers," which are beginnings (or "leads") of articles constructed to grab the reader by the hair. *Time* is good at zingers. Here are three opening sentences from one issue:

> The United States was founded on a complaint.

> When the young Chinese woman heard a mysterious voice asking, "What's under your pillow?" she felt sure that the answer was a "biological radio apparatus" put there by a special agent who suspected her of crimes against the state.

> Professor Jürgen Zerche was lecturing on political science one day this spring when a band of some 70 young leftists barged into his classroom at the Free University of Berlin and began shouting curses at him.

All immediately involve our interest, and none has a preamble. One begins with a startling short sentence, the other two with arresting anecdotes.

Much serious writing begins with what we might call a quiet zinger, something exciting or intriguing and at the same time relevant to the material that follows. When Homer begins the *Iliad*, about the anger of Achilles and its consequences, the first word in the long poem means "rage." Here are the beginnings of three books:

> On top of everything, the cancer wing was Number 13.
> Alexander Solzhenitsyn, *Cancer Ward*

> Who does not know Turner's picture of the Golden Bough?
> J. G. Fraser, *The Golden Bough*

> Harold Ross died December 6, 1951, exactly one month after his fifty-ninth birthday. In November of the following year the *New Yorker* entertained the editors of *Punch* and some of its outstanding artists and writers. I was in Bermuda and missed the party, but weeks later met Rowland Emett for lunch at the Algonquin. "I'm sorry you didn't get to meet Ross," I began as

we sat down. "Oh, but I did," he said. "He was all over the place. Nobody talked about anybody else."

James Thurber, The Years with Ross

In this last example, the first sentence is a conventional way to introduce a biographical memoir. Then Thurber shifts abruptly to anecdote, showing (not telling) in his first paragraph how important and fascinating Ross was to his staff. This showing points to the focus of the book.

At other times and in other kinds of books, a definition of the subject may be essential before we can begin:

> "In its widest possible extension the title of this book— *Adventures of Ideas*—might be taken as a synonym for The History of the Human Race. . . ."

A. N. Whitehead, Adventures of Ideas

Whitehead builds a swift bridge into his topic. Purpose and context determine the kind of beginning. But in any piece of writing, the beginning focuses our writing, it requires special attention, and requires brevity and incisiveness. We *need* some information quickly; information which may be pertinent but not wholly necessary should be suppressed; information which is both pertinent and necessary, but which might make a tedious beginning, can often be put off until later in the essay, when its relevance becomes obvious and it ceases to seem tedious.

One kind of opener is often boring, the overt announcement of what is to be done: "I am going to show that the government of the United States is split into three branches, the executive, the legislative, and the judicial." Papers may be constructed analytically, by delineating parts, but they should show and not tell. The paper that begins with the sentence above will generally develop by taking a paragraph each for the three branches, and end, as boringly as it began, "I have shown that the government of the United States is comprised of the executive, the legislative, and the judicial branches." It is essay structure for people who have difficulty following the story line of Mighty Mouse.

Endings: Concluding the Topic

Endings are nearly as important as beginnings, and the same cautions apply. We often make them too long, summarize facts that are already obvious, reargue a point already established, say abstractly what we have shown concretely—and by all these methods dilute the intensity of our conclusion. Our endings often drag and decline into blank space, dwindling instead of concluding. This diminishment is bad organization. Usually the dwindling can be cut, just as most bridges at the beginning can be removed. If the dwindling qualifies the conclusion, the qualification can come before the conclusion.

There are exceptions. In a long and complicated argument, we may be pleased to find a succinct summary at the end of the author's argument. It is like seeing an aerial photograph of country we have just walked through. But the short paper—the kind in which we are most interested in this book—rarely profits from summary and often withers by it. We should point the whole essay toward the last sentence, and when we have written it, stop writing. Often we conclude an essay—and then continue writing. The essay writer must develop the confidence to let his facts and arguments stand by themselves without epilogue. People who moralize at the end of a story, or summarize at the end of an argument, are the same people who kill jokes by explaining them. In a short paper about an experience she had while babysitting, a student concluded:

> After that third phone call, the breathing, and the hanging-up, I sat huddled in a big chair and shaking, waiting for the Bakers to come back. For a while I turned out the lights, thinking that a dark house might not seem so inviting to any fiend prowling around. But the darkness scared me.
>
> It was about three-quarters of an hour before they came back. In that time, I thought through everything I could do if I was attacked. I could scream—but the neighbors were all away. I could run—but then I was leaving Ginnie. My mind went over and over everything. I even started to wonder which dress I ought to be buried in.
>
> When I heard the car stop I was petrified. But then I heard Mrs. Baker saying something when she opened the garage door. My heart slowed down. When they came in, I told them all about the phone calls, my parents being out of town, the houses dark next door. I guess I thought they'd give me a medal.
>
> Instead, they looked puzzled.
>
> "Why didn't you call *us?*" said Mrs. Baker.
>
> Then I realized that I had been dumb to sit there scared in the dark, waiting for the breather to knock down the door,

with the telephone number written on the pad beside the phone. While the phone had rung three times, I had simply become more and more panicked, and I had never thought of the easiest thing to do. I must have been too scared. Well, I thought, that's one mistake I won't make again.

Here, the essay dwindles like an explained joke. She might have ended it:

"Why didn't you call *us?*" said Mrs. Baker.

Or, if she had wanted to add another idea, and a detail, she might have extended herself for one sentence.

I began to wonder if I had enjoyed my fear so much that I forgot the pad of paper beside the telephone which had a phone number on it.

At any rate, her paper would have improved if she had crossed out her last paragraph.

Usually we should conclude a topic without seeming to draw attention to the conclusion. Part of the paper's unity is the sense of resolution, all details organized toward an end, a coda felt by the reader. Paradoxically, this sense of resolution can be violated by the obviousness of a resolution. Anything that feels tacked on destroys a sense of unity. E. M. Forster begins "What I Believe" with a paradox that takes our attention: "I do not believe in belief." After six or seven pages, he is able to move smoothly into his conclusion, which resolves and completes all that has gone before, at the same time including new material:

These are the reflections of an individualist and a liberal who has found his liberalism crumbling beneath him and at first felt ashamed. Then, looking around, he decided there was no special reason for shame, since other people, whatever they felt, were equally insecure. And as for individualism—there seems no way out of this, even if one wants to find one. The dictator-hero can grind down his citizens till they are all alike, but he can't melt them into a single man. That is beyond his power. He can order them to merge, he can incite them to mass antics, but they are obliged to be born separately and to die separately and, owing to these unavoidable termini, will always be running off the totalitarian rails. The memory of birth and the expectation of death always lurk within the human being, making him separate from his fellows and consequently capable of intercourse with them.

Naked I came into the world, naked I shall go out of it! And a very good thing too, for it reminds me that I am naked under my shirt. Until psychologists and biologists have done much more tinkering than seems likely, the individual remains firm and each of us must consent to be one, and to make the best of the difficult job.

When you write with the skill and fluency of E. M. Forster, you have forgotten categories like beginnings and endings—because you have learned them so well.

Middles: the Structure of Thought

Beginnings and endings are the most obvious points of attention when we concentrate on shape, on narrowing, and on focus. But obviously, the passage from beginning to ending must create an order that is lucid and expressive. The revision of Marian Hart's theme in Chapter One achieves unity and shape by omitting unnecessary details and ordering the necessary ones. The remarks on unity, sequence, and coherence—in the last chapter—indicate standards for the mini-essay of the paragraph that apply to the maxi-paragraph of the essay. Remarks on transition within the paragraph, in the last chapter, apply to transition *between* paragraphs also, and therefore to the flowing development of the whole essay.

The middle is the matter. *The shape of the essay*, like the motion of the paragraph, *is the structure of our thought*. Most of the time, our matter determines our manner—or it ought to. An anecdote or a historical summary or an exposition of process must use chronological order. In an argument that advances a thesis, the order of an essay seldom depends on chronology. Instead, it is an order of persuasion—accumulating detail, proceeding by logic, and using various forms of persuasion or argument.

The structure of the middle derives from the nature of the essay. It explains, it argues, it persuades, it describes, it narrates. So it is time to look at exposition, argument and persuasion, description and narration.

EXPOSITION

Expository writing explains. It does not argue—though exposition can form part of an argument. It does not tell a story—though it might explain something essential to telling a story. Exposition exists in pure form, in whole essays of explanation. If you did an exchange year in England, you might feel called upon to write an essay explaining baseball or percolator coffee to your teacher and classmates. You could help to explain them by comparing them to cricket or tea. If you attempted to demonstrate the superiority of baseball or coffee, you would be adding argument to exposition. If you wrote a biography of Albert Einstein, you would certainly write a narrative of his life, you would probably use dialogue, and you would probably use description. Exposition would certainly be necessary also.

> But there was another consequence which Einstein now brought forward for the first time. If light is produced in a star or in the sun, an area of strong gravity, and then streams down on the earth, an area of weak gravity, its energy will not be dissipated by a reduction of speed, since this is impossible, light always having the same constant speed. What would happen, Einstein postulated, was something very different: the wavelength of the light would be shortened. This "Einstein shift," the assumption that "the spectral lines of sunlight, as compared with the corresponding spectral lines of terrestrial sources of light, must be somewhat displaced toward the red," was spelled out in some detail. However, he was careful to add the qualification that "as other influences (pressure, temperature) affect the position of the centers of the spectral lines, it is difficult to discover whether the enforced influence of the gravitational potential really exists." In fact the Döppler shift, produced by the motion of the stars relative to the solar system, was to provide an additional and even more important complication.
>
> Ronald W. Clark, *Einstein*

If you wrote a book about prose style, for that matter, you would mostly write exposition.

Expository writing carries information. When we do research on a problem, we write our results mainly as exposition. Encyclopedia entries are expository. Exposition is usually the foundation of the essay. The essayist will narrate and describe, and by contrasting passages of exposition he may argue. Argument lacking in exposition tends toward bombast or harangue.

The rules for exposition are clarity, conciseness, and vigor. Here are several passages that illustrate the variety of exposition, and the extent to which we depend upon it. They also illustrate the clarity, vigor, and conciseness we should try for. Edmund Wilson begins a book about Canada:

> The relation of Canada to the United States has always been rather peculiar. The constant slight strain it involves is to be felt in the inveterate Canadian habit, always surprising to us, of referring to us as "the Americans," as if Canadians were not Americans, too. The reason for this is apparently that at the time of our 1776 revolution "the Americans" were seditious malcontents who rebelled against their status of British colonists and set up an anti-British republic. "The Americans," for a Tory like Samuel Johnson, were always to be referred to contemptuously because they had made trouble for the monarchy. The Canadians remained British, so were never in this sense Americans, and we were for long and are sometimes still disapprovingly regarded as a society founded on disloyalty to the sovereign and the destruction of ancient traditions, and devoted to the exploits of a vulgar success which are impious in both their mutinous origins and their insolence in surpassing the mother country.
>
> Edmund Wilson, *O Canada*

Bergen Evans writes on the double negative:

> In English, two negatives in the same sentence generally reinforce one another. *I didn't say nothing* is an emphatic denial and no one who speaks English can misunderstand it. This is the normal way of strengthening a negative in all Teutonic languages, of which ours is one. In the past, double, triple, quadruple negatives were quite acceptable; Sir Launcelot was speaking the purest English when he said, *I never treacherously slew no man*.
>
> Today, this repeated negative is considered a shocking vulgarism. Negative pronouns (such as *no one* and *nothing*), negative adverbs (such as *hardly* and *scarcely*), and negative conjunctions (such as *neither* and *nor*), when used with a negative verb put a man beyond the pale, provided the sentence is short enough. No one who values public opinion can afford to say *I didn't hardly hear you* or *you didn't hear me, neither*.
>
> Bergen Evans, *A Dictionary of Contemporary American Usage*

Simone de Beauvoir gives information about abortion:

> Moreover, the law—which dooms many young women to death, sterility, invalidism—is quite powerless to assure an increase in the number of births. One thing that friends and enemies of legal abortions agree on is the radical failure of repressive legislation. In France, according to good authorities, abortions have averaged about one million per year in recent times. And of these about two thirds are attributed to married women. An unknown but large number of deaths and injuries result from these clandestine and often improperly performed operations.
>
> Simone de Beauvoir, *The Second Sex*

The philosopher Charles S. Peirce makes distinctions and definitions:

> And what, then, is belief? It is the demi-cadence which closes a musical phrase in the symphony of our intellectual life. We have seen that it has just three properties: first, it is something that we are aware of; second, it appeases the irritation of doubt; and, third, it involves the establishment in our nature of a rule of action, or, say for short, a *habit*. As it appeases the irritation of doubt, which is the motive for thinking, thought relaxes, and comes to rest for a moment when belief is reached. But, since belief is a rule for action, the application of which involves further doubt and further thought, at the same time that it is a stopping-place, it is also a new starting-place for thought. That is why I have permitted myself to call it thought at rest, although thought is essentially an action. The *final* upshot of thinking is the exercise of volition, and of this thought no longer forms a part; but belief is only a stadium of mental action, an effect upon our nature due to thought, which will influence future thinking.
>
> Charles S. Peirce, *Values in a Universe of Change*

A literary critic begins to define a term:

> A myth, in its simplest meaning, is a story about a god, or some being comparable to a god. Hence myths usually grow up in close association with religions, but, because they are stories, they also belong to literature, especially to narrative, fictional and dramatic literature with internal characters. It makes no difference to its relation to literature whether a

myth is believed to be true or false. Classical mythology became purely literary after the religions associated with it died,
but from a literary point of view we may speak of Christian or
Hindu mythology even when the attitude towards it is also
one of religious acceptance.

Northrop Frye, "Myth and Poetry"

A novelist has his character think about another character:

> First, I assumed that the man who had shot Drew knew that
> he had shot him. That was a beginning. I also assumed that
> he knew we hadn't all been killed in the rapids. What then?
> He might be waiting above the calm where Bobby and Lewis
> were—where I was, more or less—planning to draw down on
> them when they started out. If that were the case he would
> kill them both, though if Bobby gauged the change in the
> light well enough and set out when there was enough visibil-
> ity to use the canoe but not enough to shoot by, they might
> have a chance to get past him, through the next stretch of
> rapids—the ones now a little downstream from me—and on
> down. Our whole hope rested on our being able to second-
> guess the man, and, now that I was on top of the gorge, it
> seemed to me that we had guessed right, or as right as it was
> possible for us to do. If Bobby moved out in the very early
> half-light, the chances of making a good shot down onto the
> water would be greatly reduced, and big gaps in the upper
> part of the wall, small deep ravines such as the one I had come
> up, would keep him from getting downstream at anything
> like the speed the canoe could make. I counted on his know-
> ing this, and on the idea that he would try to solve the prob-
> lem by setting up his shots downstream at calm water, where
> the target would be moving at a more constant speed and not
> leaping and bobbing. Below me, except for one rush of white-
> ness cramped between two big hedges of stone, the rapids
> seemed comparatively gentle, in places—so far as I could
> tell—scarcely more than a heavy-twilled rippling. But even
> this would be disconcerting for a marksman because of the
> bobbing it would cause. If I were going to kill somebody from
> this distance and this angle I would want to draw a long bead.
> Under those conditions, and if he was a good shot, there was
> no reason he couldn't get Bobby and Lewis both, and within a

few seconds of each other, if he took his time and dropped the first one cleanly. That would take calm water, as slow as possible, and it would have to be downstream, out of sight around the next turn.

James Dickey, *Deliverance*

ARGUMENT AND PERSUASION

In writing expository prose, we assemble details—facts, anecdotes, descriptions—to understand and to explain, not to take a position and defend it. Much of our writing is expository: we investigate the parliamentary system of government, or an innovation in psychotherapy, or a school of artists, or a sport. On occasion, we might seem to argue the superiority of something—say, the Cubist painters over the Impressionists—when we are really only giving reasons for personal preference. If we are explaining our own likes and dislikes, we are writing exposition; we are not arguing that anyone else should feel as we do. The exposition of our preference is a valid form of exposition. When I read someone's praise of crocheting, I can enjoy and understand it, without feeling any pressure to make an afghan.

On the other hand, sometimes we write arguments, in which we try to persuade the reader of a thesis, to convince him. In an argument, we will use exposition, narrative, and description, but in addition, we will have a thesis to defend, and we will try to argue and persuade by means of clear thinking, reasonableness, and taking account of the opposition.

Most of the time, in writing an argument, we are dealing with debatable material. We cannot *prove* our thesis, as a mathematician or a philosophical logician can, by manipulating his own terms. We cannot measure our results in a cyclotron like a physicist. We are dealing with probabilities and persuasions, not certainties or proofs. Or say that we are dealing with an old-fashioned sense of the word "proof," an inexactness that we might call "the agreement of reasonable men." We have an opinion; we may feel it strongly; we may believe it is true. But we must recognize that other people have other opinions, and respect their differences, if we are going to try to persuade them.

The honest writer avoids some forms of persuasion, or attempted persuasion. "The rhetorician would deceive his neighbors,/The sentimentalist himself"—as I quoted before from W. B. Yeats—and in much dishonest writing the writer is both sentimentalist and, in Yeats's sense, rhetorician. The loaded word—when National Guardsmen shoot "unarmed civilians" or "a traitorous rabble"—or loaded syntax—when the beer company asks, "As a lawyer, what do you think of Fitz's?"—can combine to make a whole essay into loaded argument, or propaganda. Arguments, ideas, or phrases seem to say one thing, and really say another. In good writing, we must avoid such subterfuge.

Clarity in Argument

To avoid fooling ourselves, and trying to fool others, we must apply to our arguments all the standards of clarity and forcefulness that we have discussed in talking about words and sentences. Misuse of the passive verb can help us avoid responsibility, and confuse an argument. Misuse of abstract nouns often involves the writer's reluctance to *see* what he is talking about; this reluctance makes a vagueness, which fuzzes over a reality that might do damage to an argument. To argue well, you must be wary of the misuse of conjunctions in the complex sentence, by which you may imply cause or sequence or another relationship that the evidence you offer will not support. Most first drafts leave us with problems in verb forms, abstract nouns, and askew syntax; but in arguments, these errors often attempt to defend us against understanding what we are saying. These errors are not merely mechanical; they are *learned* errors by which we fool ourselves. Here is some hasty thinking from an impromptu.

> Last night Blood Sweat and Tears played at the gym. I started thinking about Mr. Williams back in Harbor Springs (my counselor). Because he was forty or fifty, he hated the new music, and once a terrific trick was played on him. He was acting principle and some guys got the key to the p.a. and hooked up a two hour tape of rock and turned the p.a. up loud and jammed the lock and split. (Blood Sweat and Tears was part of the tape.) People like him should never be in high schools. They hate kids. They never remember that they were kids and they've got no sense of humor at all. In fact, middle aged people should never be allowed to teach teen-aged kids. They don't understand. This fact was true in my whole school except for Miss Casey since she never grew up anyway. Nobody at school ever heard of revelance.

Mr. Williams may well have been annoying, and the practical joke amusing, but we cannot take an argument seriously when it is so one-sided and clichetic.

Reasonableness in Argument

Most of the time, we persuade by being reasonable—and also by seeming so. The *being* is clear thinking; the *seeming* is tone. We will *be* reasonable by writing with clarity, and by avoiding typical errors of thinking which I will mention later. We will *seem* reasonable by refusing to be dogmatic, by allowing time to opposing points of view, and by a modesty that distinguishes between fact and opinion. It is not that we should continually qualify our remarks by tagging them with phrases like "in my opinion"; it is more the attitude we take. If it is factually raining, it will not be dogmatic to assert that the grass is wet. But if we look at a girl and call her pretty, obviously we are uttering a feeling of our own; nothing *necessarily* follows except within ourselves.

Of course fact and opinion are mixed; the mixture is humane and necessary. It is only obligatory for the sake of honest writing that the writer know what he is doing. A fact is information that can be documented from historical and scientific sources. ("Truth" is elusive; the scientific "facts" of one century may be illusion to the next; a "fact" is what we can reasonably accept as true.) It is also the statement of a personal experience that can be accepted as reasonable. "It rained all day, July 5th, 1971" can be fact; "Hester looked pretty" is opinion, or surmise, and not fact. When we quote the documented opinion of someone else—"her minister thought that Hester looked pretty"—we are on the border of fact and opinion. It is a pity that human life is so full of twilights; day and night are so easily distinguishable; but everything human seems to flourish in twilight.

When we quote the minister, we have quoted an outside source, which gives the appearance of objectivity; yet we have quoted only an opinion. With this sort of reference, we can write as if the reference were fact if we do not lean on it too heavily. If we made the minister's opinion the fulcrum of our essay ("But contrary to her doctor's statement, we know from her minister that Hester looked pretty. Therefore . . .") the opinion will crumble and the essay collapse. We have let ourselves seem to be unreasonable.

For persuasive argument, we must discover a tone that uses fact when it is relevant, inserts opinion modestly and reasonably, allows time and space to doubts, and builds a sequent argument by paragraph steps that the reader can follow. Here is a typical passage of argument, from the beginning of a book about "the corporate oligarch," in which the author finds a new type of businessman. It mingles fact and opinion with clarity and without loss of energy:

> That he is a major figure in the contemporary world few will deny. Contrary to popular belief, however, it is not a simple matter to identify him precisely, to define his powers, to describe his methods or to explain his motives. A massive literature exists on the subject of management, most of it published in the last fifty years. The lives of men at the top of the corporate hierarchy have been treated in novels, motion pictures, biographies and television programs. Yet the subject remains confusing and overburdened with generalizations.
>
> The problem begins with definitions.
>
> Underlying the most widely accepted definition is a belief that "the motive of business is pecuniary gain, the method is essentially purchase and sale. The aim and usual outcome is the accumulation of wealth. Men whose aim is not increase of possession do not go into business. . . ." So wrote Thorstein Veblen. This seeking after wealth would make the corporation no more than "a legal device," as A. A. Berle and Gardner Means put it, "through which private business transactions may be carried on."
>
> If this were the whole story, the subject of this book would be the men who have become rich through successful business ventures which are set up as corporations. Many of the top executives of the 1,323,180 corporations in existence in the United States at the beginning of the 1960s would consider this definition of their role correct. But observers of the modern corporation differ. To most of them corporations have become what Reinhold Niebuhr called "quasi-sovereignties," what Earl Latham called "a rationalized system for the accumulation, control, and administration of power," what others have called plutocracies or oligarchies.
>
> This suggests that the lives of the men who head corporations have changed in ways that have not been fully acknowledged. How much they have changed is unclear. For instance, it is generally agreed that the older type of businessman was an entrepreneur and that the new type of businessman is a

professional manager. But the distinction between the two is not a sharp one. No one man is all entrepreneur, none all professional manager. Every executive of modern corporations is an entrepreneur as well as a manager, since he assumes the risks of his business very much as he would if he owned it. And some of the great fortune makers, or moguls, or robber barons, of yesteryear were conscientious managers as well as entrepreneurs, since they were extremely efficient in the way they conducted their business. The change has only been one of emphasis in this respect. Many contemporary businessmen tend to give a higher priority to running a well-organized company than to making a lot of money. And it is only to dramatize the difference in emphasis that the generalizations "entrepreneur" and "professional manager" have been useful.

David Finn, *The Corporate Oligarch*

Here, exposition helps to begin a thesis about social change that is in itself an opinion—but an opinion that the author will defend with facts and with reasoning.

For a purer example of argument, we might go to the editorial page:

Highways Are for Everyone, Not Just Studded Tire Users

Studded tires are definitely out of season in July and they may be out of season permanently if legislation banning tire studs gets to the governor's desk, as now seems likely.

The News supports this legislation, not because it doubts the margin of safety that studded tire users claim is increased but because the case against their continued usage in Michigan is stronger and more economically defensible.

Even the safety factor of studded tires may be overrated. In applying the studs ban, enough senators accepted the contention that studs cut grooves in highways which, when filled with water during rainstorms, set up conditions for hydroplaning.

Hydroplaning may occur when a cushion of water builds up between the pavement and the tires, causing the driver to lose control.

Studding tears up highways, there doesn't seem to be any

question about that. Road repair programs are accelerated
under the pounding of stud wear. Instead of getting a 20-year
life expectancy out of concrete highways, Michigan motorists
may get only half that, when studded tires are permitted.

.   .   .

    All this means is that state taxpayers will be paying more
and more to keep their highways in decent shape. Snow tires
already provide some safety without the disadvantage of chew-
ing up roads. And of course, winter-time driving requires special care and restraint on the part of drivers anyway.

    Studded tires are best on glare ice, a condition that occurs
only a few times during winter. With or without studded
tires, glare ice conditions or sleet requires the utmost in
driver caution. In fact, drivers are urged not to take to the
roads in these conditions.

    Continued use of studded tires is not warranted for the few
occasions in which they work best. Do they save lives? Their
supporters say they do. But caution and restraint save lives
without the disadvantages studded tires have. Highways are
for the pleasure and utilization of all motorists, not just those
who believe in studded tires.

The Ann Arbor News, Tuesday, July 4, 1972

This editorial is pure in the sense that it contains little exposition,
little explaining, and more advocacy. Still, to advocate its points, it
must stop to explain what "hydroplaning" is, and it must refer to
facts like the life-expectancy of highways.

    Also, it must try, at least, to account for the arguments of the
opposition.

Time for the Opposition

When we hope to persuade, we should pay court to the opposition.
We should seek to imagine all possible rebuttals to our position, and
answer them. We should be both sides of the debating team, like any
good debater. Then in our argument we should deal with the most
important objections. Sometimes we can take on the objections directly. Suppose we are arguing the superiority of football to baseball,
not merely a personal preference, which would be exposition, but an
argument or a persuasion of general superiority. Recognizing a common objection to football, we might say, "People have argued that

football glorifies violence, and baseball skill, but. . . ." Then we could adduce contradictions by anecdote, by appeal to a hypothesis, or whatever. And we could do the same for other objections.

Thinking of opposition arguments is a natural system for multiplying ideas. Put yourself on the other side. Gather evidence and argument against your thesis. Counter every notion of your own, and by this means gather material. But when you write it, don't arrange it like a dialogue of disputants. A pro-con structure jerks the head from right to left to right, as if we were watching a ping pong ball. You don't need to give equal time. You need not say:

> It has been argued that middle-aged people have more experience than the young, because they have lived longer.
> But mere time does not give understanding. In fact, age seems to diminish understanding. . . .

Brainstorming the opposition argument, you can accept it and counter it in the flow of one sentence:

> Although middle-aged people obviously have more experience than the young, they don't seem to profit from it.

Similarly, you find positive ideas because you have thought up answers to negative ones. Suppose you are attacking the SST. Trying to gather arguments, you think of a proponent saying, "Time to cross the Pacific will be cut by a third." You turn this to your own purposes by saying, "Surely we do not need to spend billions of dollars in order to give businessmen three fewer hours to drink Scotch in the lounge of a 747." Of course on some occasions, the voice of the opposition, droning in the Senate of your head, may come to sound more and more reasonable. If it happens, you might as well take a deep breath, cross out your old title, and begin again: "The Necessity for Studded Tires."

Our most persuasive argument, in the long run, will be positive praise, and not attack on the opposition. We persuade by praising football more than we do by attacking baseball. If we record straightforwardly too many of the opposition arguments, we lose focus; we are spending most of our time dealing with the contrary to our thesis, even suggesting ways in which the reader might disagree with us, and our statement will become fuzzy. We lose not only unity but argument as well. Often, it is wise to deal with opposition arguments obliquely, raising them in dependent clauses, while the main clauses carry the argument, as we did in the argument above about the middle-aged and the young. This device raises the issues that the opposition would raise, but keeps a clear direction. We might say, "Although football is violent, there is a skill to its violence that is greater and more subtle than the skill of baseball."

Time for the opposition is part of tone, and it is part of the honesty of openness. We do not win many arguments by asserting that *no* other point of view is possible, and that anybody who disagrees with us is stupid. *Admit* that football is violent, that studded tires may stop a skid on glare ice, or that middle-aged people sometimes understand the young. If you don't admit these facts, you are telling lies and leaving your valid argument unsupported. Also, you are losing your reader, especially if he is the one you want to reach—the idiot who disagrees with you.

The Order of Argument

When you have gathered a series of valid arguments, you must organize them. In your catalogue of argumentative points and details of evidence, some entries will make a stronger case than others, and some will be more interesting. The general rule is to save the best for last. Where narration is primarily ordered by time, and description by space, argument or persuasion is ordered by increasing intensity. We can start with the arguments in which we have to concede most to our opponents, or the arguments to which we hear our mental adversary objecting, "But . . . but. . . ." Then while he is still spluttering, we pin him to the ground with our best points. The persuasive effect derives from the crescendo. Suppose we are arguing for the institution of a national educational television network, parallel in budget to NBC, CBS, and ABC. We might list:

> success of BBC
> annoyance of advertisements
> higher cultural level
> pressure of advertisers
> guards against government control
> expense small compared to other expenses of govt.
> public service broadcasts
> service for minorities

Of course the relative weight of each item, in this limited list, would depend on the evidence and argument the writer could adduce in support. A writer might find a different order more persuasive.

But for the sake of an example, let us speculate on what we have here. Two of the arguments are rebuttals of the imagined adversary, who tells us, "Government television will be the mouthpiece of the state," and, "All this money should go to more worthwhile uses." Perhaps the essay could begin with a general affirmation of the thesis, and then proceed to an acknowledgment that, of course, laws should provide a certainty that government could not interfere with programming. In answering the objection about the cost of the enterprise, we might be able to turn an objection in the opposite direction, and use it to further the thesis. Money spent on a national network, you could say, could be used for minority representation, and for educational programs; the network would *serve* social welfare, not *starve* it. For many an essay, this point might be strong enough for a conclusion.

You might give examples of the annoyance that advertising causes; anecdote could supply detail. Anecdote from research might also indicate pressure from advertisers, and this topic might lead to the content of commercial television in contrast to the possible content of public television. In one writer's scheme, his final point might be the example of the BBC. "You say it will never work? Here it is, and it works."

My point is not that there is only one way of doing it. Each of us has a way to order our argument *best*, according to our best material. In general, the crescendo is the right kind of noise. In the essay imagined above, an alternative conclusion might be to talk about the high cost of the network—as if one were giving away a point—and then turn it around and say that, despite the cost, the social effects would be so great that the network was cheap at any price. One would certainly *not* end it, after the BBC example of the argument about social effects, by remarking that, of course, it was essential to avoid government interference.

We should organize the arguments in ascending form. But one kind of exception might come up. Our opening—our zinger—ought to be *interesting,* and not merely our least effective argument. We might open with an anecdote about a BBC program, and not mention that institution again until the end of the essay, when we reap the crop that grew from the seed we planted. Or we might start with an anecdote about a tasteless commercial, one that annoys every-body, and will not only catch the reader's attention but engage his sympathy. In the beginning of the paper, we are most interested in holding the reader, so that we can persuade him later. At the end, we are interested in convincing him once and for all.

A relay team in track has four runners. Usually the fastest man runs last. The second fastest runs first, second is slowest, and third is third: 2, 4, 3, 1. It is a good arrangement for arguments, also.

Logic and Emotionalism

If we wish to persuade, we must avoid illogic. Logic is not the only mode of persuasion, goodness knows; poems and stories convince us; although they are sometimes logical in form, they usually convince by embodying feeling in character and image. Arguments embody feeling also, usually in anecdote and detail. But when we think publicly, and preferably when we think privately, we must under-stand logic in order not to think badly. We all know some logic without perhaps calling it that; it is common sense. Suppose I told you an anecdote about a man with long hair who hijacked a school-bus. Suppose I told it well, embodying feelings of fright and outrage. But suppose then I added, "Therefore, people with long hair are dangerous criminals." You would laugh at my thinking; and you would be right. I would have committed the logical error of general-izing from an insufficient amount of evidence. If I had been more modest in my declaration, I could at least have shown you my opin-ion without raising laughter; if I had said, for instance, "I know it is dangerous to generalize from a particular, but this sort of news item seems to me to characterize what is wrong with the United States today. At least to my prejudiced eyes, someone with long hair is always making the trouble." Here, the anecdote is used not for pseudo-argument, but as a device to introduce an opinion. There is no false logic, because there is no claim to logic.

When we decry "emotionalism" we are blaming not feelings but a misuse of them, or a misunderstanding of how to use them. Emotion-alism uses an appeal to feelings to disguise a defect of thought. If we say:

> I love this country, its history and its landscape, and I would die to defend it against an invader. I don't believe that any-one who refuses to defend his country should enjoy the rights of citizenship.

we are taking a rather extreme position, based on emotion, but we are not covering bad thinking with the camouflage of feeling. We are openly displaying our patriotism and our prejudice. We do not say that the second sentence follows *logically* from the first. It certainly depends upon it *emotionally*. But if we write,

> Cowards who run away to Canada to keep from getting a scratch in defense of their great country ought to be jailed for life because of all the brave men who have died for freedom.

we write loaded words, we beg questions, and we state an illogical cause. The errors in writing and thinking are manifold, but we may lump them together under a general label, "emotionalism pretending to argue." We find this kind of bad writing on any heavily charged issue: busing, abortion, amnesty, legalization of marijuana.

Common Fallacies of Thinking

If we wish to study logic, we should go to the philosophers. A brief definition of induction and deduction appears in the glossary. A longer introduction to logic (for essay-writing, not for the philosophy class) can be consulted in a book like Manuel Bilsky's *Patterns of Argument*. Here, we will do best to list and exemplify a few of the more common errors of thinking that everyone falls into, from time to time.

Generalizing from a Particular, or from too narrow a range of particulars, is a common error of induction. We do not collect enough evidence, and we seem to assume that because we have evidence of X being repeated twice, X will always happen. Because the one Eskimo in our circle of friends likes to read Trollope, we may generalize that Eskimos enjoy Trollope. Clearly, such an assumption is illogical. We need a greater sample, we need to spread the net wider for evidence; if we cannot support a generalization, we must abandon it, or admit its worthlessness as proof.

This advice is not to be construed as advice to avoid the particular. Often an argument takes on persuasive power because a specific bit of evidence is taken as *typical* of the generalization. The effectiveness of the argument depends upon the validity of the assertion. In the essay on public television, one began with a description of a nauseatingly boring commercial, and then said, "Therefore, we must have at least one national network without advertising," one would be illogical. If, after the particular, one listed other offensive commercials, and then perhaps gave statistics on the time devoted to commercials, one would be ready for a generalization without having relied on a single particular.

The Overinclusive Premise. In the furnace of argument, many logical errors are forged by means of the overinclusive premise. All of us are guilty. "Everybody who goes to medical school is out for money." "All people who act like that are communists/fascists." These statements are generalizations (possibly from a limited sample) which common sense will not tolerate. If we say "some" instead of "all," we are more sensible—and we have admitted that our charge is not inclusive.

Guilt by Association (or holiness by association, for that matter) is another common form of faulty thinking. The Mafia, we believe, is an Italian organization. So when we identify someone as Italian, the Mafia may cross our minds. Everyone *knows* this sort of thing is absurd; yet if we do not keep constant scrutiny over ourselves, we fall into it again and again. Politics thrives on guilt by association. Because socialists believe in free medicine, anyone who believes in free medicine is a socialist. If we attach an emotional negative to the word "socialist," we can think that we have just argued free medicine down. We have just associated emotively; we have not *argued* at all.

Begging the Question. In this error the arguer assumes the premise of an argument that his readers may question. The arguer could try to prove his assumption, but he does not. Someone might say, "The rising incidence of mongolism proves that early advocates of a test ban treaty were correct." The writer neither demonstrates that mongolism *is* rising, nor shows that nuclear testing causes mongolism. Causation asserted but unsupported is common in sloppy thinking. In an earlier example, we quoted, "Cowards who run away to Canada. . . ." Here the reader hears the assumption that anyone who went to Canada to avoid the draft is a coward. The question is not raised and explained or argued. A questionable idea is asserted. Sometimes misused conjunctions beg the question: "Although middle-aged, he wore levis."

Evading the Issue is another favorite tactic of politicians, usually introduced by an assertion that they will *not* evade this issue: "I'm glad you asked that question." Sometimes a politician will say something like, "I believe in freedom of assembly, and the freedom of all Americans regardless of race, creed, or color to assemble with people of their own choice." If we look at the context of the speech, we may see that he is not defending freedom but segregation, the rights of associations to exclude members on account of race. "Right to work" laws are laws against forms of union organizing. "Freedom of the press" is sometimes an umbrella for pornographers. Ignoring the question is frequently a deliberate illogic, an attempt to deceive the public by diverting attention from a real goal, which might seem disreputable, to a substitute goal, of which anyone might approve. Evading the issue is euphemism in paragraph form. The gap between expression and meaning is large enough to power the buses of Cincinnati for twelve years and six months.

Nonsequitur is Latin for "it does not follow." We use the term for a statement or idea that *appears* to grow out of an earlier one (by causation, by chronology, by logic, or whatever) but which upon examination fails to make the trip.

He was a doctor, and therefore an all-around man.

She left an hour ago, although her car wouldn't move.

Nonsequiturs sometimes afflict us when we are trying to make complex sentences for the sake of conciseness.

Sequence as Cause, or post hoc ergo propter hoc, is a form of the nonsequitur. The assumption is that if B follows A, A is the cause of B. This assumption is not logical. The philosopher David Hume argued that we could not *know* cause at all. Because we saw one billiard ball hit another, and the second ball move, we *assume* cause and effect, but we cannot see it.

Again, the politics of paranoia adopts the arguments of sequence as cause. "Rudolph Blast was in Newark the day before a bomb went off; therefore. . . ." Such evidence is not even circumstantial, and it does not hold up in court. If a hurricane comes after a bomb test, we are not safe to assume that the bomb test caused it. Sequence is not causation, and is inadequate evidence of it.

The Argument ad Hominem—the Latin means "at the man"—rises in us frequently when we lose our tempers. The ad hominem argument diverts attention from issue to personality, and thus it is a refinement of evading the issue, and of the nonsequitur. We ignore the issue and attack the person defending the issue or symbolizing it. When someone defends the removal of trees in order to make a parking lot, we attack him for wearing white socks. A friend says, "I believe in a socialist form of government, because the profit motive, which is basic to a capitalist system, robs us of our humanity and corrupts our intelligence to the service of materialism." We rebut him, "Your cousin sells lipstick."

Analogy as Fact. Analogies in argument are most useful. They illustrate the sense in which we mean a statement that might otherwise be too tenuous to be understood. They embody attitude and feeling, and they persuade by being exact carriers of feeling. But we can fall into another common form of illogic in arguing from analogy as if it were fact. Suppose we want to write about different civilizations, which seem to have features in common—like beginning, developing, fulfillment, and decay. To carry this idea to a reader, we invent an analogy; each civilization is like an organism: it is born, it grows up, it matures, it is old, and it dies. So far so good. We follow the abstract thought by associating it with concrete things. But many writers become so accustomed to a dominant analogy that they begin to take it literally. Arguing later that our own civilization must end, we say, "Like all organisms, our society must come to death." The argument is invalid because a civilization is not literally an organism and therefore we have not proved that what is true of an organism will be true of civilization. The analogy is not the thing itself.

The General Fallacy of Imprecision. These common fallacies are not exclusive. An issue is often evaded by a nonsequitur, or by an argument ad hominem. Our terms overlap, as our errors do. Common to all these errors is the general fallacy of imprecision.

Ambiguity is a general term that can apply to various imprecisions, to misplaced modifiers, to pronouns with uncertain antecedents, and to words used carelessly for position and for meaning. Clarity is essential to argument. One of the commonest flaws in argument is the use of one term in several senses. We can fool ourselves into thinking that we have said something profound when we are really just playing with words. Abstractions lend themselves to ambiguity more readily than specific words. Watch out for prose like this from a theme about campus politics.

> Jerry was liberal, but not so liberal as Mary Huncher. Some of the professors, even the most liberal, were conservative when it came to Mary Huncher, who claimed that they weren't liberal at all.

With ambiguity, or question begging, or whatever, we fall into fallacies unless we examine ourselves. By self-serving, or laziness, or in anger, we commit sloppy thinking, and when we think carelessly we lose the argument, if our reader is thinking well. We must discipline ourselves to honest clarity in thought, or we lose not only arguments but much more. The careless thinker is a liar. He will never learn to make himself clear.

DESCRIPTION

Description is a gathering of sensuous detail. We use expository description to explain what a species of whale looks like. Exposition proper conveys information in general; description is an exposition of sense data: it evolves and embodies. We use description in argument, showing for instance what becomes of a vehicle that tries to brake on glare ice without studs. Of course we use description frequently in autobiographical or fictional narrative.

The order of details, in description, is usually *spatial*. But words follow each other—they are not simultaneous in the way a picture seems to be—and we necessarily move in words from point to point in a sequence that has to be chronological. So in description we talk about space in a temporal way. In describing a scene, we can begin from the periphery and move to the center, or move from the center to the periphery. The order is not crucial: it is crucial that there *be* an order; that we do not move from center to periphery to center to periphery to periphery.

Some writers seem to think of description as filler, or padding. Not only beginning writers, but professional ones who write the less skillful stories in adventure or confession magazines—and are paid by the word. In these places, we will see description used to delay information, to tantalize:

> Rhonda turned from the window, her eyes wet. "Belinda," she said to me, "I could forgive you for Ron. I could forgive you

for Bruce. I could even forgive you for Althea. But there is one thing I can never forgive you for!"

She turned back to the window, her eyes flooded with tears. My cheeks suffused with shame. Over her shoulders, I could see the sweet meadows of home, adeck with lilacs and daisies, their sleepy heads waving in the soft breezes of June, while above, storm clouds gathered to chase away the white puff-ball clouds of early morning.

"They Had a Name for Me," *Real Romance*

In this example, the *main* function of description seems to be suspense, as a daytime television serial uses an advertisement. To be sure, it also shows a heavy-handed attempt to use description as a good writer does, *for the meaning and the feeling that images carry.* This anonymous writer has her protagonist look at the fields in an attempt to symbolize her past innocence, contrasted to the torment (storm clouds) of the sinful present.

When you write well, your description cannot seem to approach pure symbolism because then it will not seem to be real description. But there is room for invention, especially when we use comparisons (simile, metaphor, analogy) that carry feeling. Remember the discussion of the girl writing about her grandfather's funeral. "The sky turned dark" was boring. "Storm clouds gathered" would have been a pathetic and trite attempt to appeal to our emotions. But the new comparison would have worked.

In *Ulysses*, James Joyce has Stephen Dedalus look at the sea when he is feeling depressed. "The ring of bog and skyline held a dull green mass of liquid." Though the description is literal enough, it expresses Stephen's emotions. Here is a passage from a book by a doctor who spent a year in Vietnam. He describes finding some bodies washed up on the shore of a river:

Four nude, markedly swollen, water-logged bodies lay side by side on their backs. Each had a massively swollen face. Eyes seemed to try to bulge out of sockets whose contents were as big as apples. Their lips were three times normal size and each mouth was open and round like that of a fish, with a massive splitting tongue protruding skyward. A thin, bloody fluid trickled from their nostrils.

Massive edema and rigor mortis held their arms up and out in front of them with fat fingers reaching toward the clouds.

Their scrota were the size of softballs, and their swollen pe-
nises stood as if erect. Their knees were bent in identical
frog-leg positions. The smell was overwhelming and hundreds
of flies circled around those which were already busy inspect-
ing the mouths and nostrils. There was not a mark on the
front of their bodies.

John A. Parrish, M.D. *12, 20 & 5*

The accurate description has modifiers that come from observation,
not from the worn tracks: *fat* fingers, *frog-leg* positions, *massively
swollen;* it has statements of fact and measurement, like "massive
edema" and "three times normal size"; it has comparisons that embody feeling, like "scrota . . . the size of softballs," "mouth . . . open
and round like that of a fish," and ". . . as big as apples."

Statistical accuracy in description must never be confused with
emotional accuracy. Again, sometimes we must lie, to tell the truth.
A contemporary poem ends with the sudden vision of a hundred
cows in a field. Reviewing this poem, a hostile critic (carried away
by his anger into absurdity) asked *how* the poet could tell that exactly one hundred cows were in the field. He received a postcard
from the poet: "I counted the teats and divided by four." The pseu-
do-particular has a long tradition. It does not lie, because we know it
is not intended to be statistically accurate. When Wordsworth says of
daffodils, "Ten thousand saw I at a glance," we do not suspect him of
counting. If we write, "The sandwich was as thick as the toe of Italy,"
we are saying that it was "very thick"—so thick that it astounded and
delighted us. If we say, "The sandwich was two-and-five-eighths
inches thick," we are being pedestrian, and expressing little astonish-
ment. Mere accuracy is all right, but the exaggeration is a lie that is
truer to the feeling than accuracy is. Sometimes in writing, you can
be accurate in both ways at once; maybe a list of ingredients could
be literally true, and also carry an astonished reaction to abundance:
"Salami, bologna, ham, roast beef, corned beef, Swiss cheese, provo-
lone, onions, lettuce, red peppers, olive oil, vinegar, and, I believe,
oregano."

NARRATIVE

At its simplest, narrative is telling a story. At its broadest, it is any
development—in sentence, paragraph, or paper—by chronological
order. So narrative can belong to exposition, as we describe the
stages of the moon, or of a rocket ship in flight. Narration may help

us in argument, where we need anecdote or exposition. And obviously we use narrative in autobiography and in fiction.

Narrative must find its way between two extremes. It must have enough detail so that the reader knows what is happening. It must not have so much detail that the reader gets bogged down. The detail must be appropriate; it must have the right quality, as well as the right quantity. Here is a fragment from a theme:

> When I heard the doorbell, I stood immediately, my heart pounding. I knew it was her. I didn't answer it quickly, and heard the door opening toward me. I must have forgotten to lock it! I looked around for a second. Then I picked up my suitcase and climbed through the open window.

The first version had been:

> When I heard the doorbell, I placed my hands against the arms of the chair and pushed myself upright immediately. My heart pounded in my chest. I knew it was her. For some reason, I didn't move toward the door right away. I just stood there and stared, my heart pounding, my legs shaking. Then I heard a sound like the doorknob turning, and a creaky noise as she must have started to push the door open. I realized that I had forgotten to lock it when I came in from the drug store. I looked all around to see if there was any way to escape. I saw the window open beside me. Without thinking of what I was doing, I picked up my suitcase, checked the fasteners on it, set it on the windowsill and lowered it to the ground, which was only about 2½ feet down. Then I sat down on the sill myself, swinging my legs through, and pulled the rest of my body after me.

This student was commendably rich in detail; but total recall is boring. We need the essential narrative, and nothing more. The revision does it. If the writer had gone further in cutting, and written:

> When I heard the doorbell, I climbed out the window,

we would have missed some crucial information.

Here is a passage from the book about Vietnam from which I quoted earlier. It begins with exposition and ends with narrative:

> The western perimeter of the camp bordered on a "free-fire zone." Anyone or anything that moves in that area is free

game and can be shot, mortared, or bombed. All of the military maps had it marked as such and supposedly all civilians in the area had been informed.

The camp dump was in this "free-fire zone." Each morning at the same time a truck drove out to the dump and all of the tin cans, cardboard containers, wrappers, and garbage from the camp was dumped about fifty meters inside the zone. Within minutes, the dump was filled with Vietnamese from nearby villes [hamlets] gathering cans and garbage. The marines in the watchtower would fire close to them to frighten them away. A few days earlier, an eight-year-old Vietnamese boy had been wounded by these warning shots and was brought to the aid station where he was kept until his wounds were healed. One day he stole an orange soda from a marine who shot and killed him as he tried to run away.

John A. Parrish, M.D., *12, 20 & 5*

This is a good example of narrative used in exposition, and ultimately, as you can see, in an argument that does not need stating.

DIALOGUE AND QUOTATION

Dialogue belongs most obviously with narrative in the spheres of fiction and autobiography. In exposition or argument we may use *quotation*, repeating conversations to explain or to persuade, and in writing up research it sometimes lends verisimilitude to quote directly from an interview, or from a source of speeches like the *Congressional Record.*

When we have the option to manipulate dialogue (that is, when we are not quoting directly, but remembering something or making it up) we have many things to keep in mind.

Dialogue moves best with a minimum of direction markers. Here are two passages for contrast:

The door opened. Nancy stood there, wearing a white maxi-coat.

"What do you want?" inquired Jim quizzically.

"I want my ring and my record player," she spat. Her eyes flashed.

"Get out!" he exclaimed.

"Don't you care at all, any more?" she asked tearfully.

"Shut up!" he shouted, slamming the door.

Let us revise this passage by cutting it:

> The door opened. Nancy stood, wearing a white maxi-coat.
> "What do you want?" said Jim.
> "I want my ring and my record player."
> "Get out."
> "Don't you care at all, any more?"
> "Shut up!" He slammed the door.

Maybe the second example is too sparse, but it is better than the first. Beginning writers often explain things too much, telling us twice what we know the first time. (It is like speaking of "white snow.") And in dialogue, it is usually better to use varieties of "say," or to use nothing, than it is to use verbs like "growled" and "whimpered." (See H. W. Fowler, in *Modern English Usage*, on "Elegant Variation"; he says fine things about substitutes for "say.") In other contexts, we prefer the particular because it is more expressive, but these dialogue-verbs have been overused, and if the dialogue is adequate, the verb usually overexplains what we know from the speech itself. Sometimes, we might want to know that "he whispered," because we needed the information that he was trying not to be overheard. When you can, omit this information. The writer of dialogue should try to convey the tone of the speaker *within* his speech, and avoid the stage directions.

AUTOBIOGRAPHY

In the Vietnam book quoted earlier, Dr. Parrish was writing autobiography; not a book about his whole life, but about a bad year of it. We are all authors of a continual autobiography. In letters we tell what we have been doing and thinking; we confide to a diary or a journal; in conversation we tell anecdotes of experiences lived through or observed. We may even tell an old friend what we did last summer; the traditional theme is only as far as paper and ball-point pen.

Your own life is your greatest source for writing. Even when you are explaining, arguing, doing research, or writing fiction, your own experiences—eating, reading, loving, being tired, playing checkers—are what you think with, and what you argue by. Analogy and metaphor derive from experience. The problem is reaching the source, and bringing the experiences back for use. In writing out of your own life, you confront that mass of experience directly. The exercise of the imagination in recovering the past for autobiography is an aid to other writing. The same spirit that floats to recall the old summers, in autobiography, will float to discover the precise analogy, in argument.

Memories of childhood make good subjects. Many writers seem to need the distance of years—the long mellowing in the mind—before they can write fully and with feeling. Everyone alive has the material to fill a thousand books. Our minds are huge storehouses of material—the look and smell of a room on an afternoon in May, five years ago, the sun making stripes in the wood floor, the sounds of the mother in the kitchen, and the newspaper hitting the door. Nothing fully understood is trivial. Any difficulty lies in a heaviness of our spirits that will not float. We must recover in order to make new. Sometimes it helps to close the outward eyes to let the light reach the inward eyes of memory; to feel, see, hear, and taste the vivid past. Then if we hold the mental image close, we can describe it in original words, and the words will release other memories, and by a series of soft explosions we remake an old world in new words. From description we can move to action, and bring narrative into our autobiographical writing. Remembering the people we know, we hear them talk the way they talked. We write dialogue, in autobiographical prose, not as a word-for-word transcript of ancient conversations, but as imitation of style combined with memory of content. We write dialogue by ventriloquism.

In an earlier part of this chapter, I talked about "getting ideas." I have just been talking about it again. Of course our own experience should be our happiest source in writing. *It is all there.* But many young people are curiously alien to their own pasts. They write more easily about Vietnam than they do about Shaker Heights. I suspect that this happens when writing is entirely mental, and is even subsumed by the intellect. By daily writing, and by deliberate brainstorm—*by cultivating daydream*—we can learn to recover the past, and to reconstitute it by means of style. Here is a passage of reminiscence, which the author has organized by place.

> The first I heard of Runkel's Saw Mill was when the oldest Johnson boy, Dave, who was working there at one dollar a day, came home from the doctor with his arm in a sling. When the doctor looked at that arm hanging like a rope with every bone crushed into fine splinters, he told Dave he would have to cut it off up close to his shoulder and Dave said, "You

cut off my arm and some day I'll kill you. You put those bones back in place." Dave had noticed that a wide leather belt was running a bit to one side of its pulley and tried to push it back in place with his hand while it was running, and his whole arm had been pulled around the pulley. The doctor had done his best to put the bone splinters together, but he told the boy that he had no hope that he would ever have any more use of that arm. There were days and weeks when everybody thought the doctor was right, but Dave's healthy body and fine spirit fooled them all. His elbow was always stiff and bent so he appeared to be wanting to shake hands with you, but within a year he was able to do a man's work again.

My next contact with Runkel's Mill was when I dropped my new jackknife into the mill race. One of my brothers and I were fishing above the race, and I caught a small bass that had swallowed the hook so far down that I had to use my knife to cut it out. Just as I did that I dropped both the fish and my knife into water moving rapidly towards the mill wheel. When my brother saw how quickly both fish and knife disappeared he said, "Let's get away from here. If we ever fell in we'd be ground to pieces by that wheel."

It wasn't the water wheel but one of the circular saw blades that killed the mill owner. And it wasn't the big seven-foot blade used to rip lengthwise through the logs, turning them into boards and planks, but a small eighteen-inch blade used to cut boards into various lengths. Mr. Runkel had left the saw running and had gone some distance from it when the lock nut turned off and then the blade went spinning through the air, striking him across his back as he was bending down. It cut his body nearly in half and went on to embed itself in a beam on the side of the mill. It was said that his death must have been instantaneous. After that the family operated the mill a few years with hired help, but its usefulness was about at an end.

When the creek left the mill and pond it flowed on through a wide valley. About once a year, in the spring rains, it overflowed its banks and the whole valley became a shallow river. . . .

Tracy Redding, *Hoosier Farm Boy*

And the author goes on about the creek, *remembering.*

WRITING FICTION

Writing fiction is writing out of your life with imagination added. It is autobiography to write about what happened last summer. It is fiction to write about what happened next summer. Really, we are most apt to write fiction by using last summer, but revising it in our imaginations. Sometimes we write what we *wish* had happened last summer. Sometimes we write what we *fear* might have happened last summer. Suppose in reality we went swimming, were frightened by undertow, but made it safely to shore. We could write it autobiographically. Or we could "make up" a story: a character ("he") drowns trying to make it to shore; or he saves a pig from drowning / discovers a cache of perfume bottles / meets a grandmother who flies balloons. Starting from real experience, the daydream can take us anywhere. And wherever we go, we must ultimately take care that our story is formal, economical, and makes its point—just as we do in other forms of writing.

Daydream can take off from next to nothing. You are in a store, and you have an impulse to shoplift. You resist the impulse, but walking home you dramatize in a daydream what might have happened. Perhaps you get away with it and feel guilty. Then what do you do? You return the stolen goods surreptitiously. And are accused of shoplifting! Or you mail them back. Or you give them to someone who needs them, and relieve your guilt, but then wonder further about your action. On the other hand, perhaps you daydream that you are caught: police, trials, disgrace. The daydream can lead to a story in the third person. "She" does some shoplifting. You describe her, her feelings, her actions, her responses to the actions of others, and the end of her story. It all started from your own impulse and your subsequent daydream. Or the daydream can be a happy one, a wish fulfillment. You do the impossible feat, and everyone loves you. But make it "he" or "she." When the daydream is glorious, the word "I" is self-glorifying. For that matter, sometimes "he" or "she" sounds narcissistic, when the character shares obvious background with the author. Beware of writing about a noble freshman. Scrutinize your daydreams for dealing with the wholeness of a feeling. In fiction as in autobiography, we often omit a discreditable feeling because we don't want to admit it to ourselves.

Fiction by definition is a lie. But more profoundly, good fiction is telling the truth, because fiction is the embodiment of an emotional truth. The wishes and the fears of daydream are as real as tables or days of the week. Fiction *can* lie badly, and often does, when it distorts human nature to flatter the author's or reader's ego, or when it gives the reader or the author an easy way out of a real dilemma, or when it substitutes comfort for anxiety by turning birth and death into something like cotton candy. Situation comedies on television— those endless hours of cute children, cranky husbands, and kooky wives: the television family—distort our lives wholly, to manufacture a light narcotic that induces the passive consumer to buy products. Since we have all been nurtured on these lies, they are as big as mountains inside us, and we must be wary, or we will spend our lives reciting lies under the impression that we are speaking the gospel of observation. Truth to feeling requires vigilant scrutiny.

A good deal of fiction, in fact, is more autobiography than invention. Only the names are changed to protect the guilty. Good fiction is seldom written out of daydream widely detached from the author's experience. In good historical fiction, and in good science fiction, the authors are able to daydream feelings from their own experience into situations they imagine. But historical novelists know history, and science fiction writers know science. So writers do well to stick close to their own background. Northern liberals write bad fiction about southern racists *or* the black world of northern cities. Farm boys write badly about the jet set, and girls from expensive prep schools write badly about camps of migrant laborers.

We make up stories, and we use our experience as the starting point and as the continuing reference point. Making up stories is an acquired ability. If we write much fiction, we develop a story-making facility. If we see a stop sign punctuated with bullet holes, we begin to imagine the hunters who used it for target practice. We see them, we hear their dialogue, we imagine or create their motives. Imagination depends upon experience, upon understanding ourselves and the people we have known. The story-maker creates a world of strangers based upon a lifetime of friends and acquaintances.

Description, narrative, and dialogue are ingredients of fiction, but the most important ingredient is the formal imagination. The same instincts for shape that lead you to cut irrelevances in autobiography, and to distort the real for the sake of the whole and the probable, work in fiction. Many writers find it necessary, in fiction as in autobiography, to write big and to cut small. In the first draft they cannot be sure which details are going to be expressive, and which not. They float to gather. It is important for many writers not to adhere too closely to a plan. If you start to write a story about shoplifting, and then find yourself getting more and more interested in the character of the storekeeper, let it happen. You may find that you have written a story about the day of a shopkeeper, and in rewriting you can shift your attention to accord with what you find you have written. Let the characters have a life of their own. Let your imagination take over from your planning intellect. Let it ride. Then revise to make a whole.

One of the most useful ways to keep a story whole is to keep to one viewpoint: either your own, viewing all of your characters' minds as if you were God; or one of your characters, a "he" or an "I," whose mind you read. Point of view helps unity and focus, which are as important to fiction as they are to essay.

As there are clichés of adjective/noun, and of dead metaphor and of analogy, so there are clichés of plot. Though we write out of experience, we must be sure that it is our experience of people we have observed in real life, and not our experience of that television family. Formula plots fill television, movies, confession magazines, and bestsellers. Boy meets girl, boy loses girl, boy gets girl. Good man appears evil, usually by his own nobility; good man is vindicated and keeps his ranch. Be wary of pat resolutions, problems solved along commonplace lines. As with all writing—from single words to trilogies—originality is honesty/is knowing yourself/is hard-headed scrutiny *as well as* the loose invocation of dream. We arrive at the paradox of the miserly spendthrift again.

WRITING RESEARCH

Although research can support an argument, the research paper differs from an argumentative paper by paying most of its attention to assembling information. Sometimes a research paper has no thesis at all. It sets out to answer a question—by what means did the United States acquire Alaska?—and not to prove a point. Research is a way of learning, important in formal study, which we can use the rest of our lives: we can research voting records of congressmen, recipes, genealogy, precedents in zoning for the neighborhood, or types of schooling for information of the PTA. Research is a method. The research paper is a particular embodiment of the general method. It applies the results of library research, or other investigation, to the aims and forms of the essay.

First you must choose a subject. Often our choice of a subject resembles Chinese boxes, starting with a large box, moving to the smaller one inside it, then to a smaller one inside *that*, until finally we arrive at something of suitable size. We must, as always, *limit the topic*. A student named Jennifer Case, in the spring of 1971, decided she wanted to write about ecology:

> "Fine. Come back in twenty years with thirty volumes. What *about* ecology?"
>
> "I think I would like to write about animals that become extinct because of what men do."
>
> "Fine. What animals?"
>
> "I don't know. There are birds and wild animals I could do. Some are extinct and some are going to be. But I like whales best."
>
> "Fine. *What* whales?"
>
> "I don't know."
>
> "Go to the library and find out."

This dialogue, between the student and her instructor (which can happen inside the student's head, too, between student-student and instructor-student) made the preliminary narrowing of the topic. To move from "ecology" to one species of whale is to move from thirty volumes to a possible research paper. But more preliminary work remains. Jennifer Case needed to read loosely among the whale-books, looking for two things. One was a thesis or an argument; but the general tone of her argument was clear before she chose whales as a species to investigate. It was the specifics that remained, to flesh out the thesis using a special whale. The first necessity was to find the whale to write about.

The *Encyclopaedia Britannica* is a good place to start, because it gives a brief and factual overlook at a large subject, like a map of a whole country. Jennifer read the Britannica article, which talked about different types of whales, and was most attracted to two—the blue whale because it is the largest mammal of all time, and the humpbacked whale. Thinking about it later, she said that the humpback reached her because of the record, "Songs of the Humpback Whale," which she had first heard Judy Collins mention on the Dick Cavett Show, and which she had later listened to; and also because, when she saw a picture of the humpback, she was drawn to it because of its ludicrous shape; it was an ugly duckling among the graceful whales. These last details—Dick Cavett, and maternal feeling toward an underdog—are examples of the reasons we choose to write about specific subjects, reasons that are eventually irrelevant to our argument and therefore extraneous to our paper, but human feelings that are originally pertinent to the choices we make.

Jennifer went to the card catalogue of the library and looked up "whales" and "whaling." She found a hundred and fifty library cards. Libraries cross-index by subject, and usually store the books in the stacks by subject. Thus, if your library has open stacks, you can find from the card catalogue which shelves in the library contain most of the books on any subject, and then browse in this section. In the University of Michigan library, SH 381 turned out to have the most cards on whales and whaling. A 11 was also helpful, and QL.

Jennifer checked out seven books, and began reading in order to make a choice. She took few notes at this stage, writing something down only when she couldn't resist it. But for every book that she consulted, she made a bibliography card: call number, author, title, publisher, city, year. Then if she took a note from a book—either paraphrases or quotations—she wrote down the author's name in order to clue her to the bibliography card, and she wrote down the page number for her quote or reference. By this means, she saved herself time; when she needed later to check a fact or a quotation, she could refer herself back to the bibliography card and find the address of the book in the library. When she came to make her bibliography, she needed only to alphabetize her bibliography cards and type them up without the call number.

Jennifer read loosely for eight or ten hours, gradually acquiring familiarity with the humpback. She also read much of *The Year of the Whale*, a good book about the blue whale, but could not use it because her choice was the humpback. She followed her humpback through various sources, taking notes frequently now, on three-by-five-inch cards. *Whales*, by a Dutch author named E. J. Slijper, was particularly useful. At the back of books, and in footnotes, she found references to other sources of information, periodicals and government pamphlets and books. She consulted periodicals in the library, and discovered with the assistance of a librarian how to use microfilm. She consulted the *Readers Guide to Periodical Literature* for the latest publications. She built a collection of cards. Here are a few of them:

Bibliography cards for two books:

Sci. Lib.
QL
737
.64
1622
1963

Norris, K. S. *Whales, Dolphins &
Porpoises.* Berkeley: U. of Cal.
Press, 1966.
(proceedings of a symposium in
Wash. D.C. held in 1963, ed. by
Norris)

Sci. Lib.
SH
381
.A57

Andrews, R. C. *Whale Hunting.*
New York: Appleton, 1916.

A bibliography card for a periodical:

Hickel, W. S. "When a Race Breathes
No More; Extinction of 47 Species
of U.S. Wild Life"
Sports Illustrated, December 14, 1970

Three cards with information on them:

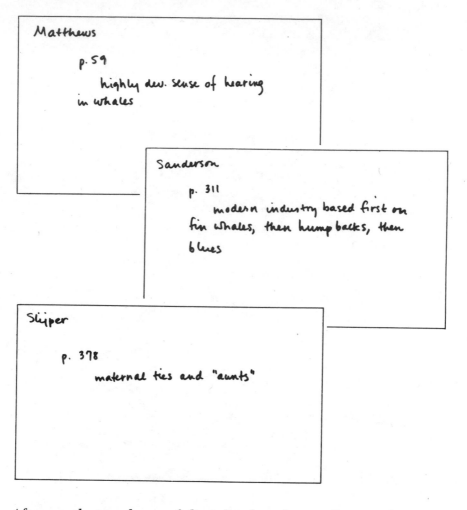

Matthews

    p. 59

      highly dev. sense of hearing
in whales

Sanderson

    p. 311

      modern industry based first on
fin whales, then humpbacks, then
blues

Slijper

    p. 378

      maternal ties and "aunts"

After another ten hours of disciplined reading and note-taking, she was ready to organize and begin writing.

In the meantime, she had developed respect for libraries. The card catalogue, the subject index, the microfilm machine, and the reference room were added to her experience. She had learned the beginnings of research in high school, but the high school library had limited resources. In the reference room were the encyclopedias, the

Who's Who's, the dictionaries of biography, indexes to the *Congressional Record*, and to *The New York Times*, yearbooks on all sorts of subjects—and a reference librarian who helped her. At first, the walled books of the stacks were threatening; how could she ever cope with such multiplicity? But gradually the library grew familiar, and she accepted the fact that she was not writing a Ph.D. thesis, and that her knowledge would remain limited.

In organizing the paper, she had only to try different orders of the three-by-five-inch cards that held her notes. A stack of three-by-five's is an instantly changeable outline. You can place them in piles according to topic, order them in each pile according to the best arrangement of facts, and then order the piles in the best sequence for the essay. Because each piece of information is a unit that might go anywhere in the paper—we cannot organize our information until we have collected all of it; when we start, we don't know where our facts will best fit our argument it is wise to keep the notes short, to write on one side of the card only, and to make a series of three-by-five's even when we are finding several things on one page in a book, rather than lumping different facts together on one card. Later, organization will be easier.

Jennifer tried different orders. She found that she worked best by starting with general information, apparently objective but gathered around ideas about maternity and protection, and then moved onward to opinion, argument, and exhortation at the end. She worried about her beginning. She had read that a prehistoric mammal, ancestor to prehistoric whales, had a long horn protruding from its head, and might be the source of our myth of the unicorn. She played with the idea of suggesting that the humpback whale might one day be as extinct as the unicorn. But it seemed elaborate and strained.

She tried beginning with an analogy.

> The great whales graze on plankton floating in the sea as the bison once grazed in oceans of prairie grass. [That certainly takes itself seriously.] As the American bison was hunted to near extinction during the last few centuries, so is the number of whales now seriously and permanently reduced.

The bracketed aside (her own, in a draft) dismissed this attempt. Then she decided to begin abruptly, without a conventional introductory paragraph, and let the title do the introducing. The cards were ordered and she was ready to begin. The first draft felt nearly right, because she had prepared and organized well. A few facts that interested her did not fit, and she put the cards aside, to see if later she could find a place for them. She set the manuscript aside for a day, corrected it for style, inserted one new paragraph, drafted her footnotes, consulted her handbook for the mechanics of footnoting and bibliography, and typed her paper.

The Protector Unprotected

Humpbacks are mammals, as all whales are; they breathe into huge lungs, bear live young, which they nurse for the better part of a year, and have vestiges of hair which scientists believe once covered the bodies of terrestrial ancestors. The shape of the humpback's body, when compared to the other great whales, is comical—rotund, with long knobby flippers, and bumps, like freckles, all over the head and snout. The dorsal fin is small, sticking out slightly from its back. Behind this fin are several more small, irregular bumps—probably the source of the humpback's name. The upper part of the body is black while the underside is usually whitish. The average length of a mature humpback is forty-five feet.

Unlike a toothed whale, like the sperm whale, which uses its teeth to catch and devour its food, the humpback is a filter-feeder, subsisting mainly on plankton, but also on any small fish unfortunate enough to be in the way. Even birds sometimes fly into the huge mouth. The humpback is a baleen whale; as it swims through the water, mouth open, tiny organisms catch in a mesh of hairy bristles called baleen, which run the length of the whale's palate.

The migration of humpbacks relates directly to their feeding habits. They feed mostly in Arctic or Antarctic waters, areas particularly rich in plankton. But when winter comes to the poles, the whales are driven toward tropical waters which are, oddly, nearly barren of the humpback's food. So while ". . . 90 per cent of captured humpback whales had their stomachs filled to capacity . . . "[1] when taken in the Antarctic (in a study done in 1942), ". . . only one out of 2,000 humpbacks (taken in waters off Australia) was found to have food in its

[1] E. J. Slijper, *Whales* (New York: Basic Books, 1962), p. 257.

stomach."[2] The tagging of humpbacks has shown that they migrate along the coasts of the continents and that there are several rather distinct populations, one of these feeding in the Arctic, the other feeding in the Antarctic. There seems to be little intermixture between the two groups.

Although humpbacks are slow swimmers, they are famous for their playful behavior. They often jump completely out of the water, unlike most of the larger whales. Christopher Ash has suggested that humpbacks jump and splash to shake off the barnacles that inevitably attach themselves to the flippers and tail of the whales.[3] According to E. J. Slijper, the humpback also:

> likes to roll on the surface, slapping the water with its flukes and wing-shaped pectoral fins as he does so. The slaps can often be heard many miles away. Moreover, humpbacks like to swim on their backs for a while and to display their white bellies. They often turn whole series of somersaults both above and under the water.[4]

Sometime during their fourth year the humpbacks mate in the warm waters of the tropics. After a long period of love-play, they swim at each other, picking up speed. At the last instant they turn toward the surface and, belly to belly, jump out of the water. Probably they copulate at this moment, although some scientists maintain that this jumping behavior does not include copulation, but is rather an elaborate part of the whale's love-play. Humpbacks also copulate while lying on the surface of the water on their sides. In this case, they glide past each other before mating, stroking and slapping with their long, wing-like flippers. While the love-play is rather long in duration, it seems that copulation lasts only a short period of time—from ten to thirty seconds. How many times the same pair of whales mates is unknown.

Eleven to twelve months later the baby whales are born, usually one calf to a mother, although there are records of multiple births among humpbacks. Humpback babies are

[2]Slijper, p. 316.
[3]Christopher Ash, *Whaler's Eye* (New York: Macmillan, 1962), p. 61
[4]Slijper, p. 97.

born, like most whale babies, tail first, and large in proportion to the size of the mother. The average mature female is forty-five feet long while the average calf is fourteen feet long at birth—nearly one-third the size of its parent. Almost immediately after the birth of the calf, the mother and perhaps one other mature female from the herd (called the "aunt") nose the baby gently toward the surface of the water where it will take its first breath.

Maternal ties are strong in whales; the mother stays very close to her calf for months after it is born, often allowing no other whale but the aunt to swim between her and her offspring. In its earlier stages, the American whaling industry capitalized upon this instinct. Whalers harpooned suckling calves knowing that the mothers would stay by their young and be easy prey. There is now an international agreement which protects calves and nursing or pregnant females.

The humpback's protectiveness is called "epimeletic" behavior. When this protectiveness is maternal, or the act of any older whale on the part of any younger whale, it is specifically called "nurturant." An article called "Epimeletic Behavior in Cetacea" includes descriptions of strong maternal affection in humpbacks. There is a report by a whaling captain of female humpbacks buoying up dead young for hours.[5] In the same article, "succorant" behavior is described. This is care-giving behavior between mature whales: remaining in the area of an injured companion, or supporting it so it can breathe, or even attacking the source of the injury. Male humpbacks display succorant behavior more often than females, but there are reports of "standing-by" in both sexes.

The most highly developed of the whale's senses is its hearing. There is no particular reason for a whale's sight to be highly developed since it often feeds at depths which are dark. The humpback's sense of hearing is used to locate food and to locate other whales.

Dr. Roger Payne has done considerable research on the sounds made by humpback whales. He believes whale songs

[5]Kenneth Norris, *Whales, Dolphins, and Porpoises* (Berkeley: University of California Press, 1966), p. 77.

like bird songs make contact with other members of the species. *Newsweek* (June 8, 1970) quoted Dr. Payne as saying that, ". . . in certain layers of the ocean, known as sound channels, humpback songs can travel thousands of miles without losing much power." Dr. Payne's recording, "Songs of the Humpback Whale," is available commercially. In the notes on the record jacket he explains that,

> Humpback whale songs are far longer than bird songs. The shortest humpback song recorded lasts 6 minutes and the longest is more than 30 minutes.

It is difficult to describe the sounds humpbacks make. Sometimes their noises are like incredible belches. Sometimes the humpbacks sound like cows bellowing or jungle birds screeching far away. The pitch and the duration vary enormously. When my cats heard the record for the first time, they paced nervously back and forth in front of the speakers and then ran out of the room to hide under a bed.

For many years the humpback was of basic importance to the American whaling industry, partly because of the whale's habit of migrating close to shore, making him easy to catch, and partly because humpbacks yield a good amount of oil for their size. In a Congressional Hearing on the Conservation of Whales (1931), Dr. A. B. Howell had this to say: "For all practical purposes it may be said that the existing whaling industry is dependent upon the Blue Whale, Finback, and Humpback . . . But at present all three species have been almost exterminated commercially in all but the most inaccessible portions of their ranges." (p. 3) The latest figure I could find on the number of remaining humpbacks is "a few thousand" (*Newsweek*, Jan. 25, 1971), down from hundreds of thousands.

Until 1963, humpbacks were only partially protected by the International Whaling Commission. In that year, the Commission forbade even the limited four-day take of humpbacks due to the near extinction of the species. As reassuring as this sounds, the humpback is still the victim of whalers not belonging to the member nations of the Commission and even, occasionally, of whalers from member nations—sometimes out of simple error and sometimes because of inadequate enforcement of the regulations. (Victor Scheffer, author of *The Year of the Whale*, would like to see enforcement of whaling regulations by the United Nations.) Another discouraging fact is that the whaling industries of various nations have turned to other endangered species, especially the fin whale, to take their quotas.

Given modern processing techniques, many products can be made from the body of a whale. Not only oil and meat come from the carcass, but cattle-feed, fertilizer, glue, glycerin, and insulin. In 1955, Georges Blond estimated the commercial value of an Antarctic blue at four to six thousand dollars.[6] I should mention that the blue whale is the largest of the great whales, in fact, the largest mammal known to inhabit the earth, now or ever.

The problem is this: either we continue whaling policies as they now exist in order to acquire what the whale affords, until we have killed off all whales, or, we develop alternative sources for the products now supplied by the whaling industry. Since we would have to find alternatives eventually, it seems sensible to look for them now, and preserve the declining population of whales in our oceans. In previous centuries, it was fashionable for women to cinch their waists with corsets stayed by whale-bone. That practice is no longer "essential." It never was. Science could make whale oil as obsolete a source of lubricants as whale-bone is obsolete in women's corsets. The same goes for cattle-feed and glue and all the rest. With proper application of the brain-power in this world we can find other means to satisfy our wants. We need not exterminate one species of animal after another.

If we should find ourselves unable to make alternatives in the laboratory, perhaps we should question how badly we need the products in the first place. Perhaps, to preserve a species, we could learn to do without things like ambergris (which comes from the sperm whale and is used in making perfume) and whale meat for cattle-feed. A T-bone steak is an

[6]Georges Blond, *The Great Story of Whales* (Garden City, N.Y.: Hanover House, 1955), p. 16.

incredible waste of matter and energy if it comes from a steer that ate a whale that ate a herring that ate some plankton that ate. . . . In the portion of a poem that follows, Gary Snyder embodies the interconnectedness of all living things. He is talking about eating shark meat but it could as well be whale steak:

> Sweet miso sauce on a big boiled cube
>   as I lift a flake
>   to my lips,
>   Miles of water, Black current,
>   Thousands of days
>   re-crossing his own paths
>   to tangle our net
>   to be part of
>   this loom.[7]

So far it seems that every generation thinks the next generation is the one that will have to stop the destruction of the ecosystem. That kind of thinking can't go on. We must protect our brother the humpback, as the humpback protects his brother. The movement toward protection of humpbacks by international agreement is a small move in the right direction.

[7]Gary Snyder, *Regarding Wave* (New York: New York: New Directions, 1970), p. 29.

Bibliography

Ash, Christopher. *Whaler's Eye.* New York: Macmillan, 1962.

"Battle of the Whales." *Newsweek,* 25 Jan., 1971.

Blond, Georges. *The Great Story of Whales.* Garden City: Hanover House, 1955.

Norris, Kenneth. *Whales, Dolphins, and Porpoises.* Berkeley: University of California Press, 1966.

Slijper, E. J. *Whales*. New York: Basic Books, 1962.

Snyder, Gary. *Regarding Wave*. New York: New Directions, 1970.

U.S. Congress. Special Committee on Conservation of Wildlife Resources. *Whales*. Washington: Gov't Printing Office, 1931.

"Whale of a Singer." *Newsweek*, 8 June, 1970.

Jennifer Case wisely limited her paper and it works well within its limits. She has a fine eye for detail, and embodies her ideas and feelings in the facts that fascinate her. As a result, she is able to interest the reader. Competent writing is the final ingredient in her paper. But we should not allow our pleasure in her writing to obscure the *basic* ingredients of research and organization. Reading and note-taking, hours and hours of them, supply us with the details we find ourselves using. We must be willing to put in the time and the thought to *accumulate* detail; then we must use our shaping intelligence to set the right details in the right order, and *eliminate* the useless, even when it is amusing or intriguing. Then we must work over our words, sentences, and paragraphs for style. It is worth it.

WRITING ABOUT WRITING

Often we are asked to write about something we have read. Sometimes we write to investigate an aspect of writing; we may analyze the argument of an essay, or the paragraph structure, or the use of narrative and description. I want to deal briefly with the kind of writing we usually call "criticism," essays that talk about the content, the form, and the value of other essays, of stories, and of poems.

When we write an essay on an essay, we judge its clarity, its persuasiveness, its unity, its interest—and we attempt to apply appropriate standards. If the essay is wholly expository—say, a disquisition on constructing golf courses—we are silly if we blame it for its lack of persuasiveness. If we read a polemic between a feminist and a male chauvinist, we miss the point if we don't deal with the argument. It is sensible to draw a line between explaining and evaluating. Though the two activities are not wholly separable, we should try for the sake of clarity to know what we are up to. It is perfectly possible to explain without evaluating. It is not possible to make an understandable evaluation without giving some concrete reasons for your position—without quoting or paraphrasing, examining, and explaining.

In looking at an essay—or, to a degree, at a story and a poem—it is sensible to check three questions. It helps you to avoid mistakes in reading. First, consider the purpose, moment, or occasion of the writing. Is this a reminiscence or an editorial? A recipe or a denunciation? You must ask: *What is it for?* Second, you must ask: *Who is it talking to?* Is it addressed to friends or strangers, to initiates or adversaries, to Kiwanis or the Hell's Angels? Third, *What is its tone,* or assumed vantage point? Is it the humble investigator or the omniscient intelligence? Is it sharing a discovery, piece by piece, or is it handing out the results of a discovery already consummated?

For more guidance in criticism, look at a book like Sylvan Barnet's *A Short Guide to Writing about Literature.* Here, we must be content to name two general ways of dealing with literature, to look at two common fallacies in dealing with literature, and to present a few examples of criticism from the classroom and from printed sources.

One way to deal with poems and stories is to analyze them, to separate the qualities of the work of art—a mental act of taking stock by stepping back inside your mind and looking—and report on them separately. In dealing with a story or a novel, for instance, you can analyze the author's characterization, use of setting, and development of plot. Also, you can analyze *within* these categories. The writer will show character by dialogue, by description, by action, and by the reaction of other characters. In analyzing poetry, we may of course deal with character, setting, and plot (and speaker and occasion) also. Or with sound, or imagery, or metaphor.

In analysis we dig into the methods a writer uses, in order to explain what he has done. Never worry, as so many beginning critics do, that analysis will destroy a work of art. Ten million words have been written about *Hamlet. Hamlet* still sits at the top of the shelf, looking down at all the books written about it, smiling a little.

Remember as in all essays to narrow your topic. You cannot write a six-hundred-word essay called *Hamlet* and approach your topic. If you are going to write about *Hamlet,* or *Huckleberry Finn,* or "The Love Song of J. Alfred Prufrock," find a tiny topic and be adequate about it. Write about "Mark Twain's Use of the River in Huckleberry Finn," or "Hamlet's Puns," or "Eliot on Prufrock's Character."

Another kind of critical paper is explication, line by line analysis of a short poem or a passage from a longer poem or a work of fiction. We use explication more with poems than with prose. Explication and analysis both deal with similar terms, like character and metaphor. Analysis means attempting to deal with larger units, and must be more summary. Explication is more narrow and more thorough, dealing with the words as they come—somewhat as Chapter Two of this book deals with words—and therefore lacking the overview. In a paper of explication on *Hamlet*, one might take the Queen's lines about Ophelia's death:

> There, on the pendent boughs her coronet weeds
> Clambering to hang, an envious sliver broke;
> When down her weedy trophies and herself
> Fell in the weeping brook. Her clothes spread wide;
> And, mermaid-like, awhile they bore her up:
> Which time she chanted snatches of old tunes;
> As one incapable of her own distress,
> Or like a creature native and indued
> Unto that element: but long it could not be
> Till that her garments, heavy with their drink,
> Pull'd the poor wretch from her melodious lay
> To muddy death.

and go through them line by line; you find the *use* of flowers, as a parallel to Ophelia and as a value put upon her; you also find the vivid imagery of the action—those floating clothes!—and the metaphor of drunkenness. And more.

Of course a million pitfalls await anyone writing criticism. One of the greatest is the reader's sense of the author. Too often in reading we ask ourselves silly questions: "Did T. S. Eliot really mean all these hidden meanings?" The whole notion of "hidden" meanings begs the question: who is supposed to be hiding what from whom? And the suggestion of intention is naïve. With anything complicated in our own lives, are we ever really certain of our own intentions? Then how are we able to know Eliot's intention in 1909, or Shakespeare's in 1601? We must keep our eyes on the text, not on the imagined "idea of the author." If something is *there* in the text, if we can show that it is *there*, then it's *there*—no matter if the author rises before us in ectoplasm and denies it. The only qualification we need make is historical, and governs the meanings of words at the time they were used. "King" meant something to Shakespeare it cannot mean to us. The OED is especially helpful in reading old books.

So avoid *the biographical fallacy*. First, avoid arguing from intentions, which are always unknowable. Second, avoid using the work of literature to illuminate the author's life. Of course if you are writing a biography, write a biography—and use the literature as you will. But do not write biography under the guise of criticism, as so many critics have done. People writing about a novelist try to explain the novels by referring to his first marriage, his depressions, and his isolation. But novels are novels—if they are any good—and we learn nothing about them by learning what experience *may* have informed them. Critics writing about W. B. Yeats's poems seem to run from the poems to the life as fast as they can. When a poem is about a woman, they cry "Maud Gonne!"—the name of a woman whom Yeats loved, unhappily and unrequitedly—and lift their eyes from the page. They have said nothing about the poem. So keep your eyes on the words in front of you, when you write criticism. If you love an author's work, it is fascinating to know something about his life, and nothing is wrong with this knowledge. But when you write about the work, write about the work.

The beginning critic should avoid the biographical fallacy, even if it seems artificial to avoid using what he knows. Probably it is more difficult to avoid *the autobiographical fallacy*. This kind of criticism is not really about the poem; it is about the reader's response to it. At the extreme, it can read like this passage from an examination:

> I like this poem. When I first read it I felt scary, and then when I read it over again I felt good. I like the images and the sounds and the ideas. The poem is *right on!*

There is no need to quote the poem that the student is writing about—it could be any poem. All he talks about is himself.

This kind of paper is often a result of enthusiasm, and an understandable excess. We *respond* to something! We want to tell people. We want to copy our response in our prose, making the equivalent of a printout of our heart beat, body temperature, and brain waves. We try to name our feelings. But in our enthusiasm, we have forgotten the object about which we are supposed to be enthusiastic. Our subject, instead, is I, I, I. Unwittingly, we have fallen into egotism, and we praise the poem because it was able to create such a response in us. Remember two things especially, when you write criticism: *The poem is important, not the poet.* And equally, *The poem is important, not the reader.*

Robert Frost has a poem called

Acquainted with the Night

I have been one acquainted with the night.
I have walked out in rain—and back in rain.
I have outwalked the furthest city light.

I have looked down the saddest city lane.
I have passed by the watchman on his beat
And dropped my eyes, unwilling to explain.

I have stood still and stopped the sound of feet
When far away an interrupted cry
Came over houses from another street,

But not to call me back or say good-by;
And further still at an unearthly height
One luminary clock against the sky

Proclaimed the time was neither wrong nor right.
I have been one acquainted with the night.

One student on a final examination began an "analysis" of this poem:

> I really love this poem. I chose to write about it because I know just the feeling that Frost is writing about. It reminds me especially of one night at home last summer. All afternoon I had been feeling depressed, listless. I turned on the television and turned it off. After supper I helped my mother with the dishes but then I didn't want to hang around with my brothers the way I usually did but I felt like taking a walk. It was really funny, because I never take walks, but that night I really wanted to.
>
> I didn't walk outside town, so that part isn't the same. But it rained! When I read the poem it all came back to me, so clearly! . . .
>
> .   .   .
>
> The poem is excellent because it is so realistic and so moving. Reading it, my whole body felt just what was happening. It made me remember the strangest feeling of my life, when I too was one acquainted with the night.

This reader, partly because of coincidence, will not let herself see the poem itself. Another student wrote about the same poem:

> Robert Frost's "Acquainted with the Night" recounts an experience of loneliness and of restlessness. Frost—or the man who says "I" in the poem—is all alone. He listens as if somebody might be calling for him but it is never him. It seems as if it couldn't be him, or even as if he wanted to be alone. Why does he walk back and forth in the night if he doesn't want to be alone? He is *sad* (a lane isn't sad unless you are) and he is guilty or shameful about something ("dropped my eyes, unwilling to explain")—maybe about wanting to be alone? When you come to the clock at the end of the poem, at first it seems to be some sort of symbol of what he is looking for. It is "luminary," which can just mean that it was lighted up, but which sounds mysterious and grand. And it was "at an unearthly height." What does this mean? Well, it could just mean that it was really separated from the earth a lot—as Frost (the walker) isn't, concerned with streets and lanes and feet. But it is *sort* of a hint of God or some mystery too. But just when he thinks he's going to get an answer, it turns out that the time of day isn't what matters. It's "neither wrong nor right" so the walker must be worried about right and wrong, or about not being able to tell them apart. Maybe that's why he wants to be alone?
>
> The poem has fourteen lines. It is some sort of a sonnet. It doesn't have much colorful language in it. It's mostly just what happens, but there are words (like the ones at the end I mentioned) which are really well used. "Acquainted" is a funny word, like an "acquaintanceship" not a "friendship." It sounds as if Frost knew the night *very well* but didn't like it very much. And the part I like best is when he says
>
>> stopped the sound of feet
>> When far away an interrupted cry
>> Came over houses from another street.
>
> It's so *cold,* that way of referring to your own walking by hearing it.
>
> The poem is a good one. It's more complicated than it looks. It gives a feeling—of desolateness—and a reason for it.

This sensitive examination answer, if pondered over and revised into an essay, would have made a good piece of criticism.

Here is an example of polished criticism. The paragraph is from a book about Thomas Hardy, and introduces a discussion of *Tess of the d'Urbervilles*.

> With *Tess of the d'Urbervilles* we come to one of the most contentious novels in the language. Once again the theme is preposterous human suffering, an ill-starred individual, fighting the good but lonely fight against invincible odds. But this time the sufferer is an attractive peasant girl, "a pure woman" who, although she had "passed the Sixth Standard in a National School," was still a child, still a country innocent, when she was sordidly raped. Yet in *Tess*, a transcendental purity of spirit, embracing all that is charitably humble and devotedly unselfish, survived long enough to enthrone humanity in a brief splendour. The book, too, is a commentary not only on Victorian morality but on the complexity of sexual morality as a whole. Despite the martyrdom and literary canonisation of Tess, there is no vindication of unchastity, and this is a factor not necessarily forced by the magazine-readers. All Hardy's heroines are chaste.
>
> George Wing, *Hardy*

Because this is a paragraph from a book, I do not print it as a model for a theme, but as an example of a writer beginning to cope with fiction and fictional character. It is easier to find examples of the explication and analysis of short poems or parts of poems. Here is R. P. Blackmur going to work on a few lines by a poet named Hart Crane:

> To illustrate the uniformity of approach, a few examples are presented, some that succeed and some that fail. In "Lachrymae Christi" consider the line
>
> Thy Nazarene and tinder eyes.
>
> (Note, from the title, that we are here again concerned with tears as the vehicle-image of insight, and that, in the end, Christ is identified with Dionysus.) Nazarene, the epithet for Christ, is here used as an adjective of quality in conjunction with the noun tinder also used as an adjective; an arrangement which will seem baffling only to those who underesti-

mate the seriousness with which Crane remodelled words. The first three lines of the poem read:

> Whitely, while benzine
> Rinsings from the moon
> Dissolve all but the windows of the mills.

Benzine is a fluid, cleansing and solvent, has a characteristic tang and smart to it, and is here associated with the light of the moon, which, through the word "rinsings," is itself modified by it. It is, I think, the carried-over influence of benzine which gives startling aptness to Nazarene. It is, if I am correct for any reader but myself, an example of suspended association, or telekinesis; and it is, too, an example of syllabic interpenetration or internal punning as habitually practiced in the later prose of Joyce. The influence of one word on the other reminds us that Christ the Saviour cleanses and solves and has, too, the quality of light. "Tinder" is a simpler instance of how Crane could at once isolate a word and bind it in, impregnating it with new meaning. Tinder is used to kindle fire, powder, and light; a word incipient and bristling with the action proper to its being. The association is completed when it is remembered that tinder is very nearly a homonym for tender and, *in this setting*, puns upon it.
> R. P. Blackmur, "New Thresholds, New Anatomies"

You don't have to know all the references Blackmur makes to see his method. And you don't have to write with such references to write criticism.

By and large, I suspect that it is good policy, when you are about to write a critical essay, to avoid reading critics—especially critics of the work you are writing about. (Sometimes it is useful to write a research paper on the criticism of a work of art, to sample the range of opinion. But this is another matter.) If we are going to write on Huck Finn, we can easily drown ourselves in the contradictory criticism of Huck Finn, and end by being too frightened to have an opinion of our own. I think we do better, once we have found out what we need to know about the vocabulary of a work, if it is old, to deal intensively with the work itself, and avoid the secondary material of biographers and critics.

For writing criticism is a matter, not of knowing about criticism, but of knowing about the work criticized. Committing ourselves, in our own words, to an interpretation and an evaluation of a literary work, we may find that we have to read more deeply than we have read before, and think more deeply about what we have read. So criticism helps us learn to read, while we are learning to write.

EXERCISES

1. a. Work up an idea that might be developed into a theme.

b. Accumulate details.

c. Organize details into a possible order, eliminating those which seem irrelevant.

d. Bring all material to class, to discuss collectively.

2. In class, brainstorm details for a paper on a recent local controversy. Then try to organize the details using the blackboard. Or take the details home, elaborate and organize them for the next class.

3. Analyze the following passages for the order and relevance of the details used.

a. By the early years of the 1890s, German firms had become notably prosperous. In one decade, Hamburg-Amerika alone had carried half a million passengers to New York—half again as much as either Cunard or White Star. The German companies basked in Imperial favor, were staffed by brilliant, ambitious executives and, as time would tell, competitive to the point of madness. The motto on the Hamburg-Amerika house flag was indicative: *Mein Feld ist die Welt* ("My field is the world").

The "noble example" of Germany in its surge to the forefront of maritime power had rallied the waning hopes of sea-minded Americans, and led directly to Congressional support for the rehabilitation of the American Line. "Germany has a scant foothold on the deep sea," said one patriot, "and none of the splendid nautical traditions of America. What the empire has done, the republic can do more readily. No race like ours with a grasp upon two oceans and the mingled blood of Viking and pioneer can long be cheated of its birthright."

Kaiser Wilhelm himself was caught up in the nobility of it all. After a short cruise on one of the great ships he wrote a letter to his mother. "Any man who, standing on the deck of a ship with the starlit firmament of the Almighty as his canopy and the boundless seas as the only object of his vision," said His Imperial Highness, "takes occasion to question his conscience, to weigh his responsibilities, and to contrast them with his inclination to do good and keep in the path of righteousness, will not hesitate to pronounce a sea voyage a salutary thing for himself and those depending upon him."

To put an end to the dominance of rivals like the *Campania* and the *Lucania* and to halt the leapfrog way in which Cunard alternated with White Star in claiming the fastest speed, the longest menus and the most ornate grand saloons, the North German Lloyd Company adopted Prussian measures. They went to the Vulcan shipbuilding company in Stettin with a simple, stark proposal: build us the fastest ship in the world and we'll buy it; give us anything less, and you can keep it.

John Malcolm Brinnin, *The Sway of the Grand Saloon*

b. But the Dolphin House was not grand. Hermione and I settled in, for what we thought would be a weekend, and developed, in fact, to be eighteen months, with the occasional relief of a day in the city. The head waiter, who had been born in Constantinople, actually carried our bags. Dinner that first night was exquisite. We bathed in the cool glow of a '45 Château Lafite-Rothschild which I had all but forgotten. The quarters, however, were shabby.

A walk on the beach, after lunch the next day, revealed that we had unknowingly chosen a coast that resembled, in uncanny ways, our native Dalmatia. Sigurd was to join us in a fortnight. How pleased he would be!

Hermione and I played jacks until tea, a lively American game which we had picked up during a visiting lectureship in Seattle. Tea was mediocre, as breakfast had been. We noticed that Americans were good at the more obvious things, but lacked expertise at the small ones. When did we ever see toast cut with elegance, in all this wide land?

Hermann von Kreicke, *The Migrant Swan*

c. In a rather pathetic attempt to keep her home, Scott had sent her Compton Mackenzie's book *Plasher's Mead* to read. But she didn't like it: "Nothing annoys me more than having the most trivial action analyzed and explained." She said the heroine was "ATROCIOUSLY uninteresting" and maybe she'd save the book and try to read it again in rainy weather. But she also tipped her hand more than she may have intended, for in the same letter she told him, "People seldom interest me except in their relations to things, and I like men to be just incidents in books so I can imagine their characters—" Everything, it seemed, had to revolve around her, her perceptions, her games, or she was not interested and refused to play. Certainly that letter carried a note of warning about herself, if Fitzgerald had been in any condition to receive it. But he was not. He knew the terms, they were remarkably like his own, and that exquisite egotism drew him even more completely to her.

But what he did not fully perceive, perhaps because Zelda did not, was the uncertainty within his girl. For, as worldly as she loved to seem to be, as reckless and ebullient as she was, Zelda knew nothing first hand of any world other than the protected Southern one of provincial towns and families who knew one another and were kin. For all her banter, New York, chic and fabulous, must have seemed as remote to her as the Orient.

Nancy Milford, Zelda

d. But the real failure of the theater, the real evidence of its prevailing shallowness, its lack of standards, of convictions, of courage (and of course the lack of convictions helps account for the lack of courage), has to do with what functions, not as a mass but as a class medium. The true, deep failure emerges when one has got past the anonymous faces in the audience at a run-of-the-mine opening night, when one has got past the irrelevant name of the playwright, the unfamiliar names of the backers. The true, deep failure emerges on the most high-toned of opening nights, on the Social Register and Café Society personalities in the audience; on the Dun-and-Bradstreet names of the backers; on the immensely relevant name of the playwright, and the producer, and the director, and the star. Here what passes for good taste, what preens itself as sophistication, is not only graciously pleased to be represented but couldn't be paid to stay away.

Louis Kronenberger, Company Manners

4. Take the following beginning, and revise it:

Every Easter we drove to my great Aunt's house in Troy to eat a ham for Easter dinner. Even when my father was a little boy, they had gone to Troy for Easter. Sometimes it would snow and we would be late. Once we blew a tire about half way, and the spare was soft, and we took at least an hour and a half to get it fixed.

Last year was my Senior year in high school, and my great aunt thought graduating from high school was a big deal, so I knew I would get a lot of attention when I got there. We have to pack because we actually stay over Friday and Saturday nights. Fortunately, for some reason, I packed my tennis shoes and my jeans. If I hadn't, I wouldn't have been able to play touch football decently, I wouldn't have wound up in the emergency ward, and I wouldn't have met Linda.

5. Here are two small articles from the *New Yorker*'s "Talk of the Town." What do you think of the beginnings, endings, details, and shape? If the article is argumentative, also consider the skill of persuasion here. In which paragraphs, in these articles, do you find exposition? description? dialogue? narrative?

a. Within the last half-dozen years, the mockingbird, moving north into New England and multiplying, has progressed from the status of welcome stranger and curiosity to that of nuisance. Bird people who first found the invasion from the Southland a romantic affair are beginning to group the mockingbird, in their emotions, with such long-established non-favorites as the starling and the blue jay. The main trouble is that once a mockingbird establishes itself in a territory, with its full repertoire of imitations, the amount of time left open for legitimate songbirds to make themselves heard is limited. Even the other species of mockers retire from the scene. The thrasher, which used to enliven two or three days each spring with its madcap torrent of high-branch mimicry, tends to avoid the territory. The cat-bird sits mute. Unlike the thrasher and the catbird, the first of which used to join riotously, the second modestly, in the song of other birds, celebrating their talents with some affection, the mockingbird sings occlusively. For their first few years in the North, the mockingbirds seemed to have left behind their habit of singing at night. But last year they began occasional night sessions, and this year they have developed regular midnight-to-dawn routines in imitation of the kill-deer, the meadowlark, the cardinal, and the oriole. The mimic is shut-ting the authentic music-makers out of their own songs, if not by monopolizing their singing time, then by giving their songs back to them so crudely that they become discouraged from producing the pure thing.

b. A lot was wrong with Elvis Presley's first-ever New York ap-pearance, at Madison Square Garden last weekend. Somebody in the Presley organization misjudged the desires of the crowd, and as a result Elvis was preceded by a standup comedian called Jackie Kahane. No doubt Mr. Kahane's patter knocks 'em dead in Vegas, but New York is not Vegas and the Garden is not a night club. "Kids today . . ." said Mr. Kahane gamely, and lamely, as the audience clapped in uni-son. "I have a kid. Everything this kid eats turns to hair." He was finally booed off the stage. There was fault to find with Elvis's own perfor-mance as well. Instead of a rhythm section to back him up, he had a twenty-three-piece orchestra, a six-man rock band, and an eight-member chorus—a bit too much insurance, even for the Garden. The program was rigidly arranged and planned, allowing for little in the way of spontaneity, and it consisted largely of romantic ballads and sugary, easy-listening songs. The classics that most of the audience had come to hear—"Heartbreak Hotel," "Don't Be Cruel," "Hound Dog"—occupied only fifteen minutes of a fifty-minute program. The blandness was conceptual as well as musical, as when Elvis sang a non-controversial medley of "Dixie," "All My Trials," and the "Battle Hymn of the Republic." The gyrations that made the man famous were seldom in evidence. Instead, he offered a repertoire of stereotyped actions and heroic poses.

Oddly, none of this made any difference. The audience was ecstatic throughout. (It would have been ecstatic even if Elvis had sung nothing but Gregorian chants.) During the intermission before Elvis's appearance, our companion, a young woman who still has her Elvis scrapbook packed away in a trunk somewhere, told us a story that made it all quite comprehensible. "When I was twelve years old," she said, "I was riding in the car with my mother and brother, and a song called 'I Want You, I Need You, I Love You' came on the radio. I immediately felt a certain twinge. My mother said, 'This is that Elvis Presley they're all talking about. I don't see what all the fuss is about.' My brother said the same thing. I just sat on the back seat and didn't say anything. You see, I *did* know what all the fuss was about."

The lights went down, the orchestra struck up what used to be called "Thus Spake Zarathustra" and is now called "The Theme from '2001,'" the audience began a full-throated scream, and Elvis appeared. He looked magnificent. His coal-black hair was fuller and drier than in days of old, and he wore a fantastical white costume studded with silver. He strolled back and forth on the stage, accepting the plaudits of the crowd like a Roman emperor. He looked like an apparition, and this was appropriate, because he has been a figure of fantasy for seventeen years. As the performance went on, it became impossible to avoid the conclusion that he is a consummate professional. He never cut loose, but he did not have to. The slightest gesture of his hand, the smallest inclination of his head set off waves of screams from the favored direction. The greatest ovation, except for the one that attended his initial appearance, came when he went into the first of his old songs, "Love Me." "Treat me like a fool," he sang. "Treat me mean an' crool, but love me."

Throughout, Elvis maintained a certain ironic distance from it all, sometimes engaging in a bit of self-parody. At the beginning of "Hound Dog," for example, he posed dramatically on one knee, said, "Oh, excuse me," and switched to the other knee. But he manifestly enjoyed the audience's enjoyment, even as he indicated with a smile here and a gesture there that it all had less to do with him than with their idea of him. On our way out, we asked our companion if she had liked the show. "It was bliss," she said, "I haven't felt so intensely *thirteen* since —well, since I was thirteen."

6. Here are some argumentative passages. Analyze them for their logic, order, reasonableness, and for their fallacies if they have any. Remember that these passages are excerpts.

a. A realistic discussion of the place of athletics in our educational program is long overdue. There is in both our schools and colleges today a vicious overemphasis on competitive athletics. Such overemphasis is seriously destructive of our entire educational system.

A short while ago, many Americans were disturbed because unofficial team scores showed that the Soviet Union had clearly taken first place, the United States second, in the Olympic games in Rome. These Americans were ready to argue that we must step up our concern with athletics in school and college as part of our struggle against communism. This line of reasoning needs to be examined. To understand my point, imagine that our independence as a free nation turned solely on the outcome of the next Olympic games—analogous to the ancient trial by combat between selected champions of opposing forces. Under such conditions, we would be forced to modify all our educational practices with the single aim of producing the greatest number of prize athletes.

This is pure fantasy, of course. One hardly needs to argue that we are engaged in a cold war—and in all probability, a long one. What we must have to win this real struggle are more and better scientists, engineers, doctors, lawyers, teachers, technicians. In short, we must improve the academic output of our educational system. Such being the case, overconcern with the development of prize athletes might well jeopardize our future.

That we need to have concern with the physical development of our youth goes without saying. Our society is heavily industrialized and urbanized. Our children and young people need to devote more time to effective body building and physical exercise. This problem was recognized nationally when, in 1956, President Eisenhower by executive order established the Council on Youth Fitness at the Cabinet level and the Citizens Advisory Committee. I have come to believe

that all public-school pupils should devote a period every school day
to developing their muscles and body coordination. This means that
each school needs a gymnasium of ample size. It also means, in many
schools, drastic changes in the content of the physical-education
courses. However, in many junior and senior high schools, there is not
room enough in the gymnasium to allow my recommendations to be
adopted. Too often, physical-education programs are scheduled for
all pupils only two or three days a week.

Yet, in some of these same schools, the facilities and instruction
are excellent for the relatively few on the basketball or football team
that competes in interscholastic contests. Why? Because the community
demands public entertainment in the form of winning teams. Fuzzy
thinking attempts to relate athletic spectacles to the physical well-being
of all our citizens. But there is little real concern for what is of prime
importance, namely, the physical fitness of all youth, both boys and
girls. . . .

James B. Conant, "Athletics: The Poison
Ivy in Our Schools," *Basic Writer and Reader*

b. It should be obvious that even with schools of equal quality
a poor child can seldom catch up with a rich one. Even if they attend
equal schools and begin at the same age, poor children lack most of
the educational opportunities which are casually available to the
middle-class child. These advantages range from conversation and
books in the home to vacation travel and a different sense of oneself,
and apply, for the child who enjoys them, both in and out of school.
So the poorer student will generally fall behind so long as he depends
on school for advancement or learning. The poor need funds to enable
them to learn, not to get certified for the treatment of their alleged
disproportionate deficiencies.

All this is true in poor nations as well as in rich ones, but there it
appears under a different guise. Modernized poverty in poor nations
affects more people more visibly but also—for the moment—more
superficially. Two-thirds of all children in Latin America leave school
before finishing the fifth grade, but these "desertores" are not therefore as badly off as they would be in the United States.

Few countries today remain victims of classical poverty, which
was stable and less disabling. Most countries in Latin America have
reached the "take-off" point toward economic development and competitive consumption, and thereby toward modernized poverty: their
citizens have learned to think rich and live poor. Their laws make six

to ten years of school obligatory. Not only in Argentina but also in
Mexico or Brazil the average citizen defines an adequate education
by North American standards, even though the chance of getting such
prolonged schooling is limited to a tiny minority. In these countries
the majority is already hooked on school, that is, they are schooled in
a sense of inferiority toward the better-schooled. Their fanaticism in
favor of school makes it possible to exploit them doubly: it permits
increasing allocation of public funds for the education of a few and
increasing acceptance of social control by the many.

Ivan Illich, *Deschooling Society*

c. Women are contoured by their conditioning to abandon
autonomy and seek guidance. It ought to be a priori evidence of the
synthetic nature of our concept of womanhood that it is so often
expounded. The number of women who resort to the paternal guidance of the psychoanalyst is indicative of the same fact. The existence
of continual strain in the feminine situation cannot be concealed so
it must be explained; in explaining it, traditional psychology, like the
Captain in Strindberg's *The Father,* assumes as arbitrarily as he did
that women have been subjected to conditioning which is improper
to their biological function, which is the breeding of children and
supportive work in the home. The woman who seeks academic guidance from psychologists might indeed find that some of the more
galling conflicts are lessened as a result although this is a dubious
conclusion. What she actually discovers is that the conditions against
which she chafes are sanctioned by a massive structure of data and
theory which she can only adapt to for there is no hope of shifting it.
It takes another psychiatrist to explain to her the function of observer
bias, and the essential conservatism of psychology. As far as the woman
is concerned, psychiatry is an extraordinary confidence trick: the un-
suspecting creature seeks aid because she feels unhappy, anxious and
confused, and psychology is easier to change than the status quo which
represents a higher value in the psychologists' optimistic philosophy.
If all else fails, largactil, shock treatment, hypnosis and other forms of
"therapy" will buttress the claim of society. Psychologists cannot fix
the world so they fix women. Actually they don't even manage that:
one Eysenck study (1952) reported that of patients treated by psychoanalysis, 44 percent improved; of those who were treated by other
methods (drugs, shock, etc.), 64 percent improved; and of those who
received no treatment at all, 72 percent improved. The subsequent
reports of Barron and Leary, Bergin, Cartwright and Vogel and Truax

bear out these negative results.

So much for the authority of psychoanalysis and the theory of personality. For the woman who accepts psychoanalytic descriptions of herself and of her problems there are specific perils far greater than the effects of personality prejudices on the other half of the community.

Freud is the father of psychoanalysis. It had no mother. He is not its only begetter, and subsequent structures of theory have challenged as well as reinforced his system. Probably the best way to treat it is as a sort of metaphysic but usually it is revered as a science. Freud himself lamented his inability to understand women, and became progressively humbler in his pronouncements about them. The best approach to Freud's assumptions about women is probably the one adopted by Dr. Ian Suttie, that of psychoanalyzing Freud himself. The cornerstone of the Freudian theory of womanhood is the masculine conviction that a woman is a castrated man. It is assumed that she considers herself to be thus deprived and that much of her motivation stems either from the attempt to pretend that this is not so, typical of the immature female who indulges in clitoral sexuality, or from the attempt to compensate herself for this lack by having children. Basically the argument is a tautology which cannot proceed beyond its own terms, so that it is neither demonstrable nor refutable. Ernest Jones, himself a devout Freudian, began to suspect that something was wrong with the basic hypothesis because he took the trouble to observe the sexuality of female children:

> There is an unhealthy suspicion growing that men analysts have been led to adopt an unduly phallocentric view of the problem in question, the importance of the female organs being correspondingly underestimated.

Unfortunately, the suspicion must have remained unhealthy, for it never flourished into a new theory. Psychoanalysts went on believing in the genital trauma despite evidence. Faith is not after all dependent upon evidence.

Germaine Greer, *The Female Eunuch*

d. In all previous consideration of class warfare there had been at least the assumption that the design of human beings was adequate, unbiased, functional, and not particularly in need of alteration. It was assumed that if the working class took over the functions of the ruling class, they would still be able to act with the conventional organs of men. But the ultimate logic of the sexual revolution required women to stand equal to the male body in every aspect—how could this equality prevail if women in competition with the other sex for the role of artist, executive, bureaucrat, surgeon, auto mechanic, politician, or masterful lover should have to cry quite every now and again for months of pregnancy plus years of uneasy accommodation between their career and their child, or else choose to have no children and so be obsessed with the possibility of biological harm, worse, the possibility of some unnameable harm to that inner space of creation their bodies would enclose?

One could speak of men and women as the poles of the universe, the universal Yang and Yin, offer views of the Creation in such abstract lands as seed and womb, vision and firmament, fire up a skyworks of sermon and poem to the incontestable mystery that women are flesh of the Mystery more than men—it would not diminish by a coulomb those electrics of wrath in the eyes of those women whose revolutionary principles are Jacobin. It was as if the High Grand Geist of the Jacobins had returned to state, "It was never enough to sever the heads of the aristocrats. The time is now come to get the first Aristocrat of the mall. Since He designed women at a disadvantage, such Work must be overthrown!"

What a job! Men were by comparison to women as simple meat; men were merely human beings equipped to travel through space at a variety of speeds, but women were human beings traveling through the same variety of space in full possession of a mysterious space within. In that purse of flesh were psychic tendrils, waves of communication to some conceivable source of life, some manifest of life come into human beings from a beyond which persisted in remaining most stubbornly beyond. Women, like men, were human beings, but they were a step, or a stage, or a move or a leap nearer the creation of existence, they were—given man's powerful sense of the present—his indispensable and only connection to the future; how could a woman compete if she contained the future as well as the present and so lived a physical life on the edge of the divide? What punishment traveled into the future with the pile driver's clang? whose unborn ear heard the loss of a note in the squawk of the static? The womb was a damnable disadvantage in the struggle with the men, a cranky fouled-up bag of horrors for any woman who would stand equal to man on modern jobs, for technology was the domain of number, of machines and electronic circuits, of plastic surfaces, static, vibrations, and contemporary noise. Yet through all such disturbance, technology was still built on conformity of practice. If it could adjust to rhythm, tide, the ebb of mood, and the phasing in and phasing out of energy in the men and women who worked its machines, nonetheless such adjustments were dear to technology, for each departure from a uniform beat demanded a new expensive control. The best operator was the uniform operator, and women had that unmentionable womb, that spongy pool, that time machine with a curse, dam for an ongoing river of blood whose rhythm seemed to obey some private compact with the moon. How this womb, unaccountable liaison with the beyond, disrupted every attempt at uniform behavior!

Did women get into automobile accidents? Count on it, more than half their accidents came on a particular week of the month—just before and during menstruation was the time of that week. So, too, were almost half of the female admissions to mental hospitals in that week, and more than half of their attempted suicides, half the crimes committed by women prisoners. . . .

Norman Mailer, *The Prisoner of Sex*

7. Discern and describe the flaws in the following arguments.

a. You're stupid! That's why I'm right.

b. In 1971, Paul McCartney announced that he was no longer associated with the Beatles. When he decided to destroy the association, McCartney gave no convincing reasons.

c. When Luke hit the first pitch of the game into the left-field stands, it was obvious that Mitchell could no longer pitch.

d. When we consider the question of aid to underdeveloped nations, we should always consider first that we, too, are an underdeveloped nation.

e. Since democracy died in France with the elevation of De Gaulle, one can no longer go to the French for lessons in the democratic process.

f. No one who dresses like that could possibly know Mozart from Montovani.

g. Warmongers who masquerade as friends of prisoners of war attempt to deceive the gullible.

h. Everybody who voted for Wallace was a racist.

8. Take a subject in which you have some interest. Meteorology, for instance. Set up an argumentative thesis for a paper, like, "Long range weather forecasts are futile." Collect notes for arguments. Then take the opposite tack, and try to establish argu-

ments against your original position, like "Long range weather forecasts are useful."

9. Make up examples of each of the fallacies listed in this chapter.

10. In books or magazines, find a passage of description, another of narrative, and a third of dialogue. Analyze the authors' use of these devices.

11. Looking at Jennifer Case's essay, "The Protector Unprotected," answer the following questions:

a. Does she beg the question at any point?

h. Might you have organized the material differently? Make alternative suggestions.

c. Does she use clichés? Are the sentences varied enough? Are the paragraphs well-constructed?

d. Do you find any ambiguity of language in this paper? Does information seem to be lacking in some places?

e. Are there errors in logic in this paper?

f. Is the footnoting consistent? Is everything footnoted that ought to be?

g. Is the bibliography consistent? Is everything listed that ought to be?

h. Can you see when the author has omitted connectives and transitions she might have been expected to supply? Are the omissions stylish? Are they obscure?

i. Are some details not sufficiently integrated into the whole?

j. What fundamental attitude toward the humpback whale supplies the structure of this paper?

k. Is this paper constructed more upon intellectual or emotional premises?

12. Take notes on a poem or a story and arrange them as you would if you were going to write a paper. Use these notes as a basis for class discussion.

GLOSSARY

The entries are of four kinds:

1. Rules of grammar, obligatory and optional. For instance, see *Agreement*.
2. Conventions of spelling, punctuation, and manuscript form. Some conventions promote clarity, like most uses of the comma; others are simply traditional, like most spelling.
3. Words frequently misused—clichés, commonly confused pairs of words, and words or phrases that should be avoided.
4. Grammatical and rhetorical terms, and the names of figures of speech. These appear often in the discussion of writing.

A, an

See *Article*.

Abbreviation

For the use of abbreviations in *Footnotes* and *Bibliography*, see those entries in this glossary.

In formal writing, we abbreviate only some words that go with names, like: Mr., Mrs., Ms., Dr., St. (for Saint, not street), Jr., Sr.; degrees, like Ph.D. or M.A.; and indications of era or time like A.D., B.C., A.M. and P.M. (We use the latter initials only with actual time indicated; we speak of "4 P.M.," not "it was the P.M.") We do not abbreviate Monday or August or street or road or volume or chemistry, in ordinary writing.

Some writers use no. as an abbreviation for number, but it looks out of place in formal prose. So does USA instead of "the United States," and "Penna." or "Pa." instead of Pennsylvania, "lb." instead of pound, and "oz." instead of ounce.

Some institutions are so commonly called by their initials that it is overly formal to spell them out. "Federal Bureau of Investigation" seems a pompous way to talk about the FBI. On the other hand, consider your audience; many people will need to be told that SEATO is the South-East Asia Treaty Organization.

In conjunction with a figure, mph and rpm are used in formal writing. We write of "50 mph" and "1,000 rpms." But if we write without figures, we spell them out. "It is difficult to assess the speed of a space capsule, when it is told in miles per hour."

Titles like Governor can be spelled out or shortened. Frequently, we shorten it when we give a whole name—"Gov. Nelson Rockefeller" and spell it out with a last name alone, "Governor Rockefeller." The abbreviation is not appropriate to the most formal prose.

Absolute element

An absolute element is a word or a group of words which is grammatically independent of the rest of the sentence, and which is not joined to it by a relative pronoun or a conjunction.

> **Heavens,** the gorilla, **I swear** is chasing her!
> **Come hell or high water,** I'll get to Dallas by Thursday.

Abstract, abstraction

An abstraction is a noun referring to the idea or quality of a thing, and not to a thing itself: *redness, courage.*

We use the word "abstract" relatively, referring to more general and less particular words. "Enclosure" is more general, say, than "room" or "cage" or "zoo."

For remarks on abstractions and prose style, see pages 55–56 and 254–255.

Accept, except

These words sound alike but mean different things. "Accept" means to receive something voluntarily.

I **accept** the compliment.

"Except" as a verb means to exclude.

I **excepted** Jones from the group I wished to congratulate.

Acronym

An acronym is an abbreviation, pronounced as a word, which is composed of the first letters of the words in the title or phrase abbreviated.

SAC (Strategic Air Command)
snafu (situation normal, all fouled up)

Active voice

Verbs are in the active voice when the subject of the sentence does the action the verb describes.

Bob **hit** the spider.

When the subject is acted upon, we do not have the active voice.

The spider **was hit** by Bob. (See *Passive voice*)

Adjective

Adjectives describe or limit a noun or a noun-substitute. These adjectives describe:

green onions
happiest year
The man was **old**.

These adjectives limit in a variety of ways:

indefinite:

Some men walked in the road.

demonstrative:

Those men walked in the road.

possessive:

Their men walked in the road.

numerical:

Twelve men walked in the road.

interrogative:

> **Which** men walked in the road?

relative:

> The men **who** walked in the road kept coming onward.

Nouns can be used as adjectives:

> **university** professor

For the formation of comparatives, see *Comparison of adjectives and adverbs.*

For a stylistic approach to adjectives, see pages 63–73.

Adjective clause

An adjective clause is a dependent clause used as an adjective.

> The man **who is purple** will stand out in a crowd.

Adjectives frequently misused

Try to avoid the adjective used vaguely. These words once meant specific things. "Terror" once inhabited "terrific"; now it can mean "unusually pleasant."

> What a **terrific** summer day!

Some other adjectives frequently used as vague praise, vague blame, or vague intensives:

terrible	nice	cute
funny	unique	wonderful
awful	interesting	incredible

> That **terrible** man with the **cute** name was **awful** to the **nice** girl.

Adverb

Adverbs describe or limit any words except nouns and pronouns. Adverbs work with verbs, adjectives, other adverbs, verbals, and entire clauses.

Adverbs commonly show degree:

> **extremely** hungry,

or manner:

> ran **slowly**,

or place:

> **hurried** here,

or time:

> she **then** left,

For stylistic advice on the adverb, see pages 63–73.

Adverb clause

An adverb clause is a dependent clause used as an adverb.

I'll be gone **before she starts spraying**.

The adverb clause, "before she starts spraying," modifies the verb "will be gone."

Adverbs frequently misused

Most of the adjectives frequently misused become misused adverbs, with a -ly added. "Terrible" becomes "terribly," as in "terribly comfortable." Strictly adverbial adjectives are misused also:

terrifically	actually	wonderfully	literally
certainly	very	rather	hopefully
absolutely	virtually	practically	

It **certainly** was a **very** hot day and I was **practically** done at the **absolutely** last minute when **actually** a **rather** large man **virtually** beheaded me.

Advice, advise

The first word is a noun; the second, a verb.

I was **advised** to ignore your **advice**.

Affect, effect

The two words are commonly confused. These examples illustrate proper uses of them:

Bob **affected** (influenced) the writing of Wright.

Sarah **affected** (assumed) the manner of a Greek tragedian.

The harder spray was **effected** (brought about) by an adjustment of the hose's nozzle.

The **effect** (result) of the new style was unpleasant.

Agreement

The formal correspondence of one word with another. This correspondence indicates singular or plural number; first, second, or third person; and masculine, feminine, or neuter gender.

He is so evil.

They are so evil.

Tom took **his** crocodile down to the river.

Tom and Maria took **their** crocodiles down to the river.

The car and **its** trailer rounded the corner.

Agree to, agree with

One "agrees to" a proposal or an action, one "agrees with" a person.

All ready, already

> The words differ in meaning. To say that someone is "all ready" is to say that he is prepared; the word "already" means "beforehand in time," as in "He was already there."

All right, alright

> "All right" is the correct form. "Alright" means the same thing, but is a recent creation based on the old word "already." In formal writing, avoid "alright."

Although, though

> "Although" is preferable in formal writing.

Altogether, all together

> The two do not have the same meanings.
>
> > Xavier, Abby, Frank, and Al were **all together** at the table.
> > Guy Woodhouse was **altogether** (wholly) disgusting.

Ambiguity

> Writing is ambiguous when it has more than one possible meaning or interpretation.

Amid, amidst

> Avoid these words, which are not common to the American language, and which sound stuffy and bookish.

Among, amongst

> "Among" is preferable. "Amongst" is bookish.

Among, between

> Use "between" when you are dealing with two things, "among" for more than two.
>
> > **Between** you and me . . .
> > **Among** the three of us . . .

Amoral, immoral, unmoral

> "Amoral" means outside morality.
>
> > Beauty is **amoral**.
>
> "Immoral" is contrary to codes of morality.
>
> > Benedict Arnold was **immoral**.

"Unmoral" is a near-synonym for "amoral," and is less frequently used. "Amoral" is often used when the assertion is contentious, "unmoral" when the statement is merely factual.

> Dogs and cats are **unmoral**.

It would sound pretentious or silly to accuse dogs and cats of being amoral.

Amount, number

"Amount" refers to a quantity of things viewed as a whole, or to the quantity of one item; "number" describes the separate units of a group.

> The **amount** of money in his bank account was staggering.
> The **number** of dollar bills on the floor was small.
> He took out a large **amount** of salt a **number** of times.

Analogy

An analogy is an extended comparison, used for illustration and argument. For examples and stylistic uses, see pages 80–82.

And/or

This legalism frequently occurs in nonlegal prose where "or" would do just as well.

> Cooking with pots **and/or** skillets requires nothing more than a hotplate.

Omit the unnecessary word.

Antecedent

An antecedent is a word or group of words to which a pronoun refers.

> As **K.B.C.** and **Q.R.V.** ran in, **they** dropped the gas pellets.

"K.B.C." and "Q.R.V." are the antecedents of the personal pronoun "they."

Antonym

An antonym means the opposite of another word. "Bad" is the antonym of "good."

As there are no exact synonyms, so we must not expect antonyms to be precisely opposite.

Any, any other

Be careful to use these words properly. If you say "*King Lear* is more moving than *any other* play in the English language" you are probably saying what you intend. If you say, however, that "*King Lear* is more moving than *any* play in the English language" you imply that *Lear* is not in English—or that *Lear* is better than itself, which would be nonsensical. If you say that "Sophia is sexier than *any* woman in Italy" you imply that she is not in Italy.

Anybody, anyone

The words are singular, not plural. They take singular pronouns, like *Every, Everyone, Everybody.*

> **Everyone** charges **his** meal at Alice's.

is formally correct, and not

> **Everyone** charges **their** meal at Alice's.

But an exception to this rule could make the second example the preferable form of the sentence. When a pronoun has "anybody" (etc.) as an antecedent, we may wish to use forms of the plural "they" in order to avoid deciding between "he" and "she," because "they" does not indicate gender.

> Did **anybody** call? What did **they** say?

Apostrophe

We use the apostrophe to show the possessive:

> The bag was Sara**'s**.
> It was the weather**'s** fault.

to show that we have left out part of a word:

> It**'s** a big world.
> (for It [i]s . . .)
> He doesn**'t** . . .
> (for He does n[o]t . . .)
> Ten o**'c**lock
> (for o[f the] clock)

or a number

> the **'73** model
> (for [19]73)

or to form the plurals of typographic symbols, words referred to as words, letters, and figures:

> The 7**'s** on the new office typewriter are black as e**'s**, 8**'s** are unreadable, and half the time simple the**'s** are obscure.

Notice that an apostrophe does not form part of the possessive of a pronoun.

> **Her** book.
> The book was **hers**.

When we find an apostrophe with a pronoun, part of a word has been omitted.

> **He'd** have been here by now.
> **She'll** be here.
> **It's** too late.

Notice especially that "it's" means "it is," and "its" is possessive. Never write

> **Its** too late.

or

> The dog scratched **it's** fleas.

Appositive

An appositive is a noun, or a noun substitute, which is placed next to another noun, and which explains or defines it.

> Peter, the **flying dwarf**, escorted Tarquina, his **good fairy**.

"Flying dwarf" is the appositive of "Peter," and "good fairy" is the appositive of "Tarquina."

Article

The definite article is *the*, the indefinite *a* or *an*. They are adjectives, always indicating that a noun or a noun substitute will follow.

"The" is the definite article, naming an individual; "the" table, "the" abstraction. "A" and "an" are indefinite articles, naming the member of a class: "a" table, "an" abstraction. The difference in meaning is small but indispensable.

The article "a" is used before words beginning with a consonant sound (even if the letter is a vowel): "a train," "a unit." "An" is used before words beginning with a vowel sound: "an interesting idea," "an herb."

As, like

In formal writing, we avoid using "like" as a conjunction. We use "as" instead. Instead of saying,

> I write **like** I talk.

we say

> I write **as** I talk.

At

Avoid the redundancy of "Where are you at?" "Where" means "at which place."

Auxiliaries

Auxiliaries in verb phrases indicate distinctions in tense and person. Common auxiliaries are: will, would, shall, should, be, have, do, can, could, may, might, and must.

> We **are** eating the chocolate.
> You **would have** done the same.

Balanced sentences

See pages 113–120 for a discussion of balance, and of parallelism.

Beside, besides

Each word has several meanings of its own.

> She stood **beside** (by the side of) the bureau.
> Matt was **beside** himself (almost overwhelmed) with anger.
> It's **beside** (not connected with) the point.
> No one was awake **besides** (other than) him.
> **Besides** (furthermore), it's in questionable taste.

Between

See *Among, between.*

Bibliography

A bibliography is a list of books or other printed sources that the writer has consulted in order to write a paper. Research papers depend especially on outside resources, but even an argument or a book review frequently takes the writer to the library. See the bibliography on pages 231–232, at the end of "The Protector Unprotected." At the end of any paper for which you have done any reading, list your sources alphabetically by author. If you quote or paraphrase anything without naming your source, you are plagiarizing. Bibliography and footnotes are your acknowledgment of indebtedness, your statement of research done, and your contract of honesty.

For a thorough summary of the manners of a bibliography, consult the *MLA Style Sheet*, Second Edition. Here is a brief outline.

Underline the titles of books, and enclose the titles of articles from newspapers and magazines in quotation marks. Include page numbers when you refer to periodicals, but omit them when you list a book. List publishers of books, cities of publication, number of edition when there is one, and date of publication. When you refer to a magazine, include the date and volume number, and underline the name of the magazine. When an article or book is anonymous, list it alphabetically by title, using the first word that is not "a," "an," or "the." Here are some of the possible varieties of bibliographical entry; notice punctuation.

A periodical article with an author:

> Mumford, Lewis. "The Cult of Anti-Life." *The Virginia Quarterly Review*, Vol. 46, no. 2 (Spring, 1970), 198–206.

An anonymous article from a periodical:

> "Freud on Death." *Time*, Vol. 100, no. 3, July 17, 1972, p. 33.

A book with one author:

> Graves, Robert. *Wife to Mr. Milton*. New York: Creative Age Press, 1944.

A book with more than one author:

> Cordell, Richard A., and Lowell Matson. *The Off-Broadway Theatre*. New York: Random House, 1959.

An edited book:

> *Page 2*. Edited by Francis Brown. New York: Holt, Rinehart & Winston, 1967.

An article from an edited book:

> Vonnegut, Kurt, Jr. "Science Fiction." *Page 2*. Edited by Francis Brown. New York: Holt, Rinehart & Winston, 1967.

Remember to list the edition of the book consulted, and if the book is in several volumes, give the number of volumes.

Big words

Avoid the big word where the little word will do. Never say "domicile" where you could say "house." Never say "individual" where you could say "person." Never say "utilize" where you could say "use." See *Genteel words* and *-ize endings*.

Bracket

Brackets are useful in prose especially under three circumstances, all connected with quotations. We use them when we add to a quotation material which was not in the original but which is needed for clarity. Sometimes a bracketed word supplies the antecedent to a pronoun.

> He [**O'Toole**] smashed his fist through the window of the bar.

And it can supply other information lacking in the quotation but available in the context from which the quotation comes.

> "It was in mid-June [**1972**] that the storm began."

Sometimes, in quoting the spoken word, we use brackets to enclose an indication of action, like a stage direction.

> "... and, finally, I want to ask you willingly and cheerfully to share the huge burden of responsibility which the age has thrust upon us all." [**Boos**.]

Sometimes we use brackets to correct a quotation:

> "It all happened in the early hours of September 20th [**actually September 21**] when the sun began [**to**] rise over the boardwalk."

Can, may

Both words express possibility, but can (could) express physical possibility.

> He **can** go to market because he has the car.
> She **could** eat the potato salad but she doesn't want to.

May (or might) implies that something is a chance, and often implies volition:

> He **may** go to Alaska (or he may not).
> She **might** be the last of the clan (or she might not).

Often we can hesitate between the two, and choose the one over the other for the precise shade of meaning. "He *could* take the exam" and "He *might* take the exam" offer different possibilities.

In conversation, and in the most informal writing, "may" tends to disappear in favor of "can," and thus a distinction disappears, which is a loss. Instead of saying, "She may read Shakespeare, or Julia Child, or *Young Lust*," we substitute the wordier, "She can read Shakespeare, or Julia Child, or *Young Lust*, depending on what she feels like." The final clause supplies the chanciness and the volition implied in "may."

In asking or granting permission, genteel prose uses "may."

> **May** I enter?
> Randolph, you **may** not.

But "may" in this usage almost invariably sounds like an effort to be refined.

Cannot, can not

These arrangements are equally acceptable. "Can not" looks more formal.

Can't hardly

Because "hardly," as Bergen Evans says, "has the force of a negation," "can't hardly" functions as a double negative, or at least as an ambiguity. Does "I can't hardly hear you" mean "I can't hear you" or "I can hear you well" or "I can hardly hear you?" Logically, the double negative should make it mean the second, but it means the last. So we should save a word, and increase the efficiency of our language, by saying simply, "I can hardly hear you." The same advice applies to "can't scarcely."

Capital letters

Capitalize people's names, the names of cities and countries, titles of people, books, plays, names of religious or national groups, languages, days of the week, the months, holidays, organizations and their abbreviations, names of events in history and important documents, and names of specific structures like buildings and airplanes and ships. For example:

> John Doe
> Great Britain
> Berlin
> Mayor John Lindsay
> *Moby-Dick*
> *The Importance of Being Earnest*
> Methodist
> Polish or European or Bostonian
> Monday
> June
> Memorial Day
> General Motors
> G.M.
> Marathon Oil Company
> Declaration of Independence
> Empire State Building
> the Winnie Mae
> the *Titanic*

Do not capitalize the seasons, the names of college classes (freshman, senior), or general groups like "the lower classes" or "the jet set."

Adjectives are capitalized when they derive from proper nouns and still refer to them, like "Shakespearean." Other nouns or adjectives, which derive from names but no longer refer to the person himself, lose their capitals: boycott, quisling.

The title that is capitalized before the proper noun—Mayor Hermann Garsich—loses its capital when it is used outside of its titling function, as a descriptive word placed after the proper noun—Hermann Garsich, mayor of our town.

Sections of a country may take capitals—the West, the South—but the same words take the lower case when they are directions. "Go west, young man."

Sentences begin with capitals.

Case

See *Inflection*.

Circumlocution

Circumlocution is taking the long way to say something, using clichés, verbs combined with other parts of speech instead of simple verbs, and filler words and phrases. In

> **Notwithstanding the case of** the seamstress, it is **going to be** obvious that **in general, in a manner of speaking, we do well to remember the observation that a man who** is always in a hurry will lose **something or other in the long run.**

the circumlocution is general, and phrases typical in circumlocution are in boldface. Notice that the last seventeen words might be rendered

> Haste makes waste.

Cite, sight, site

"Cite" means to quote or to refer to.

> They **cited** the constructive things they'd done.

A "sight" is a view;

> a moving **sight**

or vision itself.

A "site" is a location:

> a building **site**.

Clause

A clause is part of a sentence with a subject and a predicate. It may be principal (or main or independent) or it may be subordinate (dependent on a whole clause).

> The year ended and the year began.

In this sentence, two whole clauses are made into a compound sentence by "and."

> The year ended **when it had just begun**.

In this sentence, the boldface clause is subordinate or dependent.

Collective noun

See *Noun*.

Colon

Colons direct our attention to what comes after them. Usually, they follow an introductory statement that leads us to expect a follow-up, though sometimes the introduction is implicit, or the colon itself reveals that the clause preceding it was introductory. Here are some explicit introductions:

To a long quotation, either included in the text in quotation marks, or indented without quotation marks:

> E. B. White wrote of his old Professor: "In the days when I was sitting in his class he omitted so many needless words, and omitted them so forcibly and with such eagerness and obvious relish, that. . . ."

To a list:

> He narrowed his choices to three: Mary, Elizabeth, or Karen.

Less elegantly, to an appositive at the end of a sentence:

> He narrowed the field until he arrived at one name: Zona.

A comma, here, would be just as correct, and perhaps less prone to melodrama.

Sometimes a colon occurs between two main clauses, like a semicolon; it implies that the second clause is a result of the first:

> The hands of the clock seemed never to move: she had never been late before.

Here the colon adds a meaning that the semicolon would lack. The semicolon would present the two statements as closely connected, but without the implication that the second clause derived from the first.

Comma

Commas are the most common mark of punctuation, and the most commonly misused. Subsequent entries in this glossary list the main functions of the comma—to separate items in a series; to separate main clauses with some connectives; to set off asides and parenthetical expressions, including quotations; to set off introductory phrases; and to avoid ambiguity. Then an entry lists a few common errors in the overuse of commas.

Most of the commas we use are required by the conventions of prose, for the sake of clarity. They separate parts of sentences that we need to perceive separately for understanding. The comma indicates a short pause in speaking, or, in parenthetical expressions, a change in pitch. At other times we use or omit commas according to our sense of rhythm and style. Examples, here and on pages 98–100, will show obligatory commas and optional ones.

Comma to avoid ambiguity

Sometimes we need a comma to indicate a pause which the voice would make, in speech, for clarity, but which is not otherwise obligatory.

> Outside the fields spread to the river.

is more clear with a pause:

> Outside, the fields spread to the river.

To find such potential ambiguities in your prose, sometimes it is helpful to say it aloud, pronouncing it as it is written—which means pausing when there is a comma, and *not* pausing when there is *not* a comma.

Comma fault

A comma fault (sometimes called a comma splice) occurs when the writer carelessly separates two complete sentences with a comma instead of using a period and a capital letter, making two sentences; or a semicolon.

> The woman leaped from the side of the bread truck, the man driving it put on the brakes and skidded to a stop.

could be either

> The woman leaped from the side of the bread truck. The man driving it put on the brakes and skidded to a stop.

or

> The woman leaped from the side of the bread truck; the man driving it put on the brakes and skidded to a stop.

Exceptions to this rule occur when we run short sentences together. See pages 99–100.

Commas separating items in a series

Use commas to separate words in a series,

> The dress was black, green, and purple.

to separate phrases in a series,

> She wore it to parties, in the bathtub, and at work.

and to separate subordinate clauses in a series,

> She explained that it was warm, that it needed washing, that it was comfortable, and that it was in good taste.

or whole clauses in a series,

> She shook her head, she stood up, and she left the room.

When we use "and" with each item of a series, we do not use the comma.

He touched first and second and third.

It is permissible to omit the comma before the "and," in a series of words or short phrases.

He touched first, second and third.

but it can sometimes create an ambiguity, as if the baserunner were able to straddle, and touch second and third at the same time.

Commas separating whole clauses

In the compound sentence, where two or more whole clauses are connected by *and, or, nor, for,* or *but,* use a comma immediately preceding the connective.

The faculty senate debated for three hours, but no one could resolve the issue of the blind pig.

When the main clauses are short, the comma is optional. The pause is shorter, and therefore the rhythm different. We can decide whether we prefer

The wine was old, and we drank it slowly.

or

The wine was old and we drank it slowly.

On the other hand, we have also the option to use the semicolon instead of the comma. It creates a longer pause. Sometimes we want this extra pause when the main clauses are especially long, when they themselves contain commas, or when we make strong contrast between the two parts of the sentence.

The cliff was red, solid, and perpendicular; and the car disappeared into the face of it.

Quotations are common parenthetical elements. So are phrases and words like "of course," "naturally," and "heavens to Betsy." When asides or parenthetical expressions appear at the beginning of sentences, place a comma after them. When they appear at the end of sentences, put a comma just before them:

God knows, the situation is desperate.
The situation is desperate, God knows.
Fellow Americans, I speak to you as a concerned citizen.
I am a representative of the people, of course.

Omitting commas in these examples would make the sentence ambiguous or hard to read.

God knows the situation is desperate.

Does He?

There are times when the commas can be omitted with *no* awkwardness or confusion, and the omission becomes optional. Short sentences in which word order precludes ambiguity give us this option.

> The situation was of course desperate.

On occasion one can take stylistic advantage of the rhythmic speed offered by this option.

Use a comma before and after parenthetical expressions within a sentence:

> I think you're tired, Fred, and hungry.
>
> The student worked, in a manner of speaking, for three whole days.
>
> I heard him calling, "There's my bubble gum," to the audience.

Notice that the final comma in a quoted parenthesis falls inside the final quotation mark.

A common form of the parenthesis, requiring commas, is the nonrestrictive clause. It is useful to know the difference between a restrictive and a nonrestrictive clause. A restrictive clause describes or limits its subject:

> The knight who was dressed in black won all the events in the tourney.

Here, "who was dressed in black" defines the knight, as if we were pointing a finger. Also, see:

> The building that overlooked the river was the most popular of all.

In such restrictive clauses as these, no comma separates the clause from the rest of the sentence.

Nonrestrictive clauses, on the other hand, do not define; they could become separate sentences or coordinate clauses, and unless they are very short, they take commas at both ends. It is possible to use both clauses above in sentences in which they become nonrestrictive:

> Sir Galahad, who was dressed in black, won all the events in the tourney.

This sentence, as opposed to the restrictive example above, could be broken into two sentences with no violence done to the meaning:

> Sir Galahad was dressed in black. He won all the events in the tourney.

Or, using the clause from the other example, we could have the sentence:

> The house, which overlooked the river, was built in 1972.

We could rewrite it:

> His house overlooked the river. It was built in 1972.

Nonrestrictive clauses take commas. If the clause is short, and there is no possible ambiguity, we may on occasion omit commas when it suits our style. We could have:

> A noodle, which was limp and cold, hung from the doorknob.

or:

> A noodle which was limp and cold hung from the doorknob.

If you omit commas around a nonrestrictive clause, you risk suggesting that it is restrictive or defining—that its meaning differs from your intention.

> The chess player, who was seventeen, beat me at ping pong.

Here, the nonrestrictive clause with commas isolates the clause as nonrestrictive, and identifies it as a casual input of information. But if I write it:

> The chess player who was seventeen beat me at ping pong.

the clause looks restrictive or defining, *suggesting* that the chess player beat me because of his age. So be cautious; here is an example of the insides of commas.

Commas setting off introductory phrases

Adverb clauses, transitional phrases, and phrases introduced by verbals or prepositions, when they come at the beginning of the sentence, usually require a comma to set them off from the main clause. The following adverb clauses need a comma:

> If a dunce applies himself thoroughly, he can dream of becoming President.
> When I turned to the left at the end of the lane, I found the old house intact.

Omission of these commas would leave the sentence hopelessly awkward and confusing. If the order of clauses is reversed, a comma, though possible, is no longer necessary.

> A dunce can dream of becoming President if he applies himself thoroughly.
> I found the old house intact when I turned to the left at the end of the lane.

An introductory adverbial clause, if it is short, need not always carry a comma. A comma is optional in

> If I lead he will follow.

Introductory phrases of transition, like "on the other hand," are parenthetical and usually need a comma.

> On the other hand, sometimes they don't.
> In fact they are optional.
> In fact, they are optional.

The retention of the comma is appropriate in formal writing and is acceptable in all writing. Omission of the comma is rhythmically more colloquial. Interjections like "Oh," or "shucks," almost always take the comma. They are in effect parenthetical also.

> Gosh, that's not what you said the last time.

We use a comma frequently when the sentence begins with a long phrase governed by a preposition, or with any phrase that begins with a verbal.

> In the century after the Civil War, progress in Civil Rights was minuscule.
> Being tall, he was able to reach the highest shelf.

The comma is optional, and often omitted, when the introductory prepositional or verbal phrase is short.

> At twelve she was full-grown.
> Having won they adjourned to a saloon.

Commas: using too many

In many of our first drafts, we use too many commas, or put them where they do not belong. Beginning writers often feel that something is going wrong if they haven't used a comma lately, and so they shake commas over their prose like salt. Here are some sentences, taken from themes, which have commas they either don't need, or should not have:

> But, it was not too late.
> Clarke came by, later.
> When I left she, followed me.
> The dimensions were, approximately three by five.
> I quickly saw Ed, and Sara.
> He thought she was sickly, and studious.
> The old barn was painted, red.
> A runner, who likes to win, has to train, every day.
> The agency sold, life, fire, and theft, insurance.

Common nouns

See *Nouns.*

Comparison of adjectives and adverbs

The comparison of adjectives and adverbs indicates relative

degree. There are three degrees: positive, comparative, and superlative.

positive	*comparative*	*superlative*
good	better	best
obnoxious	more obnoxious	most obnoxious
quick	quicker	quickest
quickly	more quickly	most quickly

Comparisons

For a discussion of simile, metaphor, and analogy, see pages 78–82.

Complement

A complement is one or more words that completes the meaning of a verb, or an object. A subject complement:

Phyllis is a wicked **girl.**

The predicate noun—"girl"—completes the sense of "Phyllis," which it refers to. An object complement:

The dog chewed the **raw** bone.

"Raw" modifies and completes "bone."

Complement, compliment

A complement makes something whole or complete.

Work is the **complement** of play.

A compliment is praise.

I paid you a **compliment.**

There is also an archaic meaning, in which "compliments" means something like formal politeness, and which survives in the phrase, "compliments of the season."

Complex sentence

A complex sentence contains a main clause and a subordinate clause. Here the subordinate is a relative:

I whistled at the boy who hung from the cliff.

See pages 91, 94–96, 110–112.

Compound sentence

A compound sentence includes two or more main clauses and no subordinate clauses.

The moon rose at 10:35 P.M. and the stars appeared to recede into the darkness.

See pages 90–91, 98–101.

Compound-complex sentence

This sentence type combines, as you might expect, the complex and the compound sentence. It has two main clauses, and at least one subordinate clause.

> The snow stopped falling when the sun rose, but the temperature stayed below 10°.

See page 91.

Compound word

Compound words are two or more words commonly used together as a single word.

> brother-in-law
> blackbird
> wheelbarrow
> handwriting

See a dictionary for current spelling. In this glossary, see *Hyphen*.

Conjugation

See *Inflection*.

Conjunction

Conjunctions connect or coordinate (and, but, for, or, and occasionally yet or so), or they subordinate (after, because, while, when, where, since). With coordinate conjunctions be careful to preserve unity by keeping the coordinate phrases or clauses parallel (see pp. 113–119). With subordinate conjunctions, remain aware of the habits of complex sentences (pp. 91, 94–95, and 110–113).

Conjunctive adverb

A conjunctive adverb can be used to connect main clauses: then, besides, however, therefore, otherwise.

Consider . . . as

Writers frequently misuse the verb "consider" by adding an unnecessary preposition, "as." Say "She considered him handsome," not "She considered him as handsome." Another use of the verb takes "as" appropriately. In the example above, "consider" means "believe to be." In the example below, consider means "think about" or "talk about":

> She **considered** him **as** an administrator and as a scholar.

Consist in, consist of

"Consist of" refers to the parts that make a whole:

> The government **consists of** legislative, executive, and judicial divisions.

"Consist in" refers to inherent qualities:

> The value of democracy **consists in** the responsibility with which it endows the citizen.

Continual, continuous

The two words have slightly different meanings. "Continual" describes an action that is repeated frequently.

> He called her **continually** throughout the day.

"Continuous" describes an action done without stopping.

> The bleeding was **continuous** for three hours.

Contractions

Use an *Apostrophe* to indicate the omission of one or more letters in a phrase, commonly a combination of a pronoun and a verb. "I'm," "she's," "he's," "we've," "you've," "they're," etc.; "we'd," "you'd," "he'd," "she'd"; "he'll," "she'll," "who'll," "who's."

Three of these contractions become problems. "They're" sounds like "their" and "there," and we may spell one when we mean another. "Their out working" is as incorrect as "there work" and "working their." (Correct: "They're out working"; "their work"; "working there.")

"It's" always means "it is." It is not possessive, like "its shadow." Whenever you write or see the apostrophe with these letters—"it's" —remember that the "'s *must* stand for "is." Or memorize the phrase, "It's afraid of its shadow."

"Who's" is another common contraction and once again there is a confusion. "Whose" gets mixed up with "who's." Again, the "'s" means "is," and "who's" always stands for "who is," whereas "whose" is a possessive pronoun. "Who's drinking whose soup?"

Other common contractions involve the verb and the negative: "isn't," "aren't," "doesn't," "don't," "can't," "haven't," "won't."

Coordinates

"Coordinate" means equal in rank. Two infinitives are coordinate, for instance, or two main clauses, as in a compound sentence.

Could have, could of

> The phrase is "could have." "Could of" is a mistake.
> Don't say:
>
> > She **could of** been a great actress.
>
> but say
>
> > She **could have** been a great actress.

Counsel, council, consul

> "Counsel" is advice, or a lawyer, or someone acting as a lawyer.
> Though it would be a confusing sentence, one could say:
>
> > The court-appointed **counsel** gave his client **counsel.**
>
> A different spelling, with the same pronunciation, gives us the
> word "council," which is a legislative group.
>
> > Harris for City **Council**!
>
> A "consul" represents his government in another country where he
> keeps residence.
>
> > The vice-**consul** was out to lunch.

Cutting words from quotations

> See *Ellipses.*

Dash

> Use dashes with caution—but use them. Make them on your type-
> writer by putting two hyphens next to each other.
>   In the sentence above, the dash shows a hesitation in the voice,
> followed with a rush by something that seems almost an after-
> thought. Dashes are informal. For some careless writers, dashes
> become substitutes for all other forms of punctuation; they not
> only lose any special meaning dashes may contribute, they also
> rob other punctuation of its meaning. For instance:
>
> > Yet many people use them too often—they become substitutes
> > for all other forms of punctuation—and thus lose their special
> > meaning—at the same time they rob other punctuation of its
> > meaning—
>
> Two legitimate uses of the dash are the idiomatic implication
> of afterthought, as in the first sentence above, and the idiomatic
> parenthesis. Marks of parenthesis (   ) look more formal; dashes
> give a sense of speech. These two sentences illustrate a slight,
> characteristic difference:
>
> > The myth of connotative and denotative meanings was destroyed
> > by Carnap (the logician who taught at the University of Chi-
> > cago) some twenty-five years ago.

The myth of connotative and denotative meanings was destroyed by a logician and philosopher—I think it was Carnap—about twenty-five years ago.

Declension

See *Inflection.*

Deductive reasoning

This form of thinking is the application of a general truth to a specific instance. Thus, if it is true that going through a time-warp causes pain, we may deduce that if Quasimodo goes through a time-warp he will feel pain.

Demonstratives

Demonstratives are adjectives like "this," "that," "these," and "those," used to point the finger.

This is the man who took it; **that's** my basketball.

They can be pronouns, and should have clear antecedents.

You said you couldn't read. I could not believe **that**.

Different from, different than

"Different from" is preferable, especially in formal prose.

Direct address

A noun or pronoun used to direct a remark to a specific person.

I was thinking, **Ron**, that you'd like to go up in a balloon.

Irving, close that kangaroo.

Hey **you**!

Direct object

See *Object.*

Direct quotation

The exact words of a speaker or writer, included in a paragraph, are set off by quotation marks. Put a comma at the end of the quotation before the quotation mark, or a period if the quotation ends the sentence. If the quotation ends with a question mark or an exclamation point, these marks of punctuation take the place of the comma and occur inside the quotation marks.

Al asked Wayne, "Didn't you?"

On the other hand, sometimes we quote in order to exclaim about the quotation, or inquire about the quotation. In such a sentence, exclamation point or question mark occur after the quotation marks.

> What did he mean when he said, "Good morning"?
> She had the nerve to say "Hello"!

When we quote a passage longer than fifty words, in a research paper for instance, we can use a colon to introduce the quotation (see *Colon*) and detach the quotation from the text by indenting it. Ellipses can help you avoid long, detached quotations. (See *Ellipses.*)

See *Indirect quotation.*

Discreet, discrete

The two words have different meanings. "Discreet" means "prudent in one's conduct or speech."

> She would never reveal it; she was exceptionally **discreet.**

Discrete means "distinct" or "separate."

> The words are different; they have **discrete** meanings.

Disinterested, uninterested

These words are frequently confused. To be "uninterested" is to lack fascination about something, even to be bored by it.

> I tried to arouse his enthusiasm for a game of golf, but he was **uninterested** in such a pastime.

"Disinterested" is the condition of being impartial or neutral, or of having no stake in an issue. Frequently the word is used positively as a precondition for fairness, as in the phrase, "disinterested party."

> The judge declared his **disinterest** in the matter.

This judge is proclaiming his ability to judge the case fairly. If he had claimed to be "uninterested in the matter," he would have been rejecting the appeal.

Division of words

At the right-hand side of your manuscript page, in order to keep the margin reasonably consistent, you will need on occasion to break a word with a hyphen. (See *Hyphen.*) Dictionaries usually indicate the syllables that make up a word by placing a dot between them (com · pound · ed.). Hyphenate only at the syllable break. Write com-/pounded, never comp-/ounded.

When the syllable to be isolated is only one or two letters long, avoid division (a-long; man-y, compound-ed.)

Doesn't

See *Don't*.

Don't

Goes with "I," "you," "we," and "they." It doesn't go with "it," "he," or "she." It contracts "do not." It does not contract "does not"; "doesn't" does.

Double negative

A double negative occurs in a sentence that uses two negative terms when only one is needed.

> He **didn't** say **nothing**.
> You **shouldn't never** do that to a bird.

In earlier English such doubling was thought to give emphasis, as in "I never treacherously slew no man" (Bergen Evans' example). But today such double negatives are regarded as unacceptable and illogical. If I should *not* never-do something, then by implication I should (positively) do it sometime. See *Can't hardly*.

Doubt but

Omit "but." Also omit "but" in "help but." "They couldn't doubt but that the Racquet Club was best" becomes "They couldn't doubt that the Racquet Club was best." "They couldn't help but know the worst" becomes "They couldn't help knowing the worst." And always avoid "They couldn't *doubt but* what...."

Due to

Avoid using "due to" for "because of" in adverbial phrases. "She won the race due to her long legs" sounds unnatural. It is probably best to reserve the word for finance.

Each, every

"Each" is a pronoun:

> **Each** went his own way.

And an adjective:

> **Each** package of bubble gum has five pieces.

"Each" means the individual units of a conglomerate:

> **Each** of the Boy Scouts

but "every" means the conglomerate itself:

> **Every** Boy Scout

In the Boy Scout examples above, "each" is a pronoun, "every" an adjective.

When the adjective "each" modifies a singular noun, the following verb and pronouns are singular:

Each player lifts **his** bat.

When "each" modifies a plural noun or pronoun, and comes before the verb, the pronoun and verb are plural:

They **each go their** own way.

When "each" works as a pronoun, it is usually singular:

Each goes his own way.

There are exceptions. In the example just above, if the pronoun referred to men and women, we might have written:

Each go their own way.

When "each" refers to two or more singular words, or when a plural word comes between "each" and the verb, the number of the verb is optional. We may say:

Each of the players **is**

or

Each of the players **are**

We may say:

When **Mark and Linda** speak, **each** of them **says**

or

When **Mark and Linda** speak, **each** of them **say**

The negative of "each" is "neither." Do not write "each" with a negative:

Each did not speak

but write

Neither spoke.

Egoism, egotism

"Egoism" has the connotation of a philosophy, "egotism" of a neurosis. "Egoism" is the other side of "altruism," and is a belief in the value of self-interest. "Egotism" is the necessity to use the word "I" all the time. In the argot of the day, "egotism" is an ego-trip.

Either

"Either," like "each," can be pronoun or adjective.

Either Bob or Jane . . .

Either of the twins . . .

When "either" means more than one, it takes a plural verb.

Either of you are qualified.

When it means one or the other it takes the singular.

Either Rick or Chris is lying.

Negative statements, and the pronoun "you," make "either" take a plural verb, even if the sense is singular.

He did not report that **either** of them were qualified.

When **either** of you are finished, let me know.

"Either" takes "or" and does not take "nor." "Nor" belongs to "neither."

Elicit, illicit

"Elicit" means "to bring out."

We could **elicit** no further response from the members.

"Illicit" means "not permitted."

They were having an **illicit** love affair.

Ellipses

A line of three dots . . . indicates that you have omitted something from a quotation. Use four dots if the omission occurs at the end of a sentence: three to indicate the omission, a fourth for the period.

Ellipses are useful in research papers or arguments using sources. Much of a paragraph may be irrelevant to our point. To include the whole paragraph in our text would slow the pace of argument and violate the unity of what we are saying. Therefore we piece-cut the quotation, and make it blend smoothly with our essay. Instead of writing:

Marlowe was more direct than Shakespeare, and more vigorous. As Professor William Wanger puts it:

If the *Jew of Malta* is Marlowe's *Merchant of Venice*, it is at the same time better and worse than Shakespeare's famous comedy. The lesser-known play has fewer quotable passages, perhaps, and certainly fewer that are quoted; but we must acknowledge that Marlowe's play has more energy than Shakespeare's. What it lacks in finesse it makes up in vigor, and the character of the Jew is surely more complex, and more thoughtfully observed, than the character of the Merchant.

What Professor Wanger says of two plays, we can say of all. . . .

we can write:

Marlowe was more direct than Shakespeare and more vigorous. Comparing comedies by the two men, Professor William

> Wanger found Marlowe "better and worse than Shake-
> speare . . . ," lacking "in finesse" but superior in "vigor" and
> "energy." He found Marlowe's characterization, in one com-
> parison, "more complex, and more thoughtfully observed"
> than Shakespeare's.

When we are obviously making excerpts, as with single words like "energy" and detached phrases like the last quotation, we do not need ellipses, because ellipses provide information: if we already know that quotations are excerpted, we do not need rows of dots to tell us so. But after "Shakespeare," earlier in the paragraph, when we cut between a noun and an apostrophe indicating possession, we need the ellipses.

One of the advantages of piece-cutting is visual. A paper is more attractive if it includes quotations in the body of the paragraph, rather than indenting whole paragraphs of quotation. Yet if we quote more than fifty words, we should detach them from the text. The solution is to build the quotations into the body of our paragraph.

Be careful not to use ellipses dishonestly. Compilers of advertisements for plays are skillful at dishonest ellipses. The critic wrote:

> This is a dishonest excuse for a play. There is nothing of value
> in this trash. We reach the heights of absurdity when Angelo
> Bridillo (played by someone who calls himself Alex Lucas,
> with a brilliant stupidity) attempts to rise from his wheel
> chair to provide a first act curtain. He falls, and so does the
> curtain. It would have been best if neither had risen again.
>
> Herman Hildbroner, *Lincoln Blade*

The public relations man gets busy with his ellipses, and the ad reads:

> This . . . play . . . is . . . of value . . . the heights . . . Alex Lucas
> . . . brilliant . . . best . . .
>
> Herman Hildbroner, *Lincoln Blade*

Enormity, enormousness

An "enormity" is a moral outrage. "Enormousness" is hugeness.

Etc.

This "and so forth," from the Latin et cetera, is out of place in formal prose. In whatever prose, it often trails off the end of a sentence into vagueness, and avoids extending the brain. Avoid it in formal prose. Scrutinize the use of it in any context.

Etymology

Etymology is the study of the origins and histories of words.

Euphemism

Euphemisms are fancy or abstract substitutes for plain words. We use them for social elevation, as when an undertaker becomes a mortician, or to avoid facing something frightening, as when we say that someone passed away, instead of saying that he died. See pages 32–34.

Everybody, everyone

"Everybody" and "everyone" take a singular verb.

Everybody goes to church.

The words can take a singular pronoun, especially in a formal context:

Everyone finds **his** seat and waits for the minister.

Or a plural pronoun, especially when it refers to men and women:

Everybody waited until **they** caught **their** breath.

Exclamation point

Use exclamation points only for a proper exclamation:

Oh! Zap!

or for a remark almost shouted:

It's Godzilla!

Avoid using them frequently, or they diminish in effect, like a vague intensifier.

I could not make out the face! Then I saw. It was Algernon!

Famous, notorious

To be "famous" is to be well known or celebrated. To be "notorious" is to be well known for something shady.

He was a **famous** movie star, musician, and second baseman.
He was a **notorious** pirate, extortionist, and linguist.

Farther, further

As "distance to go" the two are interchangeable. Where "further" means "more," "farther" is not a possible alternative.

We have no **further** use of him.

Few

See *Less*.

Figure

See *Numeral*.

Finite verb

A finite verb is complete, a predicate in itself.

The home **collapsed**.

Gerunds, infinitives, and participles are not finite verbs but *Verbals*.

Footnote

Footnotes name the source of a quotation in the text, or the source of information used, or on occasion qualify or elaborate a portion of the text. The last use is the least common; it can detract from the flow of a text; we use it only when some information is half-pertinent.

Footnote what you must, but omit footnotes if you feel that the material you are using is obvious. Telling us that whales are mammals, you need not footnote the *Encyclopaedia Britannica;* the information is readily available.

Footnote at the bottom of each page, rather than in a clump at the end, for the reader's convenience. To save the proper space for the appropriate footnotes takes planning ahead when you are typing. When you start a new page, in typing up your draft, estimate how many lines of manuscript you will cover, and how much space the footnotes to those lines will occupy.

For meticulous advice in footnoting, covering a multitude of contingencies, consult *The MLA Style Sheet,* second edition.

Single-space your footnotes at the bottom of each page. If there is more than one footnote, double-space between them.

Number footnotes consecutively throughout the paper; do not start each page with 1.

The number for the footnote is placed at the end of the material footnoted, and slightly above the line of the text, thus.[5]

If the name of the book or the author is given in the text, do not repeat the information in the footnote.

You can abbreviate long titles of periodicals and supply the full name in the bibliography. *The Review of Analytic Psychology* can be *RAP* in a footnote.

Here are some sample footnotes, followed by a list of shortcuts and abbreviations frequently used in footnoting.

Articles from periodicals:

[1]Leslie Raddatz, "Actress-Equestrienne with a Problem," *TV Guide,* vol. 20, no. 30 (1972), 16.

[2]Audrey F. Borenstein, "Reflections on Woman's Identity," *The Georgia Review*, vol. XXVI, no. 2 (1972), 156–158.

When a periodical has no volume number, or issue number, give the exact date and indicate the page number as p., or pp. if you refer to more than one page.

Books with one author:

[3]Germaine Greer, *The Female Eunuch* (New York: McGraw-Hill, 1971), p. 57.

It is possible to omit the publisher's name and just give the city of publication. If no author is named, begin the footnote with the book title and proceed as above. If no date is given, write "n.d." where you would have put the date. With no publisher listed, write "n.p."

Books with two or three authors:

[4]Frederick J. Hoffman, Charles Allen, and Carolyn F. Ulrich, *The Little Magazine* (Princeton: Princeton University Press, 1946), pp. 64–66.

When a book has more than three authors, use the first name and et al., which means "and others" in Latin. Or use "and others."

Books with editor:

[5]*Poets on Street Corners*, ed. Olga Carlisle (and so on).

Books with translator:

[6]Chuang T'zu, *Basic Writings*, tr. Burton Watson (New York and London: Columbia University Press, 1964), p. 33.

Encyclopedia article:

[7]"Nicaraguan Relations," *Encyclopedia of American History*, Updated and Revised Edition, 1965, p. 323.

Essay in a collection:

[8]Ned Rorem, "The Music of the Beatles," in Jonathan Eisen, ed., *The Age of Rock* (New York: Random House, 1969), p. 150.

Interview:

[9]Russell Fraser, personal interview on teaching Shakespeare, Nantucket, Mass., July 30, 1972.

Newspaper item:

[10]*The Ann Arbor News*, May 12, 1959, Section B, p. 1.

Quotation cited in a secondary source:

[11]Stanislaus Joyce, *My Brother's Keeper*, as quoted in Richard Ellmann, *James Joyce* (New York: Oxford University Press, 1959), p. 12.

Reviews:

> [12]A. Alvarez, rev. of *Delusions, Etc.* by John Berryman, *The New York Times Book Review*, June 25, 1972, p. 1.

In the last example we might have called the periodical *NYTBR* and referred the reader to the bibliography. Use initials, however, only if you footnote the periodical more than once.

Here are some short-cuts and abbreviations used in footnoting:
When you have been quoting from a book earlier in your paper, you need not repeat the whole citation of book and author after the first. If a footnote refers to the book cited in the footnote immediately previous, write:

> [2]Ibid. (in the same place), p. 20.

If you refer later in the paper to a book previously cited, and you refer to only one book by the author, you can repeat his name only:

> [3]Green, pp. 72–74.

Under the same circumstances, but with the author's name mentioned in the text, write:

> [4]*op. cit.* (in the work mentioned), p. 84.

Abbreviations frequently used and not previously explained include:
cf. (compare)
ch., chs. (chapters)
e.g. (for example)
ff. (the following pages or lines)
i.e. (that is)
il. (illustrated)
ll. (lines)
loc. cit. (in the place mentioned)

Notice that *loc. cit.* resembles *op. cit.* Usually it refers to a source further back in the text than *op. cit.* does.
ms., mss (manuscript)
n. (note)
pass. (see mentions further in text)
q.v. (see for confirmation)
rev. (revised)
v. (see)
viz. (namely)

Foreign words and phrases

Avoid them when you can. They look pretentious. In dialogue, they can be useful to characterize someone, as foreign or as pretentious. Occasionally nothing in English seems quite so apt as a foreign phrase. But look hard before you give up. If you must use one, italicize it by underlining it.

Foreword, forward

The two have different meanings. A "foreword" is a preface, the introductory statement at the beginning of a book. "Forward" is usually a direction. On occasion, "forward" means "bold" or "presumptuous."

She stuck her tongue out at him; she was very **forward.**

Gender

Gender is a grammatical indication of sex. English nouns lack gender except as their own sense indicates. That is, "sister" is feminine, "brother" masculine, and "sibling" can be either. Some pronouns have gender (he, she) and most do not (I, they, you, we). In some languages, all nouns are assigned a gender. In French, "grass" is feminine, and "time" is masculine. In English both are neuter.

Genteel words

Some words act as euphemisms by seeming socially preferable to plainer alternatives. People who use them seem to be *trying* to be genteel. Avoid them unless you are making a genuine distinction. For instance:

Genteel	*Ordinary*
perspire	sweat
wealthy	rich
home	house
luncheon	lunch

Gerund

See *Verbal.*

Go

We multiply this little word in our speech; it has small place in our writing. "I went down to get some wallpaper" is passable but wordy. In writing, it would be better to "choose" or "buy" the wallpaper.

Good, well

It is common and incorrect to use "good" as if it were an adverb.

He ran **good**.

When referring to an action "well" is the right word.

He ran **well**.

Be careful with the word "feels"; to say that a person "feels good" is to say that he is in a pleasant frame of mind; to say that a person "feels well" is to say either that he feels healthy or that his sense of touch is functioning efficiently.

Grammar

Grammar describes how words function in a language.

Guerrilla, gorilla

A guerrilla is an irregular soldier. A gorilla is an animal. "Guerrilla" is also used as an adjective, and has recently been used adjectivally to indicate activity in the service of revolution: guerrilla theater, guerrilla television.

Had ought

Avoid this combination. Instead of writing

We knew he **had ought** to come.

write

We knew he **ought** to come.

Hanged, hung

"Hanged" pertains to the execution of human beings, "hung" to the suspension of objects.

Sam Hall was **hanged** in October.

We **hung** the portraits in the hall.

He, him

See *Pronoun*.

Help but

See *Doubt but*.

Homonym

Homonyms are words that, although pronounced the same, are spelled differently and mean different things.

to, too, two	heir, air
through, threw	bare, bear
blew, blue	

Hopefully

Hopefully is an adverb frequently misused as a dangling modifier. We say

Hopefully, the plane will be on time.

when we do not mean to imply that the plane is full of hope. We could say

Hopefully, I will meet her at the gate.

We come to use "hopefully" as if it meant "I hope." The first example, above, means to say

I hope the plane will be on time.

Hyperbole

Hyperbole is extreme exaggeration to make a point.

That cat weighs a ton.

Use it with discretion.

Hyphen

We use hyphens to break a word at the right-hand margin. See *Division of words.*

We use the hyphen on occasion to join two adjectives, or words serving as adjectives, modifying a noun. They make a temporary compound word.

red-blond hair
mile-long avenue

Avoid the temptation to multiply hyphenated phrases, which can become a virulent form of adjectivitis.

The **purple-green cloud-forms sweep-crawl**

We use hyphens with some common temporary compounds. Before the two words "wheel" and "barrow" became the compound word "wheelbarrow," there may have been a stage at which men wrote "wheel-barrow." Consult your dictionary when you are in doubt. Hyphens in compounds are a matter of spelling.

We use hyphens in compound numbers from twenty-one through ninety-nine.

We hyphenate fractions used as adjectives and placed before the noun modified.

A **two-thirds** majority. . . .

but not otherwise

Three quarters of the population. . . .

We use the hyphen to avoid ambiguity. We must spell the word "re-creation" to avoid confusion with "recreation."

We use the hyphen with some prefixes and suffixes:

governor-elect
ex-wife
self-determined

We use the hyphen as a typographical device to indicate a manner of speaking, when we indicate that someone is spelling a word by writing it "w-o-r-d," or when we indicate a stammer, "w-w-word."

I, me

See *Pronoun.*

i.e.

i.e. abbreviates the Latin *id est*, or "that is." We use it sometimes to introduce an explanation or definition of a word or phrase.

She was nonessential, **i.e.,** they didn't need to employ her any more.

Usually, the expression seems overprecise, and too much like legal or scientific writing. The sentence above can omit the Latinism, and use instead a colon or a semicolon:

She was nonessential: they didn't need to employ her any more.

Immigrant, emigrant

An "immigrant" is someone who enters a country; an "emigrant" leaves one. Obviously our forefathers had to emigrate before they could immigrate.

Incredible, unbelievable

In theory, these words are synonymous. In practice, "unbelievable" holds up better.

The charges were **unbelievable**

states rather straightforwardly the disbelief.

The charges were **incredible**

suffers from the use of "incredible" as a vague intensive.

Those hamburgers were **incredible**

simply praises the hamburgers in hyperbole from which constant use has drawn the strength. "Unbelievable" undergoes some of the same diminishment

... unbelievably rare

and may also lose its utility in time.

Indefinite pronoun

See *Pronoun.*

Independent clause
>See *Clause*.

Indirect object
>See *Object*.

Indirect quotation
>We use indirect quotations when we attribute a remark without claiming to use exact words, and without using quotation marks.
>>The Congressman from Ohio then claimed that he had heard enough.
>>She said that Herbert was the nicest boy she had ever met.
>When we indirectly quote information taken from a source, we should footnote it just as we would footnote a direct quotation.

Inductive reasoning
>This form of thought draws general conclusions from particular examples or evidence.
>>As a result of these experiments we conclude that if the temperature of water falls below 32 degrees it will freeze.

Inferior to, inferior than
>"Inferior than" is incorrect. Say either "inferior to" or "worse than."

Infinitive
>See *Verbal*.

Inflection
>Inflection is the change in the form of a word to indicate a change in meaning or grammatical relationship. The inflection of nouns and pronouns is called "declension"; of verbs "conjugation"; and of adjectives and adverbs "comparison."
>Inflection of nouns indicates number and case:
>>aardvark, aardvarks; aardvark's, aardvarks'; man, men; man's, men's
>Inflection of pronouns indicates case, person, and number:
>>she, her, her, hers; who, whom, whose
>Inflection of verbs indicates tense, person, and mood:
>>bore, boring, bores, bored
>>spring, springing, springs, sprung
>Inflection of modifiers indicates comparison and number:
>>thin, thinner, thinnest
>>this dog, that dog, these dogs, those dogs

In regard to, in regards to

"In regard to" is preferable, but when either can be avoided, it ought to be.

Intensive pronoun

See *Pronoun*.

Intransitive verb

An intransitive verb neither has an object nor is passive in form.

I **was** at Annette's house in Santa Fe at the time.
Quaker **has been waiting** on the flagpole for hours.

Irregardless

Use "regardless." "Irregardless" is a redundancy, made in error on the model of "irrespective."

Italics

When we type, or write by hand, we show italics by underlining the word, italics. It comes out in type looking like cursive, *italics*.

Use italics for the names of ships: the *Niña*; for the titles of books, films, and plays: *War and Peace*; for the titles of magazines: *Sports Illustrated*; and for foreign expressions: *faute de mieux, in medias res*.

Also, we use them to indicate a special use of a word. "We might call the directory an *encyclopedia* of has-beens." We use them, from time to time, to indicate emphasis. "Do you really *mean* that?" However, the use of italics for emphasis is tricky. Italics are a vague gesture, an attempt to register a tone of voice that often fails because it cannot indicate a *specific* tone of voice. When a writer relies on emphatic italics often, he is being lazy; a more careful choice of words, a more precise context, and his emphasis will be clear without italics.

Its, it's

See *Apostrophe*.

-ize verbs

Avoid making new verbs ending in -ize, like "tomato-ize the spaghetti." Avoid using some recent coinages too: "utilize" (say "use"); "personalize."

Jargon

"Jargon" is the argot of a profession, or a peer group, like educationists' jargon, or astronauts', or rock musicians'. Businessmen fall into a jargon frequently. Sometimes they "firm up" a deal before they "finalize" it. Sometimes two negotiators are "not in the same ballpark."

Slang makes jargon too. The hip-revolutionary talk of the late sixties was jargon:

> Right on, man. Split, the fuzz. Do you dig it? Heavy.

Jargon is a language by which we attempt to prove that *we* are the initiated, and to keep noninitiates in confusion and befuddlement. It is language, not to communicate, but to exclude.

Jargon has a real purpose when it is the precise shorthand of a science. But for most of us most of the time, jargon has a tendency to be considerably vaguer than the larger language we share.

Kind of

This phrase is misused, and even used properly is often not helpful. When we say "kind of big" we are qualifying "big," as if we said "rather big." It is a misuse of the word, in speech and in writing. In correct use, kind means species. "It is a kind of pine tree." This usage works, but we often slide into vague species-making. "She is a kind of blonde I can't stand." The sentence cannot be rewritten; it must be rethought. What exactly is it that you cannot stand? Name it. "I do not like a blonde who has red eyebrows."

The same remarks apply to "sort of."

Lay, lie

Lay/laid/laying applies to: she is laying an egg; you laid the book on the table; I lay my pen on this pad. "Lay" takes a direct object. The past tense is "laid."

> He **laid** the pool on the lawn.

"Lie" takes the past tense "lay," which is a source of confusion. Lie/lay/lying applies to: I lie on the grass; she lay on the bed all day; we were lying in the sun. "Lie" never takes a direct object.

Lead, led

"Lead" is present tense, "led" is past, and "lead"—pronounced like "led"—is the metal.

Leave, let

"Leave" means "to go away"; "let" means "to allow."

> **Leave** me. (Go away from me.)
> **Let** me. (Allow me to.)
> **Leave** me out. (Don't include me.)
> **Let** me out. (Allow me to go.)

Less

This word is frequently misused where "fewer" would be correct.

There are **less** flowers in the vase today.

should be

There are **fewer** flowers in the vase today.

"Fewer" refers to actual numbers; "less" refers to general quantity.

The powerful nations are **fewer** than they used to be.

Like, as

See *As, like.*

Likewise

This expression is a clumsy transition, almost always a piece of bone in the hamburger. Try to avoid it.

Linking verb

A linking verb expresses the relationship between the subject and the predicate noun or predicate adjective. The principal linking verbs are "appear," "be," "become," "seem," and verbs used for sensations.

Lorca **is** magnificent.

Rose **became** a mother.

Joe **looks** sick.

The steak **smells** rotten.

Literally

We often say "literally" when we mean the opposite: "figuratively." We use a metaphor, but we realize that it is dead and we play Dr. Frankenstein to the monster by applying the cathodes of "literally" (or "literal").

She was **literally** big as a house.

He was a **literal** man of straw.

He hit the ball **literally** a thousand miles.

The monster never walks.

Literal means "according to the letter" or "as it actually appears." Never use it unless you mean it literally. When you find yourself misusing it for the purposes above, you can either omit it and settle for the corpse of your metaphor, or you can make a new metaphor. "She was as big as. . . ."

Litotes

Litotes is understatement. "It's not a beauty" may mean "It's ugly."

Little

Often we misuse this word—which is necessary to common speech in its literal meaning—as a vague qualifier.

He's a **little** late.

We misuse "pretty" in the same way, without considering its meaning. James Thurber once tormented his editor on the *New Yorker* by writing that something was "a little big" and "pretty ugly."

Logic

See *Deductive reasoning* and *Inductive reasoning*.

See pp. 196–210 for some remarks about persuasion, and an account of some common errors in thinking.

For further reading, consult Manuel Bilsky's *Patterns of Argument*.

Luxuriant, luxurious

"Luxuriant" means "abundant in growth"; "luxurious" means "seeking the pleasures of the senses" or providing such pleasure.

Her **luxuriant** hair was golden red.

It was done in a **luxurious** gold and leather edition.

Manuscript form

Type if you can.

Double-space on one side of white 8½ by 11 inch twenty-pound bond paper. Never use erasable paper; it won't take inked corrections, it smudges, it sticks together, and it is altogether unpleasant to read. Instead, use Correct-O Type or a similar easy device for corrections.

Always make a carbon or a Xerox. The most careful graders occasionally lose a paper. The corporations providing stolen papers for rich students make off with manuscripts when they can. Keep a copy to protect yourself.

Make margins of 1 inch to 1½ inches at top, bottom, and sides.

Number pages consecutively, including notes, appendices, and bibliography.

Put your name in the upper left-hand corner of the first page.

Type the title, upper and lower case, two or three inches down from the top of the first page. Do not underline or add a period to your title.

If quoted material is short—up to fifty words of prose, or two lines of poetry—place it within the paragraph, and use quotation marks. With lines of poetry, use a slash mark (/) to indicate line breaks, and follow the capitalization of the poem. "Of man's first disobedience, and the fruit / Of that forbidden tree...."

If quoted material is longer than fifty words or two lines of poetry, detach it from the text. Indent the quotation half an inch to the right of the place where you begin paragraphs, and single-space the quotation. Do not use quotation marks.

Man who . . .

A common circumlocution uses a noun (like "man" or "woman" or "person" or "Senator" or "typist") in a relative clause when the extra words serve no function.

He was **a man who** drank half a bottle of Scotch before breakfast.
She was **a woman who** knew better.
She was **a Senator who** always filibustered.

If this last sentence gave us the information that she was a Senator, it would be justified.

He was **a typist who** never typed more than twenty-seven words a minute.

These sentences can become

He drank half a bottle of Scotch before breakfast.
She knew better.
She always filibustered.
He never typed more than twenty-seven words a minute.

May, can

See *Can, may*.

Metaphor

See pp. 78–80.

Metonymy

Metonymy is a figure of speech in which one term suggests another to which it is related. For instance, "fifty swords" (for fifty soldiers), "wheels" (for automobile), "Madison Avenue" (for media advertising).

Modifier

Any word or group of words that describes or qualifies another word or group of words.

Momentary, momentous

"Momentary" has to do with time. It means something that lasts only a moment, or happens at any moment. "Momentous" means of extraordinary importance, as in the cliché, "a momentous occasion."

The affliction was **momentous.**
She looked West, awaiting his **momentary** arrival.

Mood

The mood (or mode) of the verb indicates an attitude on the part of the writer. The mood may be indicative, imperative, or subjunctive. The indicative mood states a fact or asks a question.

Rocky Colavito **is** here.
Was Luis Aparicio there?

The imperative mood gives a command, gives directions, or makes a request.

Beware of darkness.
Turn right at Golgotha.
Mend my parachute, please.

The subjunctive mood may express uncertainty, contradiction, wishfulness, regret, or speculation.

I would feel better if Bizarre **were** there.
If I **had** my way, I would tear this building down.

Morale, moral

"Moral" is a matter of ethics, "morale" of high or low spirits.

Their **morals** were low, but their **morale** was high.
Murder is not **a moral** act, usually.

Neither

See *Either.*

None

"None" can be either singular or plural, but is singular in more formal writing.

None of the other guys **were** going to the game.
None of his fellow senators **was** likely to take so strong a stand on the war.

Nonrestrictive modifier

A nonrestrictive modifier is a parenthetical expression that does not limit the noun or pronoun modified. It can be a nonrestrictive clause:

> The Buick, **which was a car new to my neighborhood**, was the object of fascination.

or a phrase:

> The banana, **a fruit new to our taste**, was divided evenly.

No one, nobody

These words take a singular verb. Third person pronouns, singular and plural, can refer to them: he, his, him, she, hers, her, they, them.

Not un-

Avoid the habit of writing "not un-'s."

> A **not un**distinguished gentleman, in a **not un**elegant dinner jacket, **not un**gracefully strode past the **not un**chic lady.

Noun

There are several types of nouns. *Common* nouns refer to one of a class of people, places, or things (woman, country, table). *Proper* nouns are names of specific people, places, or things (Max von Sydow, Liv Ullman, Casablanca, Ann Arbor, *The New York Times*). *Concrete* nouns name something that can be perceived by the senses (acid, trees, eggs, horses). *Abstract* nouns name a general idea or quality (terror, love, harshness, agony). *Collective* nouns refer to a group as a unit (band, tea, council, league). These categories are not mutually exclusive; a word like "tree" is both common and concrete.

Nouns, whatever their functions in a sentence, retain the same form, varying only in forming the plural and the possessive. The plural in most nouns is formed by adding -s to the singular, the possessive by adding an apostrophe and an -s to the singular, or an apostrophe after the -s of the plural: hen, hens, hen's, hens'; house, houses, house's. Some nouns add -es for the plural: hero, heroes, hero's, heroes'. A few nouns change their internal spelling: man, men; woman, women; here, the possessive is formed by an apostrophe and an -s, in singular and in plural. Other nouns with an irregular plural are listed in *Spelling*.

For stylistic advice about nouns, see pp. 53–60.

Nouns commonly used as blanks

Many nouns, which are perfectly useful when spoken with care, are frequently used imprecisely, wordily, and without utility—

nouns used as blanks: aspect, case, character, factor, fact, element, effect, nature, manner, respect, and feature.

> Some **aspects** in the **case** of Rumpelstiltskin have the **character** of **elements** that seem sinister in **nature.** The **fact** that the enraged dwarf was a **factor** in the **nature** of the King's **manner** is a **feature** with **respect** to which we can not distinguish the **effect.**

This paragraph has the consistency of mud or an annual report.

Noun substitute

A noun substitute, clause or phrase or pronoun, functions as a noun.

Number

See *Inflection.*

Numeral

In dealing with decimal points and highly precise or technical figures, it is wise to use numerals: "69.7 decibels." It is acceptable to print dates in numerals also: "June 14, 1971." The same goes for population figures and addresses: "104,000 inhabitants" and "1715 South University Avenue."

Print out the figures except when they are long to the point of being ridiculous. If you can write that a town has "one hundred and four thousand inhabitants," write it. If necessity requires precision, "104,627" will do, and "one hundred and four thousand, six hundred and twenty-seven" might look precious.

Never begin a sentence with a numeral: "97.6 mph showed on the speedometer." Here you can turn it around to "The speedometer showed 97.6 mph." "30 people stood up" should certainly be spelled out as "*Thirty* people stood up."

It is unnecessary, unless you are a lawyer, to include both spelled-out numbers and figures. Do not write "The building was at least twenty (20) stories tall." Either will do—preferably the written-out word—but both together belong only to legal or business documents.

Object

A complete sentence needs a subject and a verb; it need not have an object. "The cat screeched" is a complete sentence. "The cat clawed Herbert" includes an object. An object is something a verb acts upon.

Objects are direct and indirect.

Direct object: Any noun (or noun-substitute) that answers the question What? or Whom? after a transitive verb. Direct objects are the objects of the verb's action.

> She toppled **the giant.**
> He knows **what she wants**.

Indirect object: A noun or noun-substitute which is indirectly affected by the verb's action and which tells to whom or for whom the action is done.

> She gave **him** a karate chop.

"Him" is the indirect object, "karate chop" the direct object.

Of

We often use "of" when we don't have to:

> outside **of** the house
> off **of** the ground
> inside **of** the room

The phrases read more stylishly as

> outside the house
> off the ground
> inside the room

Exceptions occur when the extra preposition changes meaning. "Outside of" can mean "to the exclusion of," and we are correct to say, "Outside of scientific speculation, there is no use for such calibration." "Inside of" can mean "in less than." "Inside of an hour, he had finished the work."

One, you

Be careful not to use "one" in place of "you" so much that it sounds awkward or pretentious. Avoid lines like:

> Should **one** be careful to avoid the use of the word "one" when **one** is speaking to a woman whom **one** loves?

As suggested by this example, context is important when you consider using "one." It is useful at times, but it has a way of seeming affected. Never use it as an obvious disguise for the word "I."

> **One** took an amusing jaunt to Cedar Point last summer.

One of the most . . .

This cliché is drained of meaning.

> She is **one of the most** lovable people in the world.
> The rodeo last summer was **one of the most** exciting experiences of my life.

Parallelism

> See pages 113–118 on *Parallelism.*

Parentheses

> Use parentheses to enclose material which digresses or interrupts the main idea of the writing, or which explains something but remains a detachable unit.
>
> > The minister continued to pace up and down **(though he normally slept through the night)** and to stare out the window into the darkness.
> >
> > De Marque points out **(not only in the Treatise, but in the Harmonics as well)** that Jolnay was ignorant of Graf.
> >
> > Fred Papsdorf **(Charles Laughton bought his paintings)** lives on Jane Street, near East Detroit, in a small bungalow.
> >
> > She complained that she weighed ten stone **(140 lbs.; a stone, an English measure of avoirdupois, is fourteen pounds)** and had been seven stone six months ago.
>
> Also, use parentheses for numbers or letters that divide.
>
> > There are three reasons, **(1)** . . . , **(2)** . . . , **and (3)**. . . .

Participle

> See *Verbal.*

Passive voice

> A verb is in the passive voice when it *acts upon* the subject.
>
> > Kaline **was hit** by the wild pitch.

Period

> Periods end sentences. Periods indicate abbreviations (Mr., no., st., St., etc., i.e., Mass., U.S.A.).
>
> > See *Ellipses.*

Phrase

> Phrases function as a part of speech, and do not have a subject and a predicate.
>
> An infinitive phrase:
>
> > I studied **to learn Greek.**
>
> A prepositional phrase:
>
> > The flower grows **in the mountain.**
>
> A verb phrase:
>
> > The zebra **is catching up.**
>
> A participle phrase:
>
> > **Sliding into second,** Zarido tore a ligament.

Plagiarism

Plagiarism is using other people's work, whether it is a published source used without acknowledgment or a friend's old paper or a term paper bought from an entrepreneur.

Possessive

For the possessive of nouns, see *Noun*. For the possessive of pronouns, see *Pronoun*.

Predicate

A predicate is the part of the sentence *about* the subject. It includes verbs, and, on occasion, objects, indirect objects, and clauses attached to the predicate.

Preposition

Prepositions show the relationship between a noun or noun-equivalent and another word in the sentence. Some of the most commonly used prepositions are: across, after, at, behind, between, by, for, from, of, on, over, to, under, and with.

Tom hid **in** the attic.

The preposition "in" relates the noun "attic" to the verb "hid."

Presently

This word means "in a little while," and not "now." Say:

He is **at present** a milkman.

not:

He is **presently** a milkman.

But say:

He will come back to Chicago **presently.**

Pretty

See *Little*.

Principal, principle

Principle is a noun meaning a general truth (the *principles* of physics) or moral ideas (she had the highest *principles*). The adjective "principal" means the foremost. Thus, one could speak of the "principal principle" of a science or a philosophy. The noun principal means the chief officer, as in "the principal of a school."

Pronoun

A pronoun is a word used in place of a noun.

> Personal pronouns: I, you, he, she, we, etc.
> Relative pronouns: who, which, that.
> Demonstrative pronouns: this, that, these, those.
> Indefinite pronouns: each, either, any, some, someone, all, etc.
> Reciprocal pronouns: each other, one another.
> Reflexive pronouns: myself, yourself, himself, etc.

Proper noun

See *Noun.*

Prophesy, prophecy

The word with the "s" is the verb, the word with the "c" the noun.

> The priest **prophesied** doom.
> It was an accurate **prophecy**.

Punctuation

See the names of the marks of punctuation: *Comma, Period, Colon, Semicolon, Exclamation point.* Also see *Direct quotation* for punctuation connected with quotations.

Quotation marks

See *Direct quotation.*

Rational, rationale

"Rational" means reasonable and sensible. It is an adjective. "Rationale" is a noun meaning the whole system of reasons behind an idea, a position, or an action.

> His arguments were **rational**.
> Her **rationale** for the program was easy to discern.

Real, really

Conversational usage accepts "real" as an adverb, but it will not do in writing. Write:

> The boat was **really** handsome!
> Josephine seemed to be a **really** happy girl.

and avoid:

> The boat was **real** handsome.
> Josephine seemed to be a **real** happy girl.

"Real" as an adjective survives.

> It was a **real** boat.

Relative clause

> See *Subordinate clause.*

Relative pronoun

> See *Pronoun.*

Respectfully, respectively

> "Respectfully" is an adverb that modifies an action full of respect.
>
> > I remain, yours **respectfully,**
>
> "Respectively" pertains to each of a number, in an order:
>
> > He swore that he saw Ted and Joan wearing a flower and a bowler, **respectively**.
>
> Therefore to end a letter "Yours *respectively*" makes little sense.

Restrictive clause or modifier

> A restrictive modifier is a clause or a phrase essential to the identity of what is modified. (See *Nonrestrictive modifier* for contrast.)
>
> > Everybody **who wants** can get to the top.

Rhetorical question

> The rhetorical question is a frequent device of argument or persuasion. One asks a question, not to be answered, but to affect the listener or reader.
>
> > Are we born, to suffer and to die, only to satisfy the whims of rich warmongers?
> >
> > Must we write themes forever?

Satire

> Satire is a form of literature, either prose or poetry, which uses ridicule to expose and to judge behavior or ideas that the satirist finds foolish, or wicked, or both.

Seldom ever

> This phrase is redundant. "Seldom" will do.
>
> Avoid:
>
> > He **seldom ever** brushed his hair.
>
> Say:
>
> > He **seldom** brushed his hair.

Semantics

> The study of the meanings of words, especially through association. See S. I. Hayakawa, *Language, Thought, and Action.*

Semicolon

Semicolons separate whole clauses, making a pause longer or more emphatic than a comma, but shorter and less definite than a period. The semicolon indicates a close connection between the clauses.

It may be used between two (or more) balanced and equal clauses:

> The sun rose; the sky lightened; day had come.

Or it can be used between clauses of unequal length and different construction.

> The sun rose; instantly, the air was alive with birds singing so happily that anyone who heard them could not help but smile.

These sentences are compound, the semicolon replacing the conjunction.

A semicolon used with a conjunction shows more separation or pause between clauses than the comma would show.

> He flew to Denver that night; and we were glad he did.

Adverbs acting as conjunctions in compound sentences (besides, nevertheless, also, however, indeed, furthermore, still, then) take a semicolon. So do transitional phrases in mid-sentence (on the other hand, in fact, in other words, on the contrary).

> Let us take the matter in hand; however, we must not be foolhardy.
> The sun rose in a clear sky; in fact, the sky was painfully bright.

Sometimes, in a long sentence, semicolons separate series or divisions, making the divisions clearer than commas would, particularly if commas are already within the divisions.

> There were three sorts of students waiting on table at the Inn: fraternity boys who were dating expensive girls; girls from Detroit whose Daddies cut off their allowances because they had moved in with their boy friends; and street people, boys and girls, working for a week or two until they got tired of it.

Semicolons also separate incomplete clauses when a verb in one of the clauses is omitted but understood. "Poetry is one thing; verse another."

Sensual, sensuous

The two words have different meanings. "Sensual" has unfavorable connotations and means "preoccupied with or inclined to the gratification of the senses or appetites."

> He was wholly **sensual** in his priorities; his gluttony came before all else.

"Sensuous" has complimentary connotations and describes things that give pleasure to the senses.

> The passage is one of the most **sensuous** in all literature.

Sentence fragment

See pp. 91–93.

Sentence types

See *Compound-complex sentences*
Compound sentences
Complex sentences
Simple sentences

Shall, will

In common speech and most writing, we make small distinction between the words.

Formally, "I shall" expresses a person's belief about his future.

> I **shall** be twenty-one in December.

"I will" expresses his willpower, his wish.

> I **will** get to Japan before I die!

Should, would

"Should" can express obligation.

> You **should** be ashamed.

It is confused with "would" when it is used in other senses. When we make a conditional statement, in formal prose we use "should" instead of "would."

> I **should** not have reached Chicago without your loan.

Also, when we use the past of "shall" in an indirect quotation, formal prose requires "should" instead of "would."

> I said that you **should** be ready before eight.

"Would" commonly expresses habitual activities.

> He **would** visit the lake and fish from dawn to dusk.

When another phrase (like "every summer," if it were added to the last sentence) expresses habit, we can drop the "would" and use the past tense alone.

> He visited the lake every summer, and fished from dawn to dusk.

Should have, should of

The words are "should have," which can be pronounced "should've." "Should of" does not make sense.

Sic

Pronounced "sick," this Latin word is used in brackets to signify that an error of quotation was made in the source material, not by the writer copying the quotation.

> Studebaker writes, "I would rather be Thoreu [sic] unhappy than a contented pig."

Simple sentence

A simple sentence has one main clause and no subordinate clauses.

> She barked at the full moon.

Sort of

See *Kind of*.

Spelling

Spelling is irregular and irrational in English. There are a few rules of thumb, but the rules always have exceptions. We memorize to learn to spell. By memory we write "there" when it is fitting and "their" when it is fitting. By memory we spell "plough," "although," "enough," and "slough."

Here are some problems in spelling, and some suggestions about overcoming them:

Each of us has problems of his own, and sometimes we can make up our own ways to remember the correct spelling. Suppose you have trouble with the *ite/ate* ending. "Definate" is a common mistake for "definite." Maybe you can remember that it resembles the word "finite"; or the third "i" in "infinity" will help you. Or maybe you write "infinate" by mistake. Remember the antonym "finite" and remember separate, as in "separate rooms," and not "separito."

I/e, e/i: People mistakenly write "concieve" instead of "conceive," and "beleive" instead of "believe." The old recipe

> I before E
> Except after C

is useful. Examples, both ways: achieve, niece, piece; receipt, ceiling, receive. Exceptions: either, seize, weird, leisure, species.

Variant plurals: Some words change spelling in moving from singular to plural: wife/wives (like knife, life, calf, and half); man/men (like woman, milkman, etc.); Negro/Negroes (like tomato, potato, hero).

Dropping a final -e before a vowel: Most words ending with a silent -e drop it when we change them to a participle or other form that begins with a vowel. We spell the verb "move," and we spell the participle "moving." The silent -e usually remains when the added form begins with a consonant. Exceptions to both generalizations occur (argue/argument: mile/mileage), but they are infrequent and the rule is an unusually safe one.

The final -y: When y is a final vowel after a consonant (dry) it turns to -ie before -s, and to -i before other letters, except when the ending is -ing, in which case the y remains: dries, drier, drying. Beauty/beautiful. When the y follows another vowel, it generally remains -y, as in joys and grayer, with occasional exceptions, as in lay/laid.

Doubling consonants: Usually we double a final consonant before -ed, -ing, -er, or -est. We do this when the original verb or noun ended with a short vowel followed by a single consonant. "Hop" becomes "hopping." When the vowel is long or a diphthong, we usually show it by a silent -e after the single consonant, and a single consonant with the suffix. "Hope" becomes "hoping." Notice the difference between plan/planning, plane/planing, slip/slipping, sleep/sleeping.

Here are some words frequently misspelled:

accept	definite
accommodate	desert
acknowledgment	dessert
advice	divide
advise	embarrass
all right	exaggerate
allusion	explanation
annual	existence
argument	friend
arrangement	fulfillment
beginning	grammar
believe	height
business	hypocrisy
capital	irritable
capitol	its
coming	it's
committee	library
complement	lonely
compliment	loneliness
decide	necessary

nuclear	separate
obstacle	shining
occurred	similar
piece	succeed
possession	surprise
principal	than
principle	then
privilege	their
probably	there
professor	they're
precede	to, two, too
proceed	villain
quantity	who's
quite	whose
receive	writing
referred	written

Stationary, stationery

"Stationary" is an adjective that means "standing still." "Stationery" means "writing materials."

Style

See Chapters One to Five. See also Strunk and White, *The Elements of Style*; and Bergen Evans, *A Dictionary of Contemporary American Usage*; and *A Dictionary of Modern English Usage* by H. W. Fowler, rev. and ed. by Sir Ernest Gowers. See also *The Modern Stylists*, ed. Donald Hall, a collection of some of those writers and essays and excerpts by George Orwell, Ernest Hemingway, Ezra Pound, Edmund Wilson, James Thurber, and others.

Subject

A subject is a noun, or a noun substitute, about which something is stated or questioned. The subject usually comes before the predicate. The complete subject is the subject and all the words (modifiers, etc.) that belong to it.

> **The grinning barbarian, his teeth clenched,** looked into the barnyard.

"Barbarian" is the simple subject; the first six words make the complete subject.

Subjunctive

See *Mood*.

Subordinate clause

A subordinate (or dependent) clause cannot stand by itself and make a whole clause or sentence. It depends upon a main clause.

> I cannot see **who it is**.
> The claws are not lethal, **because he was de-clawed**.

Substantive

A substantive is a word or group of words used as a noun; they may be nouns, pronouns, phrases, or noun clauses.

Syntax

Syntax is the way in which words are put together to form larger units, phrases, clauses, or sentences. Or it is that part of grammar which describes this putting together.

That, which

We use the word "that" in a number of ways.

It is a demonstrative, as in "that cat."

Many writers are confused about when to use "that" and when to use "which" in introducing clauses. Nonrestrictive (nondefining) clauses take "which."

> The old car, **which** was struggling through the winter, seemed younger when spring arrived.

When the clause is restrictive or defining, we use "that" when it is possible, which is most of the time.

> The old car **that** Mr. Hornback owned was struggling up the hill.

"Which" is possible in this last sentence, but seems overprecise or rigid, and is stylistically inferior. However, when a sentence requires several restrictive clauses in a row, "that" can become confusing, and we had better revert to "which."

> The old car **which** Mr. Hornback owned, **which** had one head-light dangling loose, and **which** smelled perpetually of gasoline, chugged struggling up the hill.

Remember that "who" applies to people, whether the clause is restrictive or nonrestrictive, and "which" never applies to people.

> The folks **which** lived next door.

is incorrect. Some writers, informally, substitute "that" for "who" on occasions when the person is seen as if from a distance.

> The man **that** stood outside the door was tall and fortyish.

Toward, towards

Either is possible. "Toward" is more formal.

Transitive verb

A transitive verb *must* have a direct object to fill out its meaning.

He **put** the book down.

Try and

Like "take and."

Try and see if she's home.

is a long way to say:

See if she's home.

Type

Type is another word to avoid. Even used grammatically, it is usually filler.

It was a strange **type** of animal.

boils down nicely to

It was a strange animal.

Occasionally, as with "sort" or "kind," we actually mean something by the word.

Never use it next to a noun, without the preposition "of" coming between. It is useless to say

a new **type** soft drink

a long **type** Buick

their **type** business

that **type** handsomeness

In all these examples, an "of" would make the phrases more acceptable; but in the first three, omission of "type" would be the better solution. We save a word. In the fourth example, the idea of "type" (or "sort" or "kind") has more meaning.

Unthinkable, inconceivable

Something that is literally unthinkable is probably literally unmentionable. We use "unthinkable" as hyperbole, usually to describe something that we deplore.

His conduct was **unthinkable**.

"Inconceivable" seems to mean the same thing. In use, it means "impossible to imagine or explain."

Her absence was **inconceivable**.

Until, till

We say "till," but we write "until." "Till" looks stilted and literary on the page.

Used to, use to

The correct form is "used to": ⸳

I **used** to see her every morning at 9 o'clock.

Probably because of our slovenly pronunciation, we sometimes drift into

I **use** to see her every morning at 9 o'clock.

when we write it down. We should use the correct form, to make temporal sense.

Verb

For advice on style and the verb, see pp. 41–48.

In this glossary, see *Mood, Object, Predicate,* and *Passive.*

Verbal

Verbals are words derived from verbs but used as nouns or adjectives, and sometimes as adverbs. Verbals are gerunds, participles, and infinitives.

Gerunds always end in -ing and are used as nouns.

Flying is fun.

Running is good exercise.

Neal and Liz have benefited from their **running**.

Participles are used as adjectives.

This **flying** manual is essential.

His **shattered** hip was mending slowly.

"The **rising** cost of living" is a common phrase.

Infinitives are used primarily as nouns, but sometimes as adjectives or adverbs. They are composed of "to" and a verb, but in use the "to" can occasionally be omitted.

We started **to run from Godzilla**.

To fail is a pleasure he can't afford.

He dropped out **to begin his career as a clown**.

They helped [to] **eat** the submarine.

Vocative

See *Direct address.*

When

Don't use "when" as an introduction to definitions.

Loneliness is **when** you play the radio just to hear the announcer's voice.

This usage is unacceptable.

Where

See *When.* The same injunction applies.

Which, that

> See *That, which.*

While

> The word means "at the same time" or "during the time that."
> Somtimes writers use it in place of "although," and it can work.
>
> > **While** John is large, his stomach is not excessive.
>
> But this usage is prone to ambiguity.
>
> > Winter is warm in the southern hemisphere, **while** summer is
> > cold.
>
> Think about this sentence for a moment, and it is absurd.

Who, whom

> Who is a subject, whom an object. "Who's on first?" "To whom
> should I deliver the testimony?" In the last sentence, "whom" is
> the object of the preposition "to." In formal writing, always say
> "whom" when It Is an object of a verb or of a preposition.
>
> Sometimes position leads us into error. When a pronoun pre-
> cedes a verb, it sounds as if it were a subject; it isn't always. We
> may be tempted to write,
>
> > From **who** is the noise coming?
>
> but the phrase is "from whom," and "the noise" (not "who") is the
> subject of "is." We should write,
>
> > From **whom** is the noise coming?
>
> Sometimes a clause separates the subject "who" from its verb, and
> we misuse "whom" for "who." We write,
>
> > Herbert, **whom** she said would be here at 6:30, strolled In at
> > 8:00.
>
> In this sentence the three noun-verb combinations make a box
> within a box within a box. "Herbert . . . strolled" is the outside box,
> "who . . . would be here" is the middle box, and "she said" the in-
> side box. When "whom" comes before a preposition of which it is
> the object, it is correct but highly formal:
>
> > **Whom** am I looking at?
>
> Here, we always write "who" in informal writing. Frequently,
> "whom" will sound *too* formal even in an essay that is mostly
> formal. Use your judgment. The position of the pronoun makes
> the problem, which comes up when it is the object of a verb as well
> as when it is the object of a preposition:
>
> > **Whom** do I see?
> > **Who** do I see?

The first is correct and the second incorrect—technically—but it would take a highly formal context to accept the "correct" formulation without creating a moment of stuffiness.

-wise

Stylewise, avoid this syllable in combination with words with which it has not been combined before. *Clockwise* and *otherwise* are parts of the language. Avoid literarywise, poetrywise, intelligence quotientwise, Septemberwise, costwise, Sallywise, ecologywise—and anything similar.

INDEX

A passage from an author's work quoted in the text is designated by (q).

A, an (see Article)
Abbreviations, 254
Absolute element, 254
Abstract:
  defined, 254–255
  and particular nouns, 55–56
Abstractions:
  defined, 254–255
  elimination of, in beginnings and
    endings, 56
Academic jargon, examples of, 3–4, 46
Accept, except, 255
Acronym, 255
Active voice, 255
Ad hominem argument, 209 (see also
  Argument)
Adjective(s), 63–73
  automatic, 66–68
  clause, 256
  and the cliché, 64
  dangling, 110
  frequently misused, 256
  function of, 255–256
  with prepositional or comparative
    phrase, 94
  verbs with nouns and, 42–43
Adverb(s), 63–73
  clause, 257
  as connectives, 101
  dangling, 110
  frequently misused, 257

function of, 256
Advertising, and made-up verbs, 48
Advice, advise, 257
Affect, effect, 257
Agee, James:
  "A Mother's Tale," 73–74 (q)
  "Southeast of the Island: Travel
    Notes," 84–85 (q)
Agreement:
  defined, 257
  grammatical, 112
Agree to, agree with, 257
All ready, already, 258
All right, alright, 258
Although, though, 258
Altogether, all together, 258
Ambiguity, 258
Amid, amidst, 258
Among, amongst, 258
Among, between, 258
Amoral, immoral, unmoral, 258–259
Amount, number, 259
Analogy(ies), 80–82
  defined, 259
  as fact, 209
  looking for, 83–85
And/or, 259
Ann Arbor News, The, 200–201 (q)
Antecedent, 259
Antonym, 259
Any, any other, 259–260
Anybody, anyone, 260
Apostrophe, 260–261
Appositive, 94–95
  defined, 261
  noun phrase, dangling, 109
Argument:
  clarity in, 197–198
  order of, 203–205
  and persuasion, 196–210
  reasonableness in, 198–201
  (see also Logic and emotionalism;
    Thinking, common fallacies of)
Article, 261
As, like, 261
Ash, Christopher, 227, 231
Association, versus connotation, 28
At, 261
Auden, W. H., The Enchafed Flood,
  96–97 (q)

Audience:
  and self, 38–39
  and subject, 131–132
Autobiography, 215–217
Auxiliaries, 262

Balance, 118, 119–120 (*see also*
  Parallelism)
Balanced sentences (*see* Balance;
  Parallelism)
Baldwin, James, *Nobody Knows My
  Name,* 61–62 (q)
Barnet, Sylvan, *A Short Guide to
  Writing about Literature,* 233
Beauvoir, Simone de, *The Second Sex,*
  194 (q)
Beck, Jim, 7–10, 11, 39, 65
Beginnings, 185–188
  elimination of abstractions in, 56
  (*see also* Endings)
Bergman, Ingmar, *Four Screenplays of
  Ingmar Bergman,* 136 (q)
Berkeley Tribe, 41
Beside, besides, 262
Between (*see* Among, between)
Bibliography:
  cards, 222–224
  examples of, 231–232, 262–263
Big words, 263
Brackets, 263–264
Bilsky, Manuel, *Patterns of Argument,*
  206, 295
Blackmur, R. P., "New Thresholds, New
  Anatomies," 238–239 (q)
Bleibtreu, John N., *The Parable of the
  Beast,* 107 (q)
Blond, Georges, 230, 231
Bloom, Harold, *The Visionary Company,*
  134 (q)
Borges, Jorge Luis, "Death and the
  Compass," 107 (q)
Brinnin, John Malcolm, *The Sway of the
  Grand Saloon,* 240–241 (q)
Brown, Norman O., *Life Against Death,*
  60 (q)
Browning, Robert, 38
Buckley, William F., Jr., "Roy Cohn's
  Book," 50 (q)
Business jargon, example of, 57
Butkus, Dick, 28

Camus, Albert:
  "Encounters with André Gide,"
    163 (q)
  The Stranger, 108 (q)
Can, may, 264
Cannot, can not, 264
Can't hardly, 264–265
Capital letters, 265–266
Case, Jennifer, 221–232
Case (*see* Inflection)
Cavendish, Richard, *The Black Arts,*
  106–107 (q)
Chaucer, Geoffrey, 38
Churchill, Sir Winston, 106 (q)
Circumlocution, 266
Cite, sight, site, 266
Clark, Ronald W., *Einstein,* 192 (q)
Clause, 266 (*see also* Subordinate
  clause)
Cleaver, Eldridge, *Soul on Ice,* 49 (q),
  141–142 (q)
Clichés, 3–4, 20, 64, 76
Coles, Robert, *Children of Crisis,*
  23–24 (q)
Collective noun (*see* Noun, types of)
Collier, John, *Indians of the Americas,*
  170 (q)
Colon, 267, 278
Comma(s):
  to avoid ambiguity, 268
  and compound sentences, 98–100
  with direct quotation, 277
  fault, 268
  function of, 267
  separating items in a series, 268–269
  separating whole clauses, 269–271
  setting off introductory phrases, 271–
    272
  using too many, 272
Common nouns (*see* Nouns, types of)
Comparison, 76–85
  of adjectives and adverbs, 272–273
  revising for, 85
  for transitions, 164
  unintended, 82–83
  (*see also* Analogy; Metaphor; Simile)
Complement, 273
Complement, compliment, 273
Complex sentence, 91
  conjunctions and unity in, 110–112

defined, 273
and subordinate phrases and clauses, 94–96
(*see also* Sentence, long)
Compound sentence, 90–91
defined, 273
and punctuation and variety, 98–101
(*see also* Sentence, long)
Compound-complex sentence, 91, 274
(*see also* Sentence, long)
Compound word, 274
(*see also* Hyphen)
Conant, James B.,"Athletics: The Poison Ivy in our Schools," *Basic Writer and Reader*, 245–246 (q)
Confucius, 6, 7
Congressional Record, 225
Conjugation (*see* Inflection)
Conjunctions, 110–112, 274
Conjunctive adverb, 274
Connotation, versus association, 28
Conroy, Frank, *Stop-Time*, 14–16 (q), 18, 22, 52 (q)
Consider . . . as, 274
Consist in, consist of, 275
Contiguity, 112
Continual, continuous, 275
Contractions, 275
Contrast, for transitions, 164
Coordinates, 275
Cosell, Howard, 83
Could have, could of, 276
Counsel, council, consul, 276
Cousins, Norman, 73 (q)
Cousteau, Jacques, *The Silent World*, 74 (q)
Crane, Hart, Blackmur on, 238-239
Criticism, 232–240
Cronkite, Walter, 34–35 (q)
Cutting words from quotations (*see* Ellipses)

Daily writing (diaries, journals, note-books), 19–21
Dangling modifiers (*see* Modifiers, misplaced)
Dash, 276–277
Declension (*see* Inflection)
Deductive reasoning, 277 (*see also* Argument; Thinking, common

fallacies of)
Demonstratives, 277
Description, 210–212
Detail:
accumulating, 181–182
cutting, 184–185
extraneous, 150–151, 182
organizing, 182–184
(*see also* Paragraph; Unity)
Detroit Free Press, 171–172 (q)
Dialogue, and quotation, 214–215
Dickey, James, *Deliverance*, 195–196 (q)
Diction:
mixing formal and informal, 132–133
unity of, 132–133
Dictionaries, use of, 28–29, 36–37
Different from, different than, 277
Dillard, R. H. W., "Even a Man Who Is Pure at Heart: Poetry and Danger in the Horror Film," 135 (q)
Direct address, 277
Direct object (*see* Object)
Direct quotation, 277–278
Discreet, discrete, 278
Disinterested, uninterested, 278
Division of words, 278 (*see also* Hyphen)
Doesn't (*see Don't*)
Don't, 279
Double negative, 279
Doubling consonants, 308–309
Doubt but, 279
Due to, 279

-e, dropping final, before a vowel, 308
Each, every, 279–280
Ecclesiastes, 24 (q), 139 (q)
Orwell's parody of, 126
Eckhart, Meister, 120 (q)
Egoism, egotism, 280
Einstein, Alfred, 192
"Eisenhowese," 128–129
Either, 114–115, 117, 280–281
Elicit, illicit, 281
Eliot, T. S., 38, 234
"The Love Song of J. Alfred Prufrock," 233
Ellipses, 278, 281–282
Emphasis, 118–119

Encyclopaedia Britannica, 221
Endings, 188–191
  elimination of abstractions in, 56
  (*see also* Beginnings)
Enormity, enormousness, 282
Erikson, Erik, *Childhood and Society,*
  142 (q)
Etc., 282
Etymology, 283
Euphemism, 11, 32–34, 76, 127, 283
Evans, Bergen, 68–69, 264
  *A Dictionary of Contemporary
    American Usage,* 193 (q)
Everybody, everyone, 283
Exclamation point, 277–278, 283
Exposition, 191–196

Famous, notorious, 283
Fanon, Frantz, *The Wretched of the
  Earth,* 61 (q)
Farther, further, 283
Faulkner, William, 64
  "Go Down Moses," 74 (q)
Feeling, honest and dishonest, 2–5
  (*see also* Logic and emotionalism)
Few (*see Less*)
Fiction writing, 218–220
Fields, W. C., 29, 48, 133
Figure (*see* Numeral)
Finite verb, 284
Finn, David, *The Corporate Oligarch,*
  199–200 (q)
Fischer, Louis, *Gandhi: His Life and
  Message for the World,* 157 (q),
  159 (q)
Fitzgerald, F. Scott:
  notebook of, 20 (q)
  Tender Is the Night, 97 (q), 105, 122
Footnotes, 284–286
  example of use of, 226–231
Foreign words and phrases, 287
Foreword, forward, 287
Formal writing, 123–125
  mixed with informal, 132–133
  paragraphing within, 146
  poor use of, 126–127
  sentence structure of, 128
  (*see also* Informal writing)
Forster, E. M., "What I Believe,"
  190–191 (q)

Fowler, H. W., *Modern English Usage,*
  143–144 (q), 215
Fraser, J. G., *The Golden Bough,*
  187 (q)
Freud, Sigmund, "The Relation of the
  Poet to Daydreaming," 135 (q)
Frost, Robert:
  "Acquainted with the Night,"
    236–238 (q)
  Selected Prose of Robert Frost,
    141 (q)
Frye, Northrop, "Myth and Poetry,"
  194–195 (q)

Galbraith, John Kenneth, *How to
  Control the Military,* 152 (q)
Gender, 287
Genteel words, 287
Gerassi, John, *The Great Fear in Latin
  America,* 88 (q)
Gerund (*see* Verbal)
Go, 287
Goffman, Erving, *The Presentation of
  Self in Everyday Life,* 140 (q)
Goldston, Robert, *The Civil War in
  Spain,* 176 (q)
Good, well, 288
Gourmet, 71 (q)
Grammar, 288
Graves, Robert, 36
Greer, Germaine, *The Female Eunuch,*
  247–248 (q)
Guerrilla, gorilla, 288

Had ought, ought, 288
Hanged, hung, 288
Hamlet, 233, 234 (q)
  Quiller-Couch's parody of, 127 (q)
Hamlet's soliloquy, 30 (q), 126 (q)
Hardy, Thomas, *Tess of the
  d'Urbervilles,* 238
Harrington, Michael, *The Other
  America: Poverty in the United
  States,* 151–152 (q)
Hart, Marian, 10–14, 191
Hassler, Alfred, *Saigon, U.S.A.,* 136 (q)
Hayakawa, S. I., *Language, Thought,
  and Action,* 304
He, him (*see* Pronoun)
Heath-Stubbs, John, 66

Heilbroner, Robert L., *The Worldly Philosophers,* 136 (q)
Help but (see *Doubt but*)
Hemingway, Ernest, 39
  "Big Two-Hearted River," 74 (q)
  "In Another Country," 16–17 (q), 18, 69–70 (q), 120–121
  "Monologue to the Maestro," 140–141 (q)
Hester, J., 37
Higham, Charles, *The Films of Orson Welles,* 157–158 (q), 158–159 (q)
Hildbroner, Herman, *Lincoln Blade,* 282 (q)
Hitler, Adolf, 33
Hodin, J. P., *Edvard Munch,* 176 (q)
Homer, *Iliad,* 187
Homonym, 288
Hopefully, 289
Hopkins, Gerard Manley, 69
Howell, Dr. A. B., 229 (q)
Hume, David, 208
Hutchins, Robert M., "How Should a University Administrator Respond to Radical Action?" 155 (q)
Hyperbole, 289
Hyphen, 289–290 (see *also* Division of words)

I, me (see Pronoun)
i.e., 290
i/e, e/i, 307
Illich, Ivan, *Deschooling Society,* 149–150 (q), 177, 246–247 (q)
Images:
  defined, 78
  examples of, 16, 31
Immigrant, emigrant, 290
Incredible, unbelievable, 290
Indefinite pronoun (see Pronoun)
Independent clause (see Clause)
Indirect object (see Object)
Indirect quotation, 291
Inductive reasoning, 291 (see *also* Argument; Thinking, common fallacies of)
Inferior to, inferior than, 291
Infinitive, "to" with, 117 (see *also* Verbal)
Inflection, 291

Informal writing, 123–125
  mixed with formal, 132–133
  paragraphing within, 146
  poor use of, 128–131
  sentence structure of, 128
  (see *also* Formal writing)
In regard to, in regards to, 292
Intensive pronoun (see Pronoun)
Intransitive verb, 292
Irregardless, 292
Italics, 292
Its, it's (see Apostrophe)
-ize verbs, 292

James, William, "The Dilemma of Determinism," 136 (q)
Jamesy, Paul, *Delivery,* 175
Jargon, 292–293
Jaspers, Karl, *General Psychopathology,* 136 (q)
Jensen, Oliver, "The Gettysburg Address in Eisenhowese," 128–130 (q)
Jesus Christ, 135 (q)
Jones, Leroi, *Home,* 142 (q)
Joyce, James, *Ulysses,* 211 (q)
"Jumbo Fish-tails," 106 (q)

Kafka, Franz, "Jackals and Arabs," 74–75 (q)
Kazantzakis, Nikos, *Zorba the Greek,* 175–176 (q)
Kent Ravenna Record-Courier, 40 (q)
Kent State University (Ohio), shootings at, 34–35, 40–41
Kerouac, Jack, *The Dharma Bums,* 140 (q)
Kind of, 293
Kreicke, Hermann von, *The Migrant Swan,* 167–169 (q), 241 (q)
Kronenberger, Louis, *Company Manners,* 242 (q)

Lagerkvist, Pär, *The Sybil,* 101–102 (q), 103
Laing, R. D., *Self and Others,* 48–49 (q)
Langseth-Christensen, Lillian, "Naples," 71–72 (q)

Lao-Tzu, 135 (q)
Last Whole Earth Catalogue, The,
    87-88 (q)
Lawrence, D. H.:
    "Pornography and Obscenity,"
        170–171 (q)
    The Rainbow, 49 (q)
Lay, lie, 293
Lead, led, 293
Leave, let, 293
Less, 294
Lewis, C. S., "At the Fringe of
        Language," 149 (q), 177
Library, use of, 222–225
Like, as (see As, like)
Likewise, 294
Lilly, John Cunningham, *The Mind of
    the Dolphin,* 54 (q)
Lincoln, Abraham, "Gettysburg
        Address," 130 (q)
    parody of, in "Eisenhowese," 128–129
Linking verbs, 294
Literally, 294
Literalness, and metaphor, 30
Litotes, 294
Little, 295
Logic, and emotionalism, 205–206 (*see
    also* Argument; Deductive
    reasoning; Inductive reasoning;
    Thinking, common fallacies of)
Lorca, Federico Garcia, "The Duende:
    Theory and Divertissement,"
    158 (q)
Luxuriant, luxurious, 295
Lydgate, John, 36 (q)

Machado, Antonio, 120 (q)
Macrorie, Ken, *Uptaught,* 4–5 (q)
Mailer, Norman:
    The Armies of the Night, 102–103 (q)
    The Naked and the Dead, 49–50 (q)
    Of a Fire on the Moon, 25–26 (q), 27,
        31 (q), 39
    The Prisoner of Sex, 248–250 (q)
Male chauvinism, 35
Mann, Thomas, "Death in Venice,"
    161 (q)
Manuscript form, 295–296
Man who . . . , 296
Marlowe, Christopher, 281–282

Marvell, Andrew, "To His Coy
        Mistress," 36 (q)
Mattingly, Garrett, *The Defeat of the
        Spanish Armada,* 97-98 (q), 105,
        122
May, can (see Can, may)
McCartney, James, 172
Mead, Margaret, *Male and Female,*
        161–162 (q)
Memory, and originality, 80
Mencken, H. L.:
    "The Artist," 52 (q)
    "Mr. Justice Holmes," 87 (q)
Metaphor:
    and literalness, 30
    and simile, 78–80
    (*see also* Analogy; Comparison)
Metonymy, 296
Milford, Nancy, *Zelda,* 241–242 (q)
Modifiers, 63–73
    defined, 296
    good use of, 69–72
    misplaced, 109–110
    nonrestrictive, 297–298
    nouns as, 68–69
    restrictive, 304
    revising, 73
    that weaken nouns, 64–65
    as weak intensives, 65–66
Momentary, momentous, 297
Mood, 297
    passive, 43–45
Moore, Henry, 19
Morale, moral, 297
Morris, Desmond, *The Naked Ape,*
        164 (q)
Morris, Wright, *The Territory Ahead,*
        124 (q), 140-141 (q)
Myrdal, Jan, *Confessions of a Disloyal
        European,* 163 (q)

Nabokov, Vladimir, *Speak Memory,*
        22 (q)
Narrative, 212–214
Neither (see Either)
Neologism, 58
Newspaper writing:
    paragraphing in, 146
    question of objectivity in, 32
Newsweek, 32

New Yorker, The, 81, 88 (q),
   243–245 (q)
New York Times, The, 225
Nietzsche, Friedrich, *Beyond Good
   and Evil,* 176 (q)
None, 297
Nonrestrictive modifier, 297–298
Nonsequiturs, 208
No one, nobody, 298
Norris, Kenneth, 231
Not un-, 298
Noun(s), 53–60
   abstract and particular, 55–56
   bad, made from verbs, 57–58
   commonly used as blanks, 298–299
   fancy, 58
   function of, 298
   invisible, 56–57
   as modifiers, 68–69
   revising, 58–60
   substitute, 299
   types of, 298
   verbs with adjectives and, 42–43
Number (*see* Inflection)
Numeral, 299

Object, 299–300
OED (*see Oxford English Dictionary*)
Of, 300
One, you, 300
One of the most . . . , 300
Originality, 76–85
Orwell, George, 58
   his parody of passage from
      Ecclesiastes, 126 (q), 127, 139
   "Politics and the English Language,"
      33–34 (q)
   The Road to Wigan Pier, 86–87 (q)
Owl and the Pussycat, The, 47
Oxford English Dictionary (OED),
   36–37, 39, 235

Pacific Hawk, 61 (q)
Paragraphs, 143–163
   coherence of, 153
   focusing with, 144–146
   length of, 146–150
   narrative, 154
   revising, 166
   sequence of, 151–153

   topic sentences for, 154–157
   transitions between, 160–166
   unity of, 150–151
   uses of, 143–144
   ways of developing, 157–160
Parallel constructions, 162–163 (*see also*
   Parallelism)
Parallelism, 113–118 (*see also* Balance;
   Emphasis)
Parentheses, 301
Parody:
   defined, 17
   examples of, 126–129
Parrish, John A., M.D., *12, 20 & 5,*
   211–212 (q), 213–214 (q), 215
Participles:
   dangling, 109, 110
   as modifier, 63
   past and present, 95–96
   verbs with, 43
   (*see also* Verbal)
Passive mood, 43–45
Passive voice, 301
Payne, Dr. Roger, 228–229 (q)
Peirce, Charles S., *Values in a Universe
   of Change,* 194 (q)
Period, 99–100, 301 (*see also* Ellipses)
Periodic sentence:
   defined, 118
   examples of, 119, 121
Phrase, 301
Plagiarism, 302
Plato, 7
Plimpton, George, *The Bogey Man,* 53
Political rhetoric, 33–34, 35, 44, 48
Porter, Katherine Anne, "Flowering
   Judas," 75 (q)
Possessive, of nouns, 298
Pound, Ezra, 184 (q)
   Patria Mia, 173 (q)
Predicate, 302
Preposition, 302
Presently, 302
Pretty (*see Little*)
Principal, principle, 302
Professional writing, 14–17
Pronoun, 303
Proper noun (*see* Noun, types of)
Prophesy, prophecy, 303
Punctuation, 98–101

with direct quotation, 277–278
(*see also* Colon; Comma; Exclamation
point; Period; Question mark;
Semicolon)

Question mark, with direct quotation,
277–278
Quiller-Couch, Sir Arthur, his parody
of Hamlet's soliloquy, 126–127 (q),
139
Quotation:
and dialogue, 214–215
direct, 277–278
indirect, 291

Rational, rationale, 303
Readers Guide to Periodical Literature,
222–223
Real, really, 303
Real Romance, 211 (q)
Redding, Tracy, *Hoosier Farm Boy*,
216–217 (q)
Relative pronoun (*see* Pronoun)
Repetition:
for balance, 119
for emphasis, 118
in parallel constructions, 113, 116, 119
as transitional device, 161–162
for unity, 7
Research writing, 220–232
bibliography for, 231–232
choosing a subject for, 221
defined, 220–221
example of, 226–231
reading and note-taking for, 221–225
Resolution, 121–122 (*see also* Rhythm)
Respectfully, respectively, 304
Restrictive clause or modifier, 304
(*see also* Nonrestrictive modifier)
Revision, 6–7
for comparison, 85
for conciseness, 103–104
of modifiers, 73
of nouns, 58–60
of paragraphs, 166
of sentences, 103–104
themes and, 7–14
for unity, 133
for variety, 103–104
Rhetorical question, 304

Rhodes, Gov. James, 40
Rhythm, 120–121 (*see also* Resolution)
Roethke, Theodore, notebooks of,
19–20 (q)
Roget's Thesaurus, 28–29, 36
Ross, Harold, 81–82, 85 (*see also*
Thurber, James, *The Years with
Ross*)
Roth, Philip, "Eli, the Fanatic," 108 (q)

Saint Exupéry, Antoine de, *Wind, Sand
and Stars*, 177–178 (q)
St. John, 25
Sanders, Ed, *The Family*, 88 (q)
Santayana, George, "Poetry and Prose,"
134 (q)
Satire, 304
Saturday Review, 73 (q)
Scheffer, Victor, *The Year of the Whale*,
222, 230
Scientific prose, 44
Seldom ever, 304
Self-deceit, avoiding, 34–35
Self-examination, 5–6
Semantics, 304
Semicolon, 98–101, 305
Sensual, sensuous, 305–306
Sentences, 89–133
complex, 91, 94–96, 110–112, 273
compound, 90–91, 98–101, 273
compound-complex, 91, 274
concluding, 122–123
incomplete, 91–93
long, 96–98
periodic, 118–119, 121
revising, 103–104
simple, 89–90, 307
style and, 89
topic, 154–157
types of, 89–93
mixing, 101–103
variety of, 94–104
(*see also* Formal writing; Informal
writing; Sentence structure; Unity)
Sentence fragment (*see* Sentence,
incomplete)
Sentence structure, 101–103
formal and informal, 128
Sentimentality, 31
Shakespeare, William, 30, 234, 235,

281–282
As You Like It, 139 (q)
Hamlet's soliloquy, 126 (q)
Shall, will, 306
Should, would, 306
Should have, should of, 307
Sic, 307
Simile, and metaphor, 78–80 (*see also*
Analogy; Comparison)
Simple sentence, 89–90, 307
Singer, Isaac Bashevis, "The Gentleman
from Cracow," 121 (q)
Slijper, E. J., *Whales,* 222, 227 (q), 231
Snyder, Gary, 231, 232
Sociological jargon, 69, 126
Socrates, 5
Solzhenitsyn, Alexander, *Cancer Ward,*
187 (q)
Sort of (*see Kind of*)
Spelling, problems in, 307–309
Spengler, Oswald, *The Decline of the
West,* 81
Stalin, Josef, 33
Stanislavski, Constantin, *Creating a
Role,* 136 (q)
Stationary, stationery, 309
Steiner, George, "Gent," 88 (q)
Stone, I. F., *The Haunted Fifties,*
136 (q)
Subject, 309
Subjunctive (*see* Mood)
Subordinate:
clause, 94–96, 310
phrase, 94–96, 100
Substantive, 310
Synonyms, 27–30
Syntax, 310

Tenses, consistency of, 113
That, which, 310
Themes, 7–14
Thesaurus (*see* Roget's Thesaurus)
Thich Nhat Hanh, *Lotus in a Sea of
Fire,* 107 (q)
Thinking, common fallacies of, 206–210
Thoreau, Henry David, "On the Duty
of Civil Disobedience," 60–61 (q),
178–179 (q)
Thurber, James, 295
on Harold Ross, 81–82 (q), 85

The Years with Ross, 124–125 (q),
139, 187–188 (q)
Time, 32, 35 (q), 187 (q)
Times Literary Supplement (London),
82–83 (q)
Tomkins, Calvin, *Merchants and
Masterpieces,* 72 (q)
Toward, towards, 310
Transitional words and phrases, 163–164
Transitions, 160–166
implicit, 164–166
overt, 160
Transitive verb, 311
Try and, 311
Twain, Mark, *Huckleberry Finn,* 233
Type, 311

Unintended comparison, 82–83
Unity, 108–133
of diction, 123–133
grammatical, 109–113
of paragraphs, 150–151
revising for, 133
structural, 113–123
Unthinkable, inconceivable, 311
Until, till, 311
Updike, John:
"The Crow in the Wood," 26–27 (q),
31, 39, 70 (q), 75
Rabbit Run, 60 (q)
Used to, use to, 312
U.S. News and World Report, 32

Variant plurals, 307
Verbal, 312
Verbs, 41–48
action, and choice of style, 41–42
false color in, 46–47
fancy, 18
finite, 284
intransitive, 292
invisible, 46
-ize, 292
linking, 294
made-up, 48
making bad nouns from, 57–58
with nouns and adjectives, 42–43
with participles, 43
particular, 45
and the passive, 43–45

Vietnam War, 33
Vocative (*see* Direct address)
Vonnegut, Kurt, 180

Wakefield, Dan, *Island in the City*,
    61 (q), 105–106 (q)
Wanger, Prof. Walter, 281–282
Watts, Alan W., *The Way of Zen*,
    87 (q)
When, 312
Where (see *When*)
Which, that (*see That, which*)
While, 313
White, E. B., 70–71 (q)
    The Elements of Style, 141 (q)
    The Second Tree from the Corner,
    132–133 (q), 174 (q)
White, Theodore H., *The Making of the
    President 1960*, 157 (q), 159 (q)
Whitehead, A. N., *Adventures of Ideas*,
    188 (q)

Who, whom, 313–314
Who's Who, 225

Wiesel, Elie, *A Beggar in Jerusalem*,
    92 (q)
Williams, Thomas, *Town Burning*,
    40 (q)
Wilson, Edmund:
    O Canada, 193 (q)
    A Piece of My Mind, 39–40 (q)
Wing, George, *Hardy*, 238 (q)
-wise, 314
Words, 25–39
    big, 263
    as blanks, 37
    collecting, 35–37
    genteel, 287
    and meaning, 37–38
    misusing the insides of, 31–34
    original, 76–85
    sense, 31
    (*see also* Adjectives; Adverbs;
        Diction; Nouns; Verbs)
Wordsworth, William, 212

-y, final, 308
Yeats, W. B., 31, 108, 196–197 (q)

To the student:

As publishers, we realize that one way to improve education is to improve textbooks. We also realize that you, the student, largely determine the success or failure of textbooks. Although teachers choose books to be used in the classroom, if the students do not buy and use them, those books are failures.

Usually only the teacher is asked about the quality of a text; his opinion alone is considered as revisions are planned or as new books are developed. Now, Little, Brown would like to ask you about Donald Hall's *Writing Well:* how you liked or disliked it; why it was interesting or dull; if it taught you anything. Would you fill in this form and return it to us at: Little, Brown and Co., College Division, 34 Beacon Street, Boston, Mass. 02106. It is your chance to directly affect the publication of future textbooks.

School: _____

Course title: _____

Other texts required: _____

1. Did you like the book? _____

2. CONTENT: Was it too easy? _____

    Did you read it all? _____

    Which chapters did you like most? _____

    Which chapters did you like least? _____

3. FORMAT: Did you like the cover design? _____

    Did you like the trim size? _____

    Did you like the type size? _____

(over)

4. Were the exercises useful? _____

   How might they be changed? _____

   _____

   _____

5. Did you like the examples? _____

   How might they be improved? _____

   _____

6. Do you feel the professor should continue to assign this book next year?

   _____

7. Will you keep this book for your library? _____

8. Please add any comments or suggestions on how we might improve this book, in either content or format.

   _____

   _____

   _____

   _____

   _____

9. May we quote you, either in promotion for this book, or in future publishing ventures?   _____ yes   _____ no

   _____   _____
   date   signature

   _____
   address

   _____
   instructor's name